Problem frames

ACM PRESS BOOKS

This book is published as part of the ACM Press Books – a collaboration between the Association for Computing Machinery and Addison-Wesley. ACM is the oldest and largest education and scientific society in the information technology field. Through its high-quality publications and services, ACM is a major force in advancing the skills and knowledge of IT professionals throughout the world. For further information about ACM contact:

ACM Member Services
1515 Broadway, 17th Floor
New York NY 10036-5701
Phone: +1 212 626 0500
Fax: +1 212 944 1318
Email: acmhelp@acm.org

ACM European Service Center
108 Cowley Road
Oxford OX4 1JF
United Kingdom
Phone: +44 1865 382338
Fax: +44 1865 381338
Email: acm-europe@acm.org
URL: http://www.acm.org

SELECTED ACM TITLES:

Software Requirements and Specifications: A Lexicon of Software Practice, Principles and Prejudices   *Michael Jackson*

Software Test Automation: Effective Use of Text Execution Tools   *Mark Fewster and Dorothy Graham*

Test Process Improvement: A Practical Step-by-step Guide to Structured Testing   *Tim Koomen and Martin Pol*

Mastering the Requirements Process   *Suzanne Robertson and James Robertson*

Bringing Design to Software: Expanding Software Development to Include Design   *Terry Winograd, John Bennett, Laura de Young, Bradley Hartfield*

Software for Use: A Practical Guide to the Models and Methods of Usage Centered Design   *Larry L. Constantine and Lucy A. D. Lockwood*

Use Cases: Requirements in Context   *Daryl Kulak and Eamonn Guiney*

Software Blueprints: Lightweight Uses of Logic in Conceptual Modelling   *David Robertson and Jaume Agusti*

Problem frames

Analysing and structuring software development problems

MICHAEL JACKSON

An imprint of **Pearson Education**

Harlow, England · London · New York · Reading, Massachusetts · San Francisco
Toronto · Don Mills, Ontario · Sydney · Tokyo · Singapore · Hong Kong · Seoul
Taipei · Cape Town · Madrid · Mexico City · Amsterdam · Munich · Paris · Milan

PEARSON EDUCATION LIMITED

Head Office:
Edinburgh Gate
Harlow CM20 2JE
Tel: +44 (0)1279 623623
Fax: +44 (0)1279 431059

London Office:
128 Long Acre
London WC2E 9AN
Tel: +44 (0)20 7447 2000
Fax: +44 (0)20 7240 5771
Website: www.aw.com/cseng/

First published in Great Britain in 2001

© ACM Press, A Division of the Association for Computing Machinery Inc., ACM
The right of Michael Jackson to be identified as Author of this Work has been
asserted by him in accordance with the Copyright, Designs and Patents Act 1988.

ISBN 0-201-59627-X

British Library Cataloguing in Publication Data
A CIP catalogue record for this book can be obtained from the British Library

Library of Congress Cataloging in Publication Data
Applied for.

The programs in this book have been included for their instructional value.
The publisher does not offer any warranties or representations in respect of
their fitness for a particular purpose, nor does the publisher accept any
liability for any loss or damage arising from their use.

Many of the designations used by manufacturers and sellers to distinguish
their products are claimed as trademarks. Pearson Education Limited has made
every attempt to supply trademark information about manufacturers and their
products mentioned in this book.

10 9 8 7 6 5 4 3 2 1

Typeset by Pantek Arts Ltd, Maidstone, Kent.
Printed and bound in the USA.

The Publishers' policy is to use paper manufactured from sustainable forests.

for
Rachel, Noah, Rebecca, Sam,
Akiva, Amos, Alice and Shoshana

Contents

Problem frames

When you *analyse* a problem you see what kind of problem it is, and identify the *concerns* and *difficulties* you will have to deal with to solve it. The concerns in a Java compiler will be very different from the concerns in a car braking system. You have different things to think about. Different kinds of descriptions must be made, and fitted together into differently shaped arguments. Problem analysis takes you from the level of identifying the problem to the level of making the descriptions needed to solve it.

But most realistic problems are too big and complex to handle in just two levels like this. Another level is needed: *structuring* the problem as a collection of interacting *subproblems*. If your structuring is successful, the subproblems will be smaller and simpler than the problem you started with, and their interactions will be clear and understandable. Then you can analyse each subproblem separately, as a simple problem on its own, and make the descriptions it needs.

The central idea of this book is to use *problem frames* in problem analysis and structure. They help you by defining different simple problem classes. When you structure a larger, realistic problem, you choose the subproblems so that each one is a problem of the simple kind defined by some problem frame. Then, when you analyse the subproblem, you see what concerns it raises according to the problem frame that fits it. The frame shows you what you must do to solve it.

A problem frame defines the shape of a problem by capturing the characteristics and interconnections of the parts of the world it is concerned with, and the concerns and difficulties that are likely to arise. So problem frames help you to focus on the problem, instead of drifting into inventing solutions. They do this by emphasising the world outside the computer, the effects that are required there, and the relationships among things and events of the world by which your customer will ultimately judge whether those effects have been achieved.

Problem frames share much of the spirit of design patterns. Design patterns look inwards towards the computer and its software, while problem frames look outwards to the world where the problem is found. But they both identify and describe recurring situations. They provide a taxonomy within which each increment of experience and knowledge you acquire can be assigned to its proper place in a larger scheme, and can be shared and accessed more effectively. So just as in object-oriented design a familiarity with design patterns allows you to say 'we need an instance of the *decorator* pattern here', so in problem decomposition a familiarity with problem frames allows you to say 'this part of the problem is a *workpieces* problem'. Having identified a part of a problem with a recognised problem frame, you can draw on experience associated with the frame.

Preface

Software development problems

The central goal in a software development problem is to create the software for a computer system that will serve some useful purpose in the world. This book is about analysing and structuring problems of this kind.

These problems are found in many different contexts and forms. If you are doing software development you might be building a system to act as a repository and access mechanism for information about bank accounts and loans. You might be developing a telephone exchange to switch local calls. You might be creating a tool for writing and editing texts and diagrams; or a control device to maintain cruising speed in a car; or a compiling machine to transform Java programs into bytecode. Almost any part of the human and physical world can furnish the raw material and the context for a software development problem.

Because computers can serve so many purposes, and play the central role in solving so many different kinds of problem, the practice of software development is less specialised than the established engineering disciplines. For the individual developer, and the individual development project, there's a lot more variety. That's why you should usually start by describing and structuring your problem in a way that's rarely necessary in other engineering disciplines, where the diversity of problems to be solved is much smaller. The automobile engineer designing a sports car does not need to ask whether the car must be capable of carrying 15 people, travelling underwater, carrying a ten-ton load, or moving backwards at 100mph. The phrase 'sports car' specifies both the problem and its acceptable solutions closely enough to answer those questions and many others.

But as a software developer you are rarely solving an immediately recognisable and well understood problem. Usually, you must begin by asking: What kind of problem is this? What, exactly, is the problem about? What purpose is being served in the world? What behaviour and properties must the computer have to achieve that purpose? Often, software development seems to start at square one.

The problem frame idea was first published in book form in my book *Software Requirements & Specifications*, where it was sketched in outline as one of a small number of related topics. This book puts more flesh on that skeleton. A number of elementary and composite problem frames are discussed and illustrated, along with a number of flavours and variants, and some of the concerns they raise are examined. The use of problem frames in decomposing realistic problems into subproblems is also explored and illustrated.

A focused view

Some people think that this notion of software development *problems* derives from a perspective that is too sharply focused and too narrow. They point out that computer systems, and the process of software development itself, almost always exist in a complex and fluid social, political, ethical and economic environment. When you are discovering the requirements for a system you are likely to be engaged in a process of social negotiation among conflicting groups of stakeholders; when you make a decision about system functionality you may be implicitly favouring one group over another; when you enlarge the system scope you are often giving political power to one group at the expense of another; when you analyse the purposes to be served by the system you are exploring its economic and organisational consequences.

So, from this point of view, the major concerns in software development are social and political, organisational and economic. Thinking in terms of problems doesn't do justice to these concerns. It's true that these concerns are important in many developments, but nonetheless we are going to ignore them in this book. We are not going to discuss how to elicit requirements, how to make the business case, how to manage the project, facilitate meetings, or negotiate compromise. We will ignore these things, not because they are unimportant but simply because they are not the subject matter of this book. If you want to understand anything, you mustn't try to understand everything.

Instead, we are going to try to understand some more sharply focused ideas in problem structure and analysis in the context of software development. Our chief topics will be the material, observable effects that the system should bring about in the world, the computer behaviour that will achieve those effects, and the connection between them. In short, the topics that are often called functional requirements, software specifications, and the path by which you get from one to the other.

Focusing on problems

It is not easy to focus on problems in software development. One reason is that they have some precise and some imprecise aspects, all competing for your attention. Like Odysseus on his ship coming home from Troy, you are sailing between Scylla and Charybdis, and must try to steer a middle course.

Scylla and Charybdis

If you are attracted by the arguments of the people who regard our view of problems as far too formal and narrow, you may be dragged off to the right, into the world of purely human problems – the imprecise world of sociology and ethnography, where nothing is ever completely certain or completely exact. That's an important world, but it neglects the software and its development.

However, if you find that problems are less exciting than their software solutions, you are more likely to veer off to the left, towards the much more precise world of programming – of variables and methods and object classes, where boolean values are always either True or False, and never anything in between. Progamming is also important, but it won't be useful if no one has analysed the problem and worked out what the programs must do.

In the problems discussed in this book, there are plenty of precise and plenty of imprecise ingredients. We will try to do justice to both, to steer the proper course for understanding and analysing problems.

ble problem, are still being devised and sold, and seem to flourish. But if a method offers help with every possible problem, you mustn't expect it to help much with any particular problem.

Another reason for not advocating a particular development method is that most of the methods widely used today are strongly solution-oriented. You need solution-oriented methods to help you to produce solutions. But they give little help – and are often a positive hindrance – in structuring and analysing problems.

Problem frames, and the related ideas, are meant to be used as a front end to what you would do anyway; or to suggest how you might extend or modify your practice; or, perhaps, just to clarify it. If you do adopt and use these ideas, do it gradually in a piecemeal process, not in a sea-change. You may perhaps find that many of them are just giving names to ideas and intuitions that you already have. Naming them should make them more consciously accessible when you need them. And where they're new to you, they may shed light on some difficulties that you had felt but had never articulated.

Structure of the book

The key idea of the book is the decomposition of complex and realistic problems into structures of simple subproblems of kinds that fit recognised problem frames. So there's a mixture of larger and smaller problems. Some of the smaller problems are trivial, especially the problems used to illustrate the most basic elementary problem frames. Don't spurn trivial problems. They show the stripped-down essence of problem classes in their barest form: that makes it much easier for you to recognise them when they appear in fancy dress concealed by the trappings of a larger problem.

The problems are not presented in ascending order by size and complexity. That would be rational and tidy, but it would make the book frustrating to read. Instead, larger and smaller problems are interleaved, and different aspects of each problem are discussed wherever they seem relevant and provide a good illustration of the current topic.

Some topics, such as descriptive languages and notations, run through the whole book. Again, aspects of these topics are introduced where they arise.

This very informal structure is supplemented by two appendices. One summarises the descriptive languages and notations used; the second provides a glossary of the terminology. There is a consolidated list of all the bibliographic references, and an index.

Acknowledgements

Many people have contributed to the process of working out the problem frame ideas to their present stage of development.

Daniel Jackson has given me constant help, encouragement and advice since I started writing this book an eternity ago. As on a previous occasion, he has saved me from many errors and follies by careful and detailed comment. His patience and generosity have been wonderful.

Ben Kovitz came across the idea of problem frames in my earlier book *Software Requirements & Specifications*, when he was writing his delightful book *Practical Software Requirements*. He engaged me in a long and fascinating email correspondence, he made excellent suggestions about terminology, and he provided many illuminating insights into software development problems, both particular and general.

Barry Cawthorne worked with me on problem frames and some related topics. He provided a rich example from the world of academic administration, discussed it with me at length, and pointed out some obscurities and flaws in earlier versions of my ideas.

Steve Ferg provided useful ideas during the course of an email correspondence about problem frames, and made helpful comments on an earlier version of the text.

Richard Botting pointed out an error in my earlier definition of *sibling*. Now I have got it right.

Pamela Zave and I have been working together for ten years at AT&T Research, chiefly on the analysis and structuring of telecommunication services. Although we have not discussed problem frames explicity, there must surely be much in this book that I have learned from our long co-operation.

Many other people have encouraged me by their interest in problem frames, especially Dines Bjørner, Michael Caspersen, Hugo Fierz, David Garlan, Anthony Hall, Ralph Johnson, Neil Maiden, Lars Matthiassen, Jay Misra, Mary Shaw, Alistair Sutcliffe, Axel van Lamsweerde, Roel Wieringa, Jeannette Wing, Jim Woodcock and Amiram Yehudai.

I am grateful to them all. They have helped to make the book better. Its remaining defects are all my own work.

▪ Should the list of patients be held in a Java vector?

Focusing on the problem means considering questions like these:

▪ Are all intensive care patients to be monitored, or only some of them?

▪ Are different vital factors to be monitored for different patients, or the same factors for all of them?

▪ Do the medical staff specify the periods as well as the ranges, or does someone else specify the periods?

▪ In what ways do the analog devices fail? How can these failures be detected and diagnosed?

▪ Do a patient's monitoring needs ever change while the patient is being monitored?

Here's a rough sketch of another problem we'll be discussing:

Library administration problem

A system is needed to administer a lending library. Membership is required for borrowing books, but not for reading them in the library premises. Books may be ordered and can be obtained from associated libraries. Overdue books incur fines. Various management reports are required.

Focusing on the problem means considering questions like these:

▪ Are all books available for borrowing, or are some only to be read in the library?

▪ Can loans be renewed? If so, is there a limit on renewals?

▪ Can members reserve books? If so, how long is a reserved book kept available?

▪ Can non-members reserve books?

▪ Is there a membership fee? How long does membership last?

▪ Is it permissible to borrow one isolated volume of a three-volume work?

The reasons for focusing on the problem are compelling. First, it's widely recognised that many systems have failed – often very expensively or even disastrously – because their requirements were not properly determined. The hardware and software functioned correctly, but the function they performed was not what was needed. The developers' failure was in capturing and understanding the problem, not in devising or implementing a solution. A second, less obvious reason is that by focusing on the problem you can hope to identify the chief difficulties and concerns that lie in wait for you, and to address them early. In software development, a difficulty postponed is often a difficulty multiplied. It's much harder to deal with when it pops up unexpectedly after you are already immersed in detail and many decisions – which now seem dubious or even just wrong – are cast in concrete.

Any questions?

Where do these two problems come from?

The patient monitoring problem is very old. It dates back at least to W G Stevens, G J Myers and L L Constantine, *Structured Design*, IBM Systems Journal, Volume 13, Number 2, pages 115–139, 1974.

The library administration problem is an expanded version of the problem given in Richard A Kemmerer, *Testing Formal Specifications to Detect Design Errors*, IEEE Transactions on Software Engineering, Volume SE-11, Number 1, pages 32–42, January 1985.

There is a potted history of formulations of the library problem, and a critique of 12 partial specifications, in Jeannette M Wing, *A Study of 12 Specifications of the Library Problem*, IEEE Software, Volume 5, Number 4, pages 66–76, July 1988.

1.2 The computer and the world

Not only does everyone agree that you should focus on the problem before the solution; almost everyone agrees that you should focus on *what the system will do* before you focus on *how it will do it*. *What* before *how* is the motto.

But it's not a very helpful motto. It's often hard to distinguish a problem from its solution, and it's no easier to distinguish *what* from *how*. It's more helpful to distinguish *where*. That is, to recognise that the solution is located in the computer and its software, and the problem is in the world outside. Like this:

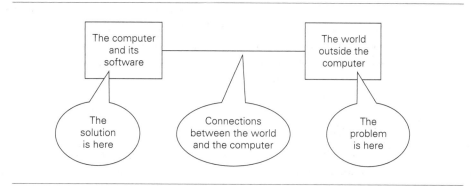

The problem and the solution

The patient monitoring problem is in the hospital ward, outside the computer. It's about the patients, the analog devices, the nurses' station, the medical staff, the specified periods and ranges. The solution – embodying the answers to questions about Java vectors and SQL statements and scheduling algorithms – is in the computer and its software. The library administration problem is in the library reading room, the associated libraries, the members, the casual readers, the books they borrow and read, the membership fees and fines they pay.

The computers can provide solutions to these problems because they are connected to the world outside. In the patient monitoring problem the computer can sense the readings at each analog device, and it can access the periods and ranges in some machine-readable form – perhaps on a separate small database; it can write to the main database where the factors are to be stored, and it can send notifications to the nurses' station. In the library administration problem the computer is less directly connected to the problem world – perhaps through magnetic card readers and barcode readers, and through on-line dialogues with library members and staff. These connections, without which the computer would be unable to play its role in the solution, are represented in the diagram by the solid line between the computer and the world.

If you're in any doubt about where the problems are, it's easy to check – at least approximately. Just ask yourself what the customers for each system might complain about if the system was not working properly. The hospital customers might complain that Mr Smith's temperature rose to 104° but the nurses' station was not notified; or that the analog device measuring Ms Jones's pulse failed and the system did not notify the failure. The library customers might complain that Ms Black reserved a copy of *Barchester Towers* but when it became available and she went to the library to borrow it, it had been lent to another member; or that Mr White's order for *The Catcher in the Rye* was never sent to the associated library that owns a copy; or that Ms Green wasn't allowed to borrow any books although at the time she was a member in good standing. These complaints are not about the computer or its software: they are about the effects that the computer and its software produce in the world outside. That's where the problem is.

1.3 Initial problem focus

You're probably thinking that this is all motherhood and apple pie. It is. Most development methods recognise that the problem is not in the computer, and show their recognition by including some relevant parts of the world in an early development description.

For example, in structured analysis the first diagram drawn is the top-level dataflow diagram, usually called the context diagram. Here is a context diagram for a small retail system:

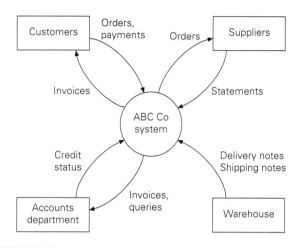

A dataflow context diagram for a retail system

The circle in the centre of the diagram represents the *system*: here, that means the computer and the software that the developers must build. The rectangles at the corners are called *terminals*. They represent the parts of the problem world that have been identified as interacting with the system: the company's customers and suppliers, and its accounts department and warehouse. The arrows represent flows of data between the terminals and the system: the system sends orders to its suppliers, receives orders and payments from its customers, and so on. The diagram is intended to show what the problem is about.

In the Rational Unified Process, the development process recommended by Rational for users of UML (the Unified Modeling Language), the initial focus is on *use cases*. The system is thought of as being surrounded by *actors,* which may be people or other systems, that interact with it. Each kind of interaction is a use case; the functionality of the system is defined by the set of use cases. The earliest depiction of a system is in terms of use cases, arranged in related groups. This diagram shows a small group of use cases:

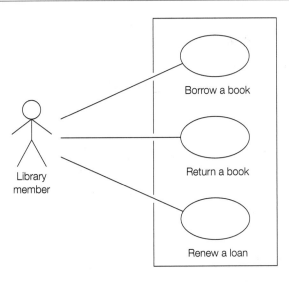

An actor and some use cases

These are use cases for a library system. The actor is a library member, and the three use cases are borrowing a book, returning a book, and renewing the loan of a borrowed book. Again, the diagram is intended to show what the problem is about.

There is an obvious relationship between these two approaches. The actors in the use cases are individuals belonging to the parts of the problem world that interact with the system; in a context diagram for the library system there would be a terminal named 'library members'. The use cases roughly correspond to individual types of interaction along the dataflows of a context diagram. For example, in a context diagram for the library system there might be a dataflow named 'borrowings, returns, renewals' flowing between the library members terminal and the system.

In both approaches, the initial focus is on the problem world and its interactions with the system: terminals and dataflows, or actors and use cases. It seems a good start.

Any questions?

Why do you give rough sketches for problems, instead of a proper requirement or specification?

Because we are trying to simulate the situation in a real project, where you start with a rough idea of what a problem is about and carry on from there. In the real project you have real customers and stakeholders and experts to consult. In a book, unfortunately, you have only the author. We're doing the best we can.

Where can I read more about Structured Analysis and the Rational Unified Process?

You can read about Structured Analysis in Edward Yourdon, *Modern Structured Analysis*, Prentice Hall International, 1989.

The original ideas of Structured Analysis are beautifully described in Tom DeMarco, *Structured Analysis and System Specification*, Yourdon Press, 1978.

The Rational Unified Process is described in these two books: Ivar Jacobson, Grady Booch and James Rumbaugh, *The Unified Software Development Process*, Addison-Wesley Longman, 1999.

Phillipe Kruchten, *The Rational Unified Process: An Introduction*, Addison-Wesley Longman, 1999.

1.4 The problem is not at the interface

Now that you have roughly identified what the problem is about, your next step must be to look into it more deeply. But where? You could look more deeply into the interface between the world and the system. For example, you could discover, decide, analyse or design more detail of the messages in the dataflows, or more detail of the dialogues for the use cases. That would be good and useful.

But there is another dimension to be explored, too. You can explore properties and behaviours of the terminals or actors that are not visible at the interface. What are the customers and suppliers, or the library members, doing when they are not interacting with the computer? Can aspects of their behaviour and properties be relevant that never play a direct part in the interface?

Yes, certainly they can. The problem is about the terminals or the actors, and there is no reason to restrict it to what can be seen at their interface with the computer. In fact, it is almost never so restricted. Over-generalising just a little, you can state this as a general principle: *the problem is not at the computer interface – it is deeper into the world, further away from the computer.*

Here is a little illustration.

The call forwarding problem

Call forwarding is a common feature in telephone systems. It allows a subscriber at one number to arrange to have incoming calls forwarded to another number: the subscriber at *n1* can set up either no call forwarding at all, or forwarding to any specified number *n2*. The problem is to develop and describe the detailed requirements for the feature.

responsibility – and what effects you would like the system to achieve – calls to A's number must reach A, and calls to B's or C's number must reach C. Again, motherhood and apple pie. No one seriously denies this.

But sometimes even apple pie is left on the plate. Studying and analysing the problem world in depth is not always easy to do. There are forces drawing you away from the task: that is, away from talking about the world towards talking about the computer instead. And there are common confusions of terminology that make it hard even to be absolutely sure what you are talking about.

1.5.1 The fascination of computers

One major force drawing you away from the world is the computer itself. To most people in software development, computers are, quite simply, irresistibly fascinating. There is something about their capacity to accept our instructions, however intricate, and, by executing them, to reveal their consequences, however surprising, that satisfies some intense common desire for the excitement and fascination of intellectual control. Few companies can persuade their employees to work 90-hour weeks, but many software companies can. Many people happily sit up writing and running programs half the night. Not many people sit up at night writing requirements documents or specifications.

The fascination with computers has a long history. Mrs Augustus De Morgan, wife of the mathematical logician who gave his name to De Morgan's Laws, accompanied Ada Lovelace on her visit 'to see Mr Babbage's wonderful analytical engine' in 1828. Ada was quite bowled over. Mrs De Morgan reported that '... Miss Byron, young as she was, understood its working and saw the great beauty of the invention'. Miss Byron soon become the world's first modern programmer.

Almost one hundred and forty years later, in 1966, the UK government carried out a small investigation into the increasing range of computer application areas for which government funding was being provided. I was the investigation consultant. One application project I looked at was the use of a computer for geological taxonomy, cataloguing the collection of specimens in a university museum. When I visited the museum curator, who was in charge of the project, I found that he had spent the previous six months rewriting the input-output software of the computer's operating system. All thought of geological taxonomy and cataloguing had evaporated in the novel excitement of programming.

For many people in software development, the computer remains far more interesting than the problem world.

Any questions?

What are De Morgan's Laws?

That 'Not (A *or* B)' is equivalent to '(Not A) *and* (Not B)', and that 'Not (A *and* B)' is equivalent to '(Not A) *or* (Not B)'.

Where is the account of the visit to Babbage to be found?

S E De Morgan, *Memoir of Augustus De Morgan, with Selections from his Letters*, Longmans, Green, 1882.

I must confess that I have not consulted this book directly. The quotation, and the information that it 'contains a few brief mentions of Babbage, and an account of a visit paid in the company of Lady Lovelace "to see Mr Babbage's wonderful analytical engine" is in B Randell, *The Origins of Digital Computers: Supplementary Bibliography* in N Metropolis, J Howlett, and Gian-Carlo Rota (eds), *A History of Computing in the Twentieth Century*, Academic Press, 1980.

1.5.2 The two meanings of 'system'

One confusion that makes it hard to know whether you're talking about the world or about the computer is the uncertain meaning of an important word: *system*. Sometimes the word *system* is used for the whole combination of the world and the computer together. In this larger sense, the *library system* includes the computer with its software and the members and books and staff and associated libraries and shelves and everything else of relevance; the *patient monitoring system* includes the computer with its software and the patients and the medical staff and the nurses' station and the analog devices and other things too. So it's quite appropriate to say that the first step is to describe the system: in this large sense, the system is where the problem is.

But the word *system* also has a smaller sense. It means the circle in the middle of the dataflow context diagram, or the rectangle containing the ovals that represent the use cases. That is, it means the computer and its software. There's room for some doubt about peripheral devices. A screen and keyboard are surely parts of the computer; the analog devices in the patient monitoring problem are surely not; the telephones in the call forwarding problem are a doubtful case. But these doubts are secondary. In its smaller sense, *system* certainly does not include the patients, or the suppliers, or the library members or the books, or the offices and the telephone subscribers. The ambiguity between the larger and the smaller sense makes it easy to claim that you are 'analysing the system' when in truth your subject matter is just the computer and its software.

1.5.3 The two meanings of 'model'

A second, crucial, confusion surrounds the word *model*. Two different meanings are important here. First, a model can be just a useful description. An economic model may be a description of a country's economy: the model is a set of differential equations describing the relationships among prices, wages, unemployment and inflation. Similarly, a model of a piece of computer software may be a description of its behaviour as a finite-state machine relating external event stimuli to changes in the internal software state. In both cases the description is useful because it lets you analyse the possible behaviour of what it describes. These descriptions are *analytic* models.

In the second meaning, a model is not a description but another reality with some similar properties. This is an *analogic* model. In some of the air battles of the Second World War, the control room on the ground used a model of the battlefield in the air. The model consisted of a large table, marked with a map of the battle area, and toy airplanes, positioned on the table to match the positions of the real airplanes. The pilots and navigators communicated with the control room by radio. As they reported their positions, and their successes and failures, ground staff in the control room moved the toy planes about the table to reflect the evolving state of the battle. When a real plane was shot down, the corresponding toy plane was removed. When real reinforcements arrived, fresh toy planes were added. The table and the toy planes formed an *analogic* model of the real air battle. By keeping the model in correspondence with the reality, the commander on the ground could see the state of the battle in the air, and could make informed tactical decisions.

In software you need to make models of both kinds. To understand the problem, you must study and describe all the relevant parts of the problem world. Those descriptions are analytic models of the world. The operational computer system may also need an analogic model – often in the form of a database or an internal structure of programming objects – of some parts of the world. In place of the analogy between real planes and toys, between airspace and the table, there may be an analogy between members and books in the library world, and member and book records in the computer's database.

Confusing these two meanings of 'model' is harmful. When you say 'we are modelling the members and books', do you mean 'we are specifying the database that will form our analogic model of the members and books'? Or do you mean 'we are describing the members and books'? In the first case you are describing something that is essentially a part of the computer and its software; in the second you are describing something in the world outside. These are very different activities with very different meanings.

Any questions?

Where does the distinction between analytic and analogic models come from?

It's in R L Ackoff, *Scientific Method: Optimizing Applied Research Decisions,* Wiley, 1962.

Ackoff also recognises a third kind of model. An *iconic* model is a graphical depiction of what it models. A map drawn to scale is an iconic model of the terrain. The boundary between iconic and analogic models is a little soft. But the boundary between analogic and analytic models is clearer and harder. In software development it's really important.

If an analogic model is like the part of the world it models, why does it matter whether we describe one or the other? Won't the descriptions be the same?

No, they won't. The model and the world are alike in some ways, but different in other ways. The battle air space is three-dimensional, but the table is two-dimensional. The toy planes come out of a box and go back into it afterwards; the real planes come out of the sky and leave the battle when they crash to the ground. The database model has behaviour and properties, such as record deletion and third normal form, that don't correspond to anything in the library. And the library has behaviour and properties, such as holiday closing, shelf locations, and the physical shape and condition of the books, that aren't reflected in the database.

1.6 Seamless development

These ambiguities in the words *system* and *model* make it hard to focus resolutely on the problem. The difficulty is greatly increased by a desire to practise *seamless development.*

Seamless development is a reaction against the older practice in which development proceeds in a sequence of clearly distinguished phases, each producing its own output document expressed in its own distinctive language and structure. In the first phase, business analysts might produce a *feasibility study* document. Then, in the second phase, systems analysts might take this as their input and produce a *requirements* document. The third phase might produce a *specification*. In a fourth phase, system designers might take the specification as input and produce a *software design*. Finally, programmers take the software design and produce the *software*.

This process had two serious disadvantages. First, the terms *feasibility study, requirements, specification* and *design* were not well defined. There was always doubt, and often conflict, about what should be in the different documents. Second, between each pair of adjacent phases there was a 'seam', where the distinctive culture, subject matter, language and structure of the earlier phase met those of the later phase. People began to talk of the document produced by each phase as being 'thrown over the wall' to the people responsible for the next phase. They meant that the phases were carried out in watertight compartments, and that the uncomfortably alien document made in an earlier phase would be largely ignored in the later phase. And that did often happen. The process did not work well.

The idea of seamless development was that development should proceed smoothly, without harmful seams between the successive phases. There should be – so far as possible – a single conceptual and notational framework within which the whole development could proceed. When the programming ideas of object-oriented languages began to influence the earlier phases of development, it seemed natural that this single conceptual and notational framework could and should be based on object orientation. Bertrand Meyer expressed it like this:

> '... This is why object-oriented designers usually do not spend their time in academic discussions of methods to find the objects: in the physical or abstract reality being modelled, the objects are just there for the picking!'

In short, Meyer was claiming that the problem world is populated by objects. Some people disagreed with him, but many agreed. The use of object-oriented notations to describe the world became very widespread; many people agreed that problems could be captured, described and analysed in terms of object-oriented notations such as those found in UML. As the development work progressed, the early object-oriented descriptions of the world would merge seamlessly with the later object-oriented descriptions of the software.

But it was hard to make the reality live up to the ambition. The idea of seamless development, combined with the conceptual haze spread about by the ambiguous words *system* and *model*, has often meant that problem description and analysis is given far too little attention. In many developments, important parts, aspects and properties of the problem world simply do not fit at all well into the straitjacket of an object-oriented view. Inevitably, those parts would be ignored, or treated only in a distorted way. The result is that many descriptions that ought to be about the world, and are offered by their makers as descriptions of the world, are really about the computer and its software and, especially, about its database and internal object structure.

1.7 Some resolutions

When you structure a problem you can't avoid moving some way towards its solution – that is, towards talking about the computer and its software. And, as we will see, to structure some problems you really do have to introduce a database or object structure as an analogic model into your analysis.

So you will sometimes find yourself talking about the computer. There is nothing wrong with that, provided that you don't neglect the problem world, and don't give a description of the computer and its software when you should be giving a description of the world. You always need to know clearly which one you are talking about. To help to be clear about this, we will adopt some firm resolutions.

■ We will try to avoid the ambiguous word *system*. Because 'the computer and its software' is rather a large mouthful, we will instead use the word *machine*. The machine is what must eventually be built and installed to solve the problem.

■ To avoid the ambiguity of the word *model*, we will use it only for analogic models. Analytic models we will call, simply, *descriptions*. We will never talk about a *modelling* activity in development, either of the problem or of a part of the world or of the machine. It's simply too confusing.

■ To avoid distorting our descriptions of the world, we won't restrict ourselves to object-oriented notations. Instead, we'll use whatever languages and notations express most directly and clearly what we want to say. Of course, sometimes an object-oriented notation will be the best choice.

Any questions?

Is the old way of doing things, with seams, the famous waterfall model of development?

Yes. The seams were where each level of the waterfall cascaded down to the next.

Where does Meyer say that objects are 'there for the picking'?

Bertrand Meyer, *Object-Oriented Software Construction*, Prentice Hall International, 1988.

Who disagreed with him about this?

Steve Cook and John Daniels, among others. They wrote:

> '... in summer lots of birds will start to sing around sunrise ... Does the sun send a message to all of the birds individually? If so, in what order? ... These are silly questions, because they are questions about software execution, not the sunrise.'

The quotation comes from their book on Syntropy (their method of software development). It's well worth reading: Steve Cook and John Daniels, *Designing Object Systems: Object-Oriented Modelling with Syntropy*, Prentice Hall International, 1994.

What is UML?

You're joking, of course, aren't you? Where have you been hiding? UML is the Unified Modeling Language. It's Rational's attempt to establish its portfolio of notations as a universal standard under the aegis of the OMG (the Object Management Group). You can read about it in these books:

Grady Booch, James Rumbaugh and Ivar Jacobson, *The Unified Modeling Language User Guide*, Addison-Wesley Longman, 1999.

James Rumbaugh, Ivar Jacobson and Grady Booch, *The Unified Modeling Language Reference Manual*, Addison-Wesley Longman, 1999.

Martin Fowler, *UML Distilled* , Addison-Wesley, 1999.

Will there be more discussion of analogic models later in the book?

Yes, there will. Definitely. It's a central topic in problem analysis. Chapter 7 is all about models.

1.8 The scope of this book

The scope of our topic – structuring and analysing software development problems – is limited by two boundaries.

■ On the machine side, we won't go further into the machine structure and mechanism than is necessary to describe what it must do to serve the purposes of the various parts of the problem. That is, we'll describe the machine's interactions with the world but not its internal mechanisms. Sometimes, to describe the problem clearly, we'll have to introduce and describe an object model or a database model, or something like that.

■ On the problem world side, we won't go further into the world than is necessary to capture and analyse the purposes of our notional customer, for whom we are building the system.

Here's how the book is arranged. Following this chapter, there are 11 more:

Chapter 2 (Locating and bounding the problem) expands and clarifies the distinction between the machine and the world, and the relationship between them. We'll always structure the world as a collection of interconnected *domains,* pictured in a *context diagram.* The problem context is bounded by your customer's responsibilities and authority. The machine you build must not change parts of the world that your customer is not authorised to change, and in analysing the problem you must not ignore relevant parts of the world for which your customer is responsible.

Chapter 3 (Problems and subproblems) starts to explore the decomposition of problems into smaller and simpler subproblems. There is an important principle here: the subproblems must be of familiar kinds because only then can you be confident that your decomposition is making the task easier. Each decomposed subproblem has its own *projections* – its partial views – of the world and of the machine, taken from the original problem. We'll show each subproblem in a *problem diagram.* That's like a context diagram with the addition of a requirement.

Chapter 4 (Basic problem classes and frames*)* introduces the idea of a *problem frame.* A problem frame captures a familiar class of intuitively recognisable problem in a generalised problem diagram. It specifies the broad characteristics of the problem domains and of the interfaces between domains and between the machine and the world. We'll look at five basic problem classes: required behaviour, commanded behaviour, information display, workpieces and transformation.

Chapter 5 (Frame concerns and development descriptions) explores the characteristic *frame concern* of each problem class. The frame concern captures the fundamental criterion of successful analysis for problems that fit the frame. It specifies what descriptions are needed, and how they must fit together to give a convincing argument that the problem has been fully understood and analysed. The frame concern, and other characteristic concerns of the frame, can be adequately addressed only if you have chosen the appropriate frame for the problem.

Chapter 6 (Frame flavours and development descriptions) refines the idea of a problem class defined by a frame to take account of different *flavours* of domain *characteristics.* For example, a transformation problem with a sequential input data stream has a different flavour from one whose input domain is an associative database. The different flavours of behaviour problem are particularly important. Domain and problem flavours are discovered and captured by making descriptions in appropriately chosen languages.

Chapter 7 (Model domains and real worlds) explores the use and design of a *model domain* – such as a database – in information problems. Model domains need special care in description and reasoning because without special care it is easy to confuse the model with the reality that it models. Model domains raise particular concerns in development, mostly about the relationship between the state of the reality and the state of the model.

Chapter 8 (Variant frames) presents some common variants of the basic problem classes. Most of these variants result from adding further domains to the problem world. For example, an *operator* may be added to a behaviour problem, or an *informant* to an information problem. Adding a *description domain* to almost any problem allows late binding of some aspect of the requirement or of a problem domain property. All these variants raise additional characteristic concerns in structuring and analysis.

Chapter 9 (Particular concerns) identifies and explores some additional concerns and difficulties that can arise in several problem frames and for several kinds of domain. They include the *overrun* concern, the *initialisation* concern, the *reliability* concern, and others. Some – for example, the *identities* concern – may sometimes force you to elaborate your view of the problem by introducing an additional domain. Others – for example, the *completeness* concern – demand only more care and better technique in domain description.

Chapter 10 (Decomposition revisited) returns to the topic of decomposing realistic problems begun in Chapter 3 (Problems and subproblems) and explores problem decomposition techniques. Some of them are essentially heuristic; some are based squarely on the explicit and systematic recognition of concerns arising for particular kinds of subproblem frame or particular kinds of domain. Some of the most important techniques are illustrated by a full decomposition of a non-trivial problem.

Chapter 11 (Composite frames) gathers together some *composite frames* that have already been identified, and identifies some new ones. A composite frame defines a familiar class of problem that demands decomposition into subproblems in accordance with a standard structure. Examples include problems that use model domains, problems with additional display domains, behaviour problems that combine default behaviour with overriding by an operator, behaviour and other problems with an auditing subproblem. Composite frames raise their own characteristic *composition concerns*.

Chapter 12 (Grown-up software development) puts the task of software development, from analysis to design, into a broader perspective. As a software developer you should always have a lively awareness of development risks – dangers of failure in developing and using the system – and should always be clear-headed about the responses that those risks demand. The fundamental goal is to write and exploit descriptions, especially descriptions of the world outside the machine, from which you can convince yourself and other people of the soundness of your problem structuring and analysis. To do this successfully you must avoid the dogmatism and pedantry that sometimes lead to the use of entirely inappropriate methods and descriptive languages. The chapter concludes with a broader perspective on the problem frame approach.

Any questions?

Aren't you going to talk about solutions?

Not really. Designing and structuring a solution is the next step after problem analysis and structure. There is something to say about it in Chapter 11, on composite frames, but it's really another complete subject. Remember, we're not doing seamless development.

CHAPTER 2

Locating and bounding the problem

The problem is located in the world outside the machine you must build. You fix the location by drawing a problem context diagram. A context diagram structures the world into the machine domain and the problem domains, and shows how they are connected. The machine domain in one context may be a problem domain in another. The context bounds the problem: the domains are the parts of the world that are relevant. You can avoid treating a problem too abstractly, or trying to serve purposes that are too remote, by focusing on the customer's needs, responsibilities and scope of authority.

2.1 The context diagram

When you set about analysing and structuring a problem, it's fundamental to determine what it is about – that is, where the problem is located, and what parts of the world it concerns. You can record what you find and decide in a *context diagram*. A context diagram is rather like the context diagrams of Structured Analysis. It shows the *machine domain* and the *problem domains*. It also shows the *interfaces* between the domains: that is, how the machine is connected to problem domains and how problem domains are connected to each other.

Here is the patient monitoring problem again:

Patient monitoring problem

A patient monitoring program is required for the ICU in a hospital. Each patient is monitored by an analog device which measures factors such as pulse, temperature, blood pressure, and skin resistance. The program reads these factors on a periodic basis (specified for each patient) and stores the factors in a database. For each patient, safe ranges for each factor are also specified by medical staff. If a factor falls outside a patient's safe range, or if an analog device fails, the nurses' station is notified.

Here's a possible context diagram for this problem:

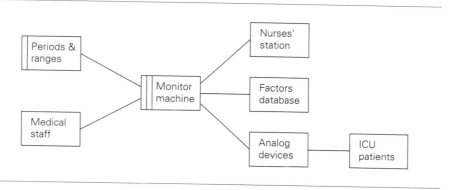

Patient monitoring: context diagram

The rectangles represent domains, and the lines represent interfaces between them. Look first at the domains. The rectangle with a double vertical stripe is the machine. Every context diagram has exactly one machine domain. In this diagram it's called the monitor machine. The other rectangles represent problem domains. One of them, periods & ranges, has a single vertical stripe, indicating that it is a domain that you, the developer, must design. The other problem domains, with no stripe, are all given as parts of the problem world.

2.2.1 Physical domains

All the domains in the context diagram are physical. The context diagram identifies the parts of the world in which your customer will check for observable effects. It's not a conceptual graph, or a semantic net, or a map of notions and ideas. So we are thinking of all the domains in a very concrete way:

■ the *machine domain* is the computer, which you must design and build by creating its software. The physical machine is a general-purpose computer, specialised by the software;

■ a *designed domain* is the physical representation of some information, for example, on a magnetic stripe card, or on a tape or floppy disk or hard disk, or even on a screen or in printed output. You show the database and periods & ranges as domains in the context diagram because you are thinking of them as physically present in the form of their representations – probably on disk drives accessible to the monitor machine. Showing the periods & ranges as a designed domain in the context diagram means that you are free to design and specify its data structure and, to some extent, its data content;

■ a *given domain* is a problem domain whose properties are given, that is, you are not free to design the domain. In some cases you can affect its behaviour by designing the machine appropriately. For example, the nurses' station will display any notifications sent by the monitor machine. Some of the other given domains – for example, the ICU patients and the medical staff – can't be affected by the machine in this kind of way.

The context diagram shows the problem world as it will be when the machine is in operation. So 'given' doesn't mean 'already in existence when you start to consider the problem'.

Any questions?

Can a designed domain be a piece of mechanical or electronic equipment? For example, could the nurses' station be a designed domain?

No. Our subject is *software* development. There's a larger discipline – *computer-based system* engineering – that includes the selection, design and development of both software and all kinds of hardware. In this book we're regarding the hardware aspects of system engineering as outside our scope. If you want to do anything properly, you mustn't try to do everything. Barry Boehm has an interesting perspective on the relationship between hardware and software development: Barry W Boehm, *Unifying Software Engineering and Systems Engineering*, IEEE Computer, Volume 33, Number 3, pages 114–116, March 2000.

Why restrict the context diagram to physical domains? Wouldn't it be helpful to include conceptual domains, too?

Well, it's certainly sometimes tempting. For example, in the library administration problem you might be tempted to include domains such as loans and reservations and memberships along with the physical domains books, staff and members. Aren't loans, reservations and memberships 'out there' in the problem world? Aren't they parts of the problem? Shouldn't they be included?

No, they shouldn't. The context diagram locates the problem in the physical world, not in a conceptual space. We want to ground our problem analysis in observable physical phenomena: this will help to check whether we're really satisfying the requirements or not. These conceptual domains of the library are not additional parts of the problem context, they are simply what the members and staff do, and what happens to the books, looked at in a rather different way.

'Membership' is just another way of talking about the events in which a person enrols in the library ('the membership is created') and later, perhaps, resigns ('the membership is terminated'), and maybe some other events in between ('the membership is suspended'). 'Reservation' is just another way of talking about the events in which a member reserves a book ('the reservation is created') and later either borrows it ('the reservation is fulfilled') or unreserves it ('the reservation is cancelled'). We'll see in a later chapter how to deal with concepts of this kind in a concrete way.

Surely, if you don't have conceptual domains, the approach can't work well for problems, like factorising large integers, in which the whole problem world is conceptual and intangible?

That's true. This is not a good approach for that kind of problem. We'll come back to the limitations of the approach in the final chapter.

2.1.2 Interfaces of shared phenomena

The domains are physical, and the interfaces between them are physical. They are also direct. Don't think of an interface as a queue or pipe or stream of messages flowing between the domains: instead, think of events and states and values as being shared between the connected domains. Each interface is an interface of *shared phenomena*.

For example, the interface between the machine and the nurses' station consists of shared *notify* events. The machine can cause a *notify* event, and both the machine and the nurses' station then participate in this same event. The participation in a shared event is like a hammer hitting a nail: there's only one event, and the hammer and the nail both take part in it simultaneously. In the interface between the machine and the analog devices, an analog device can set a value in a digital register shared with the machine. The machine can inspect this value directly because it is shared. An ICU patient has a certain skin resistance: that is a state shared with an attached analog device. There is no notion of patients sending messages to analog devices, or analog devices sending messages to the machine. In a shared state or value, both of the sharing participants can see the state or value, but only one of them can change it.

We'll come back to the subject of domain interfaces later in this chapter. Then we'll discuss the idea of shared events, states and values in a little more detail, and see how to indicate the content of each interface in the context diagram.

Any questions?

Doesn't the idea of shared phenomena – especially shared states and values – break the rules of encapsulation?

That depends on what you mean by encapsulation. If you mean 'hiding what's inside', then shared phenomena break no rules: the phenomena that are shared are not inside, by definition.

If you mean 'communicating only by method calls', then shared states and values do break the rule. But encapsulation in this sense is just a style – a widely adopted style – of object-oriented programming. There's no reason to adhere to such a rule in problem analysis. The world is not object-oriented, and you are describing the world. You can't deal with it properly if you insist on treating it as a collection of objects communicating by method calls. Encapsulation is a great idea, but it's strictly for programming.

2.2   The context diagram bounds the problem

The context diagram lays the foundation for structuring and analysing the problem by showing all the domains and interfaces that you must take into account. As you would expect, there's a circular relationship between the problem and its context. You can't decide the context without having a clear overview of the problem. You can't have much idea of the problem without knowing where it's located in the world. So in practice you must work iteratively. You include a particular domain in the context diagram; that leads you to realise that there's an aspect of the problem requirement that you hadn't considered; reconsidering the problem requirement leads you to recognise another domain to be taken into account. And so on.

Taking domains and interfaces into account means finding out about them, describing them, and reasoning about them. Showing a domain as a designed domain means that you will have the responsibility for doing the design work and the freedom that comes from being able to make design decisions. For a given domain you won't have that freedom, and your responsibility will just be to investigate and describe, rather than design. Sometimes you have to describe domain properties and behaviour that the machine must ensure – such as the appearance of notifications at the nurses' station – sometimes you have to describe behaviour and properties that are entirely independent of the machine – such as the physiology of the ICU patients. That's an important distinction. We'll return to it in a later chapter.

The context diagram locates the problem within quite an exact boundary. If you leave something out of the context diagram, you are leaving it out of the problem –

deciding that it will play no part in your work. You will never consider it, so it won't affect the outcome. If you include something, you are undertaking to give it serious attention and effort. So it's important to think carefully about the diagram, and to question the decisions it expresses.

2.2.1 The database domain

Let's start with the database. We have shown the database as a given domain. Perhaps we are regarding it as given because we have interpreted the statement 'the program reads these factors on a periodic basis ... and stores the factors in a database' to mean that the database is intended to provide information to other systems, and that its design is not our responsibility. Just as you can expect to discover the predefined properties of the nurses' station and the analog devices, so you will expect to discover the predefined properties of the database domain. If that expectation is wrong, and you must in fact design the database yourself, you need to know very soon.

The database as a designed domain

Suppose that you discover that you have made a mistake. The database should have been a designed domain: it is part of your problem task to design it. Will it be enough just to put a stripe on the rectangle representing the domain?

No, certainly not. If you are free to design the database you must ask what it is for. Perhaps its purpose is to provide information to other systems, but the developers of the other systems are giving you the task of designing it. If this answer is right, then the context diagram is definitely wrong, even after we have added the stripe on the rectangle. You can't design the database without knowing and taking into proper account the ways in which those other systems will use the database. What information will they want from it? How will they access it? Clearly, the other systems contribute some of the requirements to our problem. So they should appear in our context diagram.

Here is the relevant context diagram fragment, suitably altered:

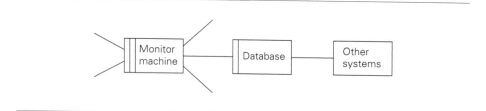

Patient monitoring: modified context diagram – 1

Excluding the database domain

But this may be all wrong. We may have made a very different mistake. We may discover that we are indeed free to design the database, but that it is not used by any other system. The statement 'the program reads these factors on a periodic basis ... and stores the factors in a database' was just a helpful suggestion from someone who thought that a database would obviously be necessary to solve the patient monitoring problem. How else, they thought, could the monitoring work?

If this is the case, you don't want the database domain in the context diagram at all. It's purely internal to the solution, not a necessary part of the problem. The decision to use, or not to use, a database, isn't one you should make now in drawing the context diagram. You should leave it to a later stage, when you come to structure the problem into subproblems. At that stage you may perhaps decide to introduce some kind of model domain, which may perhaps be properly called a database. Or you may not. But you don't want to decide now, and you don't want the database domain in the context diagram.

2.2.2   The medical staff and the periods and ranges domains

We have shown periods & ranges as a designed domain, and we have also shown the medical staff as a given domain. Do you need them both? Perhaps just one would be enough. Perhaps you don't really need either of them.

The medical staff

Let's start by supposing that you leave them both out. Then the context diagram (if you have decided to leave out the database) would look like this:

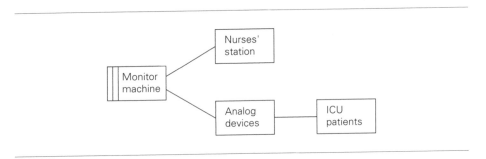

Patient monitoring: modified context diagram – 2

This would be fine if the monitoring was completely standard for all patients: the same vital factors, the same periods and the same ranges for everyone. These fixed monitoring rules would be part of the requirement. But the monitoring is not fixed. The periods and ranges are specified separately for each patient, and their current values must govern the behaviour of the monitor machine. Where can these values come from? There's nothing in this diagram that could originate them and make them available to the machine.

What about the nurses' station? It can't originate them, but it could act as the device through which they are entered into the system. If that's the case, you'll still need to show the medical staff: entry of the periods & ranges will be determined by their behaviour as users of the nurses' station. With the medical staff using the nurses' station, the context diagram will now look like this:

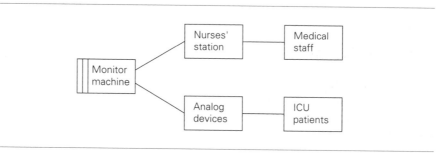

Patient monitoring: modified context diagram – 3

The medical staff domain now has no direct interface to the monitor machine. Its only direct interface is to the nurses' station; that interface essentially consists of events in which the medical staff enter period & range specifications on the keyboard at the nurses' station.

Medical staff and periods & ranges

What about the periods & ranges domain itself? If you have included the medical staff, either in this newly modified diagram or in the original diagram, do you also need to show the periods & ranges as a separate domain? This is a slightly tricky question. Here are the arguments:

- you should leave out the periods & ranges domain. You may need to introduce it later, in the problem structuring, just as you may need to introduce the database domain. But it's purely internal to the solution. In principle, the periods & ranges aspect of the problem can be stated entirely in terms of the behaviour of the medical staff: 'If the most recent event for this patient's temperature monitoring was that one of the medical staff specified . . .', and so on;

- you should include the periods & ranges domain. Leaving it out may be all right in principle, but it's horribly clumsy in practice. You'll often need to mention the currently specified periods & ranges when you talk about the requirements for monitoring. It will be ridiculously inconvenient to be forced to do all that in terms of the most recent behaviour of the medical staff. Including the periods & ranges domain will be much more convenient, even if it is, strictly, a part of the solution rather than a part of the problem.

If you want to be a purist about your context diagrams, you could leave it out. The argument for purity is that any impurity is the thin end of the wedge. If you can include a domain like the periods & ranges, surely you can include any other part of the solution that takes your fancy? Why not a list of the currently monitored patients? Or a list of the analog devices that have failed but have not yet been replaced? What about a list of the analog devices that haven't yet failed, with the time of the next check due for each one? Even if you're not a purist, you can probably see that these are definitely parts of possible solutions, not parts of the problem. You may need to introduce them at a later stage, but surely not now.

Should you be a purist? You have to use your judgement here, as in many other matters. We'll come back to the general question later in the book, when we talk about pedantry and mastery, in the last chapter. But in this particular case, purity looks more like pedantry than mastery. We'll include the periods & ranges.

Periods and ranges only

Finally, you can ask whether it makes sense to leave out the medical staff, and include only the periods & ranges domain. The question here is whether the activity of the medical staff in specifying the periods & ranges is a part of the problem world or not. The answer must definitely be: Yes. The values in the periods & ranges will certainly change – at the very least because the population of patients being monitored is changing. It's certainly not a good idea to regard the periods & ranges domain as changing spontaneously. The changes will be made by the medical staff. So the medical staff must appear in the problem context.

But they don't need to use the keyboard at the nurses' station as their data input device. We'll assume that they can enter their specifications of periods and ranges at a keyboard and screen directly attached to the monitor machine. So the final version of our context diagram will be the original version, except that we'll leave out the database domain.

2.2.3 The ICU patients domain

Finally, do you really need to include the ICU patients domain? After all, the machine is connected only to the analog devices, not to the patients.

By now, I hope you're very surprised at this question. Of course you need to include the ICU patients: they are what the whole problem is about. The problem goes deeper into the world than the analog devices. There's a chain of causality that runs all the way from a patient's vital factor to a value in a register shared by an analog device and the machine. In the case of a patient's pulse rate, it looks something like this:

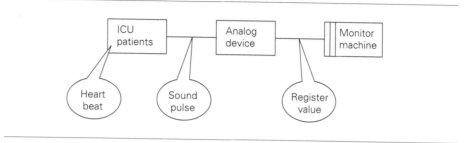

Chain of causality: patient – analog device – monitor machine

The requirement is to monitor the patient's vital factors; in this case, that means the heartbeat. The physiology of the ICU patient determines how frequently the heart can beat, and how each heartbeat is manifested as a short pulse of sound detectable by the right kind of analog device. The properties of the analog device determine how a counted sequence of detected sound pulses gives rise to a value in a register shared with the monitor machine. The central requirement in the problem is to monitor the heartbeat – not the sound pulses or the register values. You won't be able to talk about this requirement at all if you don't include the ICU patients domain.

2.3 The real problem

Over the past 50 years, we software developers have built up a reputation for solving the wrong problem. We don't listen hard enough to what our customers say. We don't take the trouble to understand their world well enough. We don't look behind what they say, and interpret what they really mean, or what they ought to be saying. We don't solve the *real problem*, which lies behind the superficial problem that they tell us about.

Well, there's some truth in all this, but it's important not to get carried away. In particular, it's important to resist two temptations. One is to generalise the problem context, and abstract away the specific details of the customer's world. The other is to generalise the requirement, to keep asking 'Why?', to try to get at the 'real problem' behind the problem the customer is talking about. Here's an example.

Zoo turnstile problem

Our customer is the visitor admissions manager of a private zoo. The zoo has bought a small turnstile system, consisting of a rotating barrier and a coin-accepting device, that can be connected to two ports of a small computer. Our job is to build the software to operate the turnstile system. The requirement is, essentially, in two parts. First, no visitor should be able to enter the zoo without having paid the entry price (which is two coins). Second, any visitor who has paid the two coins should be allowed to enter.

The obvious context diagram looks something like this:

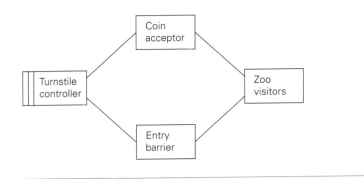

Zoo turnstile: context diagram

Generalising the problem context

The first danger is generalising the problem context and abstracting away the realities of the customer's world. The real aim is to collect entrance fees from visitors. The coin acceptor is just an implementation, which we should ignore. Would a credit card device be better? What about pre-payment by post, or on the web? We might question the whole idea of using a turnstile. Perhaps an escalator would work better? There will be an attendant near the gate. Would it not be better for the attendant to collect the entrance fee from each visitor? This personal service would be more attractive than the harsh impersonality of the turnstile. If you think like this, you're treating the turnstile and the coin acceptor as obstacles to your understanding of the true, more abstract, problem. It's a bad mistake.

Generalising the problem requirement

The second danger is to look behind the problem that's given, and to keep asking: Why? Software development always serves a human purpose, and that purpose can always be subsumed in a larger purpose. Why is the zoo collecting entrance fees at all? Because the owners want to raise revenue? Perhaps it would be better to follow the lead of some successful web businesses and let the visitors enter free, and collect revenue from advertisement hoardings placed on the animals' cages. Perhaps a zoo with free admission could form the basis of a very profitable television series. But why do they want to raise revenue? Is it to achieve a return on their investment? Perhaps they could get a higher return by demolishing the zoo and using the site for an expensive residential development. But is return on investment really the goal? Are we not all really pursuing happiness? Would the owners not be happier living a less materialistic life altogether? Why not make reservations for them at a spiritual retreat? This way madness lies.

2.3.1   The customer

There is no stopping place in this progression towards 'the real problem' unless you can anchor yourself in something reasonably firm. The firmest anchorage is with your customer.

Your customer is the visitor admissions manager of the zoo, and in that role has certain limited authority and responsibilities. Most of our imaginary questionings raise issues that lie far beyond those limits. It is no part of the admissions manager's job to reorganise the zoo's owners' lives on a more spiritual basis, or to move them into the real estate business, or even to abolish zoo entrance fees. And the reduced possibilities that then remain don't include scrapping the expensive new turnstile equipment: the visitor admissions manager has no authority to write off such an investment. So the context diagram is probably just about right, after all. A safe anchorage.

The zoo example is playful, of course. And most software developments don't have a single, easily identified person who is the customer for the problem solution. But the fundamental point remains valid. Even if your customer is purely notional – for example, the management committee that is your project's *sponsor,* or that scattered group of people who are sometimes called the *stakeholders* – you can still usefully ask yourself a vital question: Where are the limits of their combined authority and responsibility? And when you are in doubt about the location and scope of the problem, use those limits as a touchstone.

The problem requirements must not be too small in relation to the customer's responsibilities. That places a lower bound on the domains that *must* appear in its context diagram. The visitor admissions manager is not just responsible for the turnstile, but also for the way the zoo visitors are treated when they are trying to get into the zoo. How you solve the turnstile problem will certainly affect that treatment. So the zoo visitors must appear in your context diagram. And the customer's authority limits the scope of what the machine may legitimately be designed to do and on what assumptions: it places an upper bound on the domains that *may* appear in the problem context and be affected by the machine. If you're thinking of making the machine unlock the lions' cages when there are no visitors in the zoo, you have stepped outside your proper bounds. The visitor admissions manager has no authority to affect the zoo animals. Lions' cages should definitely not appear in your context diagram.

Here's the conclusion. When you are thinking of generalising, abstracting or extending the problem context or requirements, you should ask yourself: Given who the customer is, must this requirement be in scope? Can it be in scope? And what are the consequences for the context diagram?

2.3.2   How far into the world?

Identifying the customer's authority and responsibility can help you to avoid broadening the problem too far. But it can also help to avoid narrowing it too much. We included the zoo visitors domain in the context diagram for the zoo turnstile problem because the customer is responsible for visitor admissions, not just for turnstile operations. By introducing the zoo visitors into the problem, you are undertaking to study how they behave. That could save you from a serious error in your software development.

Here's how. At first sight you would expect each visitor to place two coins in the coin acceptor and then to pass through the turnstile. The sequence of events would then be:

> coin, coin, pass, coin, coin, pass, coin, coin, pass, coin, coin, pass, . . .

If the coin acceptor is very close to the barrier, this seems quite plausible. Each visitor steps up to the barrier, puts the coins in the acceptor, and passes through. You could develop your machine to enforce this sequence. But some visitors may be a little impatient, especially when the zoo is crowded or closing time is approaching. An impatient visitor may try to hurry things along a little by putting her coins in while the visitor in front has not yet passed through the barrier. And, now that we come to think of it, it's quite likely that a schoolteacher bringing 20 children to the zoo would stand at the coin acceptor putting in 40 coins as fast as possible while the children streamed through the barrier. The sequence of events might then be:

> coin, coin, coin, pass, coin, coin, coin, coin, pass, pass, coin, coin, coin, pass, . . .

The machine you need must allow this sequence too.

Without the zoo visitors domain you might perhaps think of these possibilities spontaneously, or the customer might tell you. But by putting the zoo visitors domain into the context diagram you make your development process more reliable: you impose on yourself a definite and explicit obligation to think about and describe the visitors' possible behaviour, and to analyse its consequences.

Any questions?

Do we really want to 'anchor ourselves' by the customer's responsibilities and authority? Perhaps as ethical software developers we have a responsibility to suggest that the spiritual life is preferable to the materialistic life?

If you think so, perhaps you have. But that would be in your capacity as the customer's friend and confidant, not in your capacity as a software developer.

I'm absolutely sure that I would think about the zoo visitors anyway, without putting them into the context diagram.

Of course you would. But then again, there are many software developers who might sometimes forget. This section is for them.

Will we make a model of the zoo visitors in our solution to the zoo turnstile problem?

No. Just a description. Not everything worth thinking about has to result in a piece of program text or a designed domain. And conversely, the fact that there will be no model of the visitors doesn't mean that you don't have to describe them in your problem analysis.

2.4 Domain interfaces

Domains communicate or interact only at the direct interfaces shown in the context diagram. Each direct interface is a *set* of *shared phenomena* – that is, a set of shared events, states and values. You show the sets of shared phenomena on the context diagram by writing set identifiers on the lines and giving an annotation for each identifier. Here's the zoo turnstile diagram with these annotations:

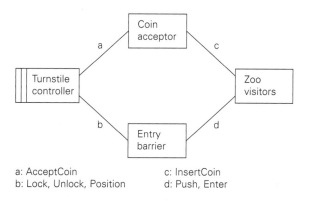

Zoo turnstile: annotated context diagram

Set *c* is *InsertCoin* events shared by the coin acceptor and the zoo visitors. Set *a* is just *AcceptCoin* events, in which the coin acceptor accepts a coin previously inserted by a zoo visitor. These events are shared by the coin acceptor and the turnstile controller. Set *d* consists of two kinds of shared event: *Push* and *Enter*. The barrier is constrained by a hydraulic mechanism. To get into the zoo, a visitor first pushes on the barrier: this is a *Push* event. Then, the barrier continues rotating until it reaches its home position, gently causing the visitor to *Enter* the zoo. Finally, in set *b* the turnstile controller can cause *Lock* and *Unlock* events, and can sense the current *Position* of the rotating barrier, which is a shared state.

Here's another example. Our current version of the patient monitoring context diagram, after annotation, is something like this:

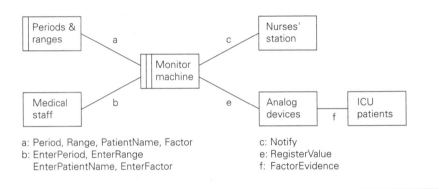

a: Period, Range, PatientName, Factor
b: EnterPeriod, EnterRange
   EnterPatientName, EnterFactor

c: Notify
e: RegisterValue
f: FactorEvidence

Patient monitoring annotated context diagram

Set *a* is shared values of *Period, Range, PatientName* and *Factor*. Set *b* is data entry events caused by the medical staff and shared by the machine. In set *a* the traffic runs in both directions: during creation and editing of the periods & ranges domain the values are determined by the monitor machine; during monitoring they are determined by the periods & ranges domain.

The analog devices convert *FactorEvidence*, such as heartbeat sound pulses, in set *f*, into *RegisterValues* shared with the monitor machine in set *e*. Finally, the monitor machine causes *Notify* events in set *c*, shared with the nurses' station.

The annotations shown here on the context diagram are scarcely more than hints and vague reminders. We will have to be much more careful and exact about the interfaces than this. In particular, we must pay a lot of attention to two questions about any shared phenomena. First, exactly what is shared between the connected domains? And second, which of the sharing domains controls the occurrences of events, or the changes in states, or the determination of values? We'll be more careful in future. But not just yet.

2.4.1 Shared phenomena are abstractions

Even with this rather vague way of talking about shared phenomena it's clear that shared events and states and values are *abstractions*, in which a lot of messy detail has been ignored. Whether it's right to make a particular abstraction to a shared phenomenon always depends on the requirements of the problem and your current purpose in the development work.

One form of abstraction is simply omitting properties of the shared phenomenon that you think are not relevant for the purpose in hand. For example, the *Notify* event, in which the monitor machine causes a notification of a failed analog device or a patient in a dangerous condition, must obviously be associated with some values that will convey the appropriate information to the nurse, but we said nothing about those values in the annotation.

Another, more important, form of abstraction is to treat a complex episode of interaction as an instantaneous event. For example, *InsertCoin* is an event shared between a zoo visitor and the coin acceptor. But on closer inspection you can see that the movement of the coin into the slot, pushing back a guard bar and activating the mechanism of the acceptor, and then passing through the acceptor's internal path, is far from instantaneous. If you were designing the acceptor mechanism, you certainly couldn't regard all this as a simple shared event. You would need to regard these episodes as the chief topic of your work, and their complexities would be your main concern. In the zoo turnstile problem, it's enough to see them as instantaneous events.

In the same way, we treated the interactions between the medical staff and the monitoring machine as consisting simply of the data entry events for *Period*, *Range*, *PatientName* and *Factor* values determined by the medical staff. But the mechanism for sharing these events and conveying the values will be based on the user interface of the data entry and editing program used by the medical staff. The events occur in elaborate dialogues in which the values are selected or constructed, and passed across. For our present purpose, these elaborate dialogues are not important: we boil them down to what we are now regarding as their distilled essence – the data entry events and the values eventually conveyed.

There are two kinds of shared event. In a *WhiteMove* event, White makes a move and sends the postcard, which Black receives; in a *BlackMove* event, Black makes a move and sends the postcard, which White receives. You are regarding each event as atomic and instantaneous, although in reality it may take as long as several days. That's reasonable because in the chess game problem, unlike the retail accounts problem, nothing significant can happen while the card is in transit. The intended recipient is next to play, but does not yet know the move that the sender has already made, and therefore doesn't know the position and can't make any move in return. The sender, similarly, doesn't know what move the recipient will make, and so can't make any further move.

2.4.4 When a connection domain can't be ignored

The general rule for including a connection domain is clear: if it materially affects the problem include it; if it doesn't, don't. Most of the ways a connection domain can materially affect a problem are obvious. Here are some of them.

Requirements about a connection domain

First, the connection domain may itself be the subject of a significant part of the problem requirement. In the patient monitoring problem, one of the explicit requirements is to notify the nurses' station if an analog device fails. If the analog devices don't appear in your context diagram, you won't be able to talk about this requirement at all. So you certainly won't be able to consider how to satisfy it.

Delayed transmission in a connection domain

The connection domain can affect a problem by introducing delays that can't be ignored. That happened in the retail accounting problem. In exactly the same way, you might need to include the Post Office after all in a more elaborate version of the postal chess problem. Suppose that the players want to keep account of thinking time, rather as is done in face-to-face chess by using a chess clock. Each player has a clock. At any time during the game, the clock belonging to the player whose turn it is to move is running, and the other is stopped. So each clock measures out the total time its owner has spent thinking while the other player is waiting. In postal chess neither player's clock should be running while the card is in the post. But postal delays are not uniform: it's not at all certain that a card posted by White to Black will take exactly as long in the post as a card posted by Black to White. So to measure thinking times fairly you must take separate account of the time while the card is in the care of the Post Office. That can only be done by recognising that posting and delivering the card are distinct events, not the same event; the Post Office is the unavoidable connection domain that relates them to each other.

Unreliable transmission by a connection domain

Another possible effect of a connection domain is unreliability. Even if there were no requirement in the patient monitoring problem to notify failures of analog devices, you would still need to include them as a connection domain. If you left them out you would be assuming that the monitoring machine shares directly the phenomena that form the external evidence of patients' vital factors. That is, you would be assuming an entirely reliable link between the patients' states and the values accessible to the machine. Ignoring the unreliability of the analog devices in this way would be unacceptable because this is a safety-critical problem. You must include them.

Conversion of phenomena by a connection domain
Finally, a connection domain may be essential to the context diagram because it converts between phenomena of one kind and phenomena of another kind. Then you must include it even if the conversion is entirely reliable with no significant delay. Look at this problem:

Checking faces

A secure door is to be controlled by a computer that recognises facial features. The face of each successive person desiring admission is captured in a video stream, and the features are compared with entries in a database of the features of people who have been cleared for entry.

Here is a simplified version of the context diagram:

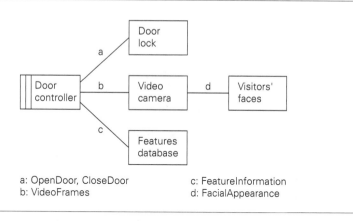

a: OpenDoor, CloseDoor   c: FeatureInformation
b: VideoFrames   d: FacialAppearance

Checking faces: context diagram

The video camera domain converts the facial appearance of a prospective visitor, captured in phenomenon *d*, to one or more digital video frames, which are shared in set *b* with the door controller. The door controller machine examines these video frames and tries to interpret them in terms of human facial features, which it then compares with *FeatureInformation* values in the features database. The conversion from the analogue *FacialAppearance* in *d* to the digitised *VideoFrames* in *b* makes solution potentially feasible. At the same time it gives the problem some of its particular character: the relationship between the facial appearance of a human being, seen from various angles, and the resulting digital images is an essential aspect of the problem. You can't capture it without including the video camera domain in the context diagram.

Any questions?

Are domain interfaces like interfaces in Java or a specification language like VDM, or UML?

No. Java is a programming language, it is not for describing the world. VDM is a specification language, but it's strongly focused on describing the machine rather than the problem that it solves.

A UML interface, like a Java interface, specifies a service as a set of *operations* provided by an object class or a program component, and invoked by users of the service. So it's an asymmetrical interface: it describes interactions between a *user*, who invokes, and a *server*, who is invoked. If the server invokes some operation of another server, that's part of another interface. Quite different from a domain interface. Interfaces in programming and specification languages are almost invariably *asymmetrical*: one side of the interface calls, the other is called.

Domain interfaces are, in general, *symmetrical* in the sense that each domain may control some of the shared phenomena of the interface. When you ignore the Post Office in the postal chess game, the interface between White and Black consists of WhiteMoves, controlled by White, and BlackMoves, controlled by Black. In the interface between the turnstile controller and the entry barrier, Lock and Unlock events are controlled by the controller, but the Position state is controlled by the barrier.

You can read about Java and VDM and UML in:

Gary Cornell and Cay S Horstman, *Core Java*, Prentice Hall, Sunsoft Press, 1996.

Cliff Jones, *Systematic Software Development Using VDM*, Prentice Hall International, 2nd Edition, 1990.

James Rumbaugh, Ivar Jacobson and Grady Booch, *The Unified Modeling Language Reference Manual*, Addison-Wesley Longman, 1999.

Is 'control of shared phenomena' just the same as input and output?

No. Input and output are about the direction of data-flow. Control is about causality: which domain causes the event to occur, or the state to change? If data does flow in a shared phenomenon, control can be upstream or downstream of the flow. The data can be 'pushed' by the 'writer', or 'pulled' by the 'reader'.

Why don't you show control in the context diagram?

We will. We're coming to that in the next chapter.

2.5 Handling a larger context

Sometimes to get a larger context under control you need to impose a containment structure on its domains. The containment structure doesn't have any formal significance: it is merely a device to bring some temporary domain abstractions to bear, so that you can make a condensed context diagram in a case where there would otherwise be too many domains to handle comfortably in one diagram. Here's an example.

Home heating control

A home heating system uses hot water radiators. Each room has a temperature sensor and control knob, an infra-red occupancy sensor, one or more radiators, and one on-off computer-controlled radiator valve. Water is heated by an oil-burning furnace. Oil admitted through a valve is blown into the combustion chamber and ignited. There is a flame sensor, a fuel-flow sensor, a blower motor speed sensor, and a water temperature sensor. A pump circulates the water through the system. There is a control panel at which the controller can be commanded manually to turn the furnace on or off; the panel also provides a display that indicates the system state and any malfunction.

The computer must regulate the behaviour of the system to maintain room temperatures as set on the control knobs. For economy, the temperature of an unoccupied room should be 5 degrees below the knob setting. The system should use information from the occupancy sensors to anticipate room use, starting to raise the temperature 30 minutes before occupancy is expected.

Here's a context diagram with only three problem domains:

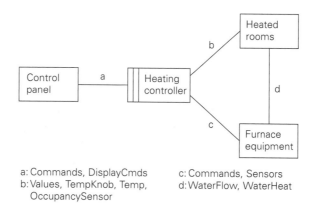

a: Commands, DisplayCmds
b: Values, TempKnob, Temp,
    OccupancySensor

c: Commands, Sensors
d: WaterFlow, WaterHeat

Home heating: condensed context diagram

We have divided the problem world into the three domains shown. Now, if you want to, you can give more detail of each one in a separate context diagram fragment. The furnace equipment domain, with its phenomena *c* and *d* shared with the heating controller machine and the heated rooms, looks like this:

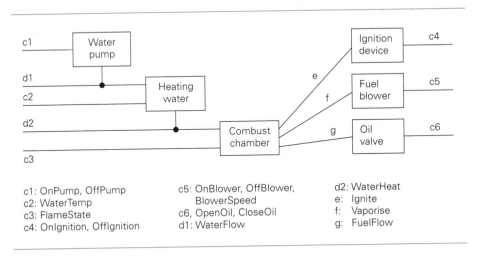

c1: OnPump, OffPump
c2: WaterTemp
c3: FlameState
c4: OnIgnition, OffIgnition

c5: OnBlower, OffBlower, BlowerSpeed
c6, OpenOil, CloseOil
d1: WaterFlow

d2: WaterHeat
e: Ignite
f: Vaporise
g: FuelFlow

Home heating: context diagram of furnace equipment domain

Think of this diagram as a fragment cut out of a larger context diagram. The only new notation is the dots on the lines marked *d1* and *d2*. The dots are needed because the phenomena of those interfaces are shared by three domains. The dot where the lines to the sharing domains meet is our notation for a 'hyperarc' connecting three or more domains. The *WaterFlow* state is shared by the heated rooms in the condensed diagram, and by the water pump and heating water in the detailed diagram. It is controlled by the water pump. The *WaterHeat* state is shared by the heated rooms in the condensed diagram, and by the heating water and combustion chamber in the detailed diagram; it is controlled by the combustion chamber.

The identifiers have been chosen in the obvious way. *c1* to *c5* are subsets of the phenomenon set *c* in the condensed diagram: commands to turn the water pump on and off; the sensed temperature of the heating water; the state of the flame in the combustion chamber; commands to turn the fuel blower motor on and off; and commands to open and close the oil valve. Similarly, *d1* and *d2* are the *WaterFlow* and *WaterHeat* subsets of set *d*. The additional phenomena *e*, *f* and *g*, which are internal to the furnace equipment, constitute the interfaces between the combustion chamber and the ignition device, fuel blower and oil valve, which all affect its state.

Nothing in *d, e, f* and *g* is directly shared with the heating controller machine. But you must represent and discuss these interface phenomena if you are to understand how the heating equipment works and how it must be controlled.

Any questions?

Where does the home heating control problem come from?

From a problem posed to a 1984 workshop on embedded systems. Statements and discussions of the problem can be found in:

S White, *Panel Problem: Software Controller for an Oil Hot Water Heating System* in Proceedings of COMPSAC 86, pages 276–277, October 1986.

Grady Booch, *Object Oriented Design with Applications*, Benjamin/Cummings, 1991.

Why do you show the shared phenomena d in home heating consisting of water flow and water heat? Aren't they private?

No, they are not private. They are important shared phenomena. The water flow and heat interface between the room and furnace equipment is not directly visible to the machine. But it is important because it captures an essential property of the problem context: to affect the temperatures of the heated rooms, the machine must affect the behaviour and state of the furnace equipment.

Why not show that the control panel affects the furnace by turning it off?

A context diagram shows only direct interfaces between domains. The connection between the control panel and the furnace is not direct. They share no phenomena. The machine is needed to connect them: in fact, this is an important function of the machine.

2.6   Machine domains

Machine domains in context diagrams raise two important questions. The first is: How much is implicitly included in the machine? The second is: How firm is our distinction between the machine and the problem domains?

2.6.1   What's in the machine?

As a general rule, we will assume that the computer has whatever ordinary hardware features are needed for our software. We will assume that it has a real-time clock if we need one; that it can respond to interrupts; that it has enough hard disk capacity for our purpose; and that it has a keyboard and screen and a printer. We'll usually – but not always – treat these peripheral devices as parts of the machine itself.

Here's an example. The requirement in the library administration problem includes the production of some simple printed outputs such as lending reports. Should you treat the printer as an implicit part of the machine, or as an explicit problem domain? Here are two alternative fragments of the context diagram for the problem:

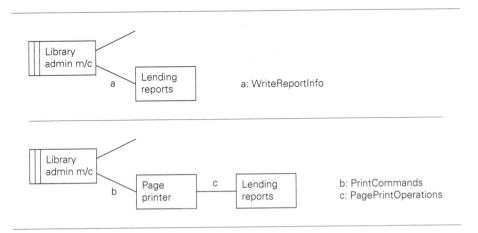

Library administration context diagram: alternative fragments

In the upper fragment the printer is an integral part of the machine; in the lower fragment it's a problem domain. Almost certainly you should prefer the upper fragment. If you choose the lower fragment you are committing yourself to examine the properties of the printer and to determine the relationship between the commands *b* issued by the machine and the page printing operations *c* that handle the paper and lay down the ink. That might be appropriate in another problem, say, scheduling and managing the intensive use of a very complex and expensive high-quality printer. But not here.

2.6.2   When a machine is a problem domain

The machine domain in a problem is always a computer. But a computer isn't always the machine domain. Sometimes a computer is the machine in one problem, but it's a problem domain in another problem.

Suppose, for example, that the monitor machine in the patient monitoring problem is thought to be overloaded. Before deciding whether to replace it or upgrade it, you want to monitor the current load. The question is: How much time does the machine spend in its idle state, and how is this time distributed over the 24 hours of each day? This is a second problem, alongside the original patient monitoring problem. Here are the two context diagrams:

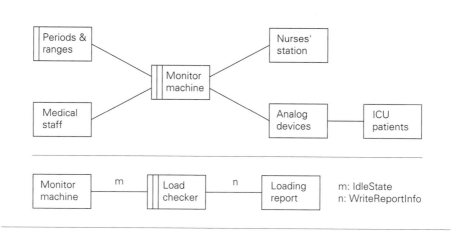

Two problem contexts: monitoring and load checking

The monitor machine, which is the machine domain in the patient monitoring problem, is a problem domain in the load checking problem. The load checking problem has its own machine domain: the load checker. Most probably, in the eventual implementation of the two problems, the monitor machine and the load checker will share one computer.

When we start to discuss problem decomposition, we'll see that one computer is usually shared among the machines that solve the subproblems. There's nothing surprising in that: it's standard to structure the solution of a problem into software parts – modules, objects, processes, components – that will be executed on the same computer.

Here's a more complex example.

System configuration display problem

A program is to be developed to display the configuration of currently installed components – BIOS, RAM and disk storage, peripheral devices, etc – in a PC. The program must also display the current assignment of IRQs and input-output ports.

> The program operates when the PC user enters a request at the keyboard. The user can select the information to be reported, and can terminate execution of the program.

At the context diagram level, there are two aspects of complexity in this problem:

- the machine you must build shares the computer with its chief problem domain – the PC of which the configuration is to be displayed. Let's call the machine to be built the system reporter, and the problem domain the configured PC;

- the screen on which the machine displays the configuration is also a device of the configured PC. You must deal explicitly with this sharing in your treatment of the problem. Let's call the shared device the system screen.

The context diagram is:

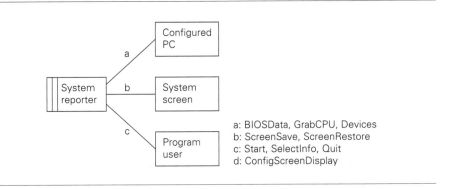

System configuration display: context diagram

The program user interacts with the system reporter machine by the shared phenomena *c* – starting the program, selecting the desired information (for example, IRQ settings or disk drive properties), and eventually selecting the *quit* option.

When the program is invoked, the screen has some pre-existing display from the program that was running at the point of invocation. Saving and restoring that display are the phenomena *b*.

The phenomena *a* shared by the system reporter machine and the configured PC allow the machine to grab and release the processor so that the state of the configured PC remains constant while its configuration is being reported. The machine can also interrogate the information stored in the BIOS and, if necessary, directly interrogate properties of devices such as modems and printers.

The screen display d that the user sees is important: it must be correctly related to the configured properties of the PC, and to the user commands c.

Any questions?

Can you have more than one machine in a context diagram?

Diagrammatically, the answer is No: there must be exactly one double-striped rectangle in each context diagram. But that double-striped rectangle can eventually be implemented by more than one computer. For example, the heating controller might eventually be implemented by three separate computers – one each to handle the control panel, the furnace equipment, and the scheduling of the room heating.

As you'll see in the next chapter, when we decompose a problem into subproblems, each subproblem has its own machine. Those subproblem machines may run on one computer or on many.

You've used the word 'requirement' a few times. What exactly does it mean?

It means the effects in the problem domain that your customer wants the machine to guarantee. The system configuration must be displayed on the screen; the nurses' station must be notified when an analog device fails; when the heated rooms are in use they must be at the temperatures set on their thermostats. That sort of thing. We'll say more about it in later chapters.

We seem to be drawing the context diagram before analysing the requirements. Is this the right way round?

Remember that you must explore the context and the requirements iteratively. We're not showing the iteration explicitly: it would make for rather tedious reading. Please remember, too, that we're not describing a fixed method, or a tightly controlled process. Keep this in mind – we won't repeat it in every chapter.

CHAPTER 3

Problems and subproblems

The context diagram answers the question: Where is the problem located? The problem diagram answers the question: What is the problem? It extends the context diagram by adding the requirement, and so provides a starting point for problem analysis. Realistic problems must be decomposed into a set of subproblems. The problems sketched in earlier chapters contain some intuitively obvious subproblem examples. Each subproblem is a projection of the complete problem, and its context is a projection of the complete context. Each subproblem must be simple enough to be shown in a problem diagram. In this chapter we are concentrating on the general nature of subproblems. In later chapters we'll discuss various recognised problem classes, and the technique and process of decomposition.

3.1 Problem diagrams

A context diagram shows the parts of the world where your problem and its solution machine are located, and the interfaces by which those parts are connected. But the problem itself – that is, the requirement – is not represented in the context diagram. The context diagram doesn't tell you anything about what the machine is required to achieve. It tells you only that the requirement is something about the domains shown in the problem context.

It's useful to show the problem requirement explicitly in a diagram. The requirement is always about the problem domains, so you need to show how it's related to those domains, and what roles the domains play in the problem. A diagram that shows these things is a *problem diagram*.

We'll start by looking at two very simple problems and their problem diagrams. Then, later in the chapter, we'll look at some more realistic problems and see how the ideas apply there. Not surprisingly, we'll find that they lead to a need for problem decomposition: for breaking a problem down into *subproblems*, each with its own problem diagram.

But first, the simple problems.

One-way traffic lights problem

When a section of road is being repaired, it's often necessary to enforce one-way traffic. Half of the road width is used for traffic and half for the repair work. The traffic is controlled by a pair of simple portable traffic light units like the pair shown here:

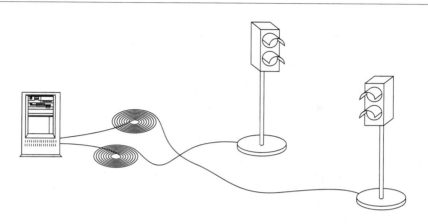

One-way traffic lights

The repairers put one unit at each end of the one-way section, and connect it to a small computer that controls the sequence of lights. Each unit has a Stop light and a Go light. The computer controls the lights by emitting RPulses and GPulses, to which the units respond by turning the lights on and off. The regime for the lights repeats a fixed cycle of four phases. First, for 50 seconds, both units show Stop; then, for 120 seconds, one unit shows Stop and the other Go; then for 50 seconds both show Stop again; then for 120 seconds the unit that previously showed Go shows Stop, and the other shows Go. Then the cycle is repeated.

3.1.1 A simple problem diagram

The problem diagram for this problem looks like this:

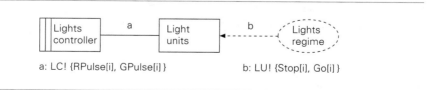

a: LC! {RPulse[i], GPulse[i] }   b: LU! {Stop[i], Go[i] }

One-way traffic lights: problem diagram

A problem diagram is like a context diagram, but a little fancier. The lights controller machine domain, the light units problem domain, and the interface connecting them are shown exactly as in a context diagram. The interface annotation is a little more informative than in a context diagram. As before, it shows the shared phenomena *RPulse[i]* and *GPulse[i]* of the interface. These are the pulse events by which the computer can affect the behaviour of the light units. It also shows, by the prefix LC!, that it's the lights controller (LC) that controls these shared events: it causes them to happen.

The requirement

The dashed oval represents the *requirement*. Here, the requirement is that the Stop and Go lights should be controlled according to a certain regime. The dashed arrow connecting the oval to the light units represents a *requirement reference*. It means that the requirement refers to certain phenomena of the light units domain. If you read the requirement description – which we have not yet formally written – you will come across references to 'Stop' and 'Go'. Because the dashed connection is an arrow and not just a simple line, it shows that the requirement reference is a *constraining reference* – the requirement doesn't just refer to the domain phenomena, it stipulates some desired relationships or behaviour involving them.

Requirement reference

A requirement reference isn't an interface of shared phenomena. The requirement itself is just a description produced in the course of development. It is not a domain. It has no physical realisation in the problem context, so it can't share phenomena with the machine or with any other domain. But we still represent and annotate it in the problem diagram in roughly the same way as we represent an interface. So the requirement reference here is represented as a set of phenomena *b* consisting of the *Stop[i]* and *Go[i]* light states of each light unit. The prefix LU! in the annotation indicates that the light units domain controls these states. If you want to think of a requirement reference as a kind of interface, imagine your customer observing the light units at this interface, checking to see whether the Stop and Go lights are showing according to the lights regime requirement.

Whenever the phenomena of an imaginary requirement interface are exactly the phenomena of a physical interface elsewhere in the diagram, you can use the same letter to mark both interfaces. It saves repetition in the annotations. So if the requirement were just to cause a particular pattern of pulse events, the problem diagram would look like this:

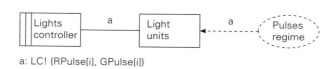

a: LC! {RPulse[i], GPulse[i]}

One-way traffic lights with required pulse events: problem diagram

The requirement pulses regime refers to the shared phenomena *a* of the interface between the lights controller and the light units. So the requirement reference is marked with the identifier *a*, and needs no separate annotation.

Any questions?

Isn't the requirement for the traffic lights problem just about the pulse events? Do we really need to refer to the Stop and Go phenomena at all?

We do. Because, as is almost always the case, the requirement is not at the interface between the machine and the problem domains. Your customer in the one-way traffic lights problem doesn't care about the pulse events. What matters is the sequence of Stop and Go light states.

If the identifiers – a, b and so on – marking the lines are really identifiers of sets of phenomena, could you write two identifiers on one line?

Yes, you could. It would mean that the phenomena of both sets are in the interface, or in the requirement reference.

Are the identifiers global to the whole development?

No. They are local to the problem diagram. But the names in the annotations referring to the phenomena – RPulse and GPulse, Stop and Go – are global.

Can phenomena be shared by three domains?

Yes. We saw one example in the home heating problem diagram in the last chapter. There's another example later in this chapter.

The phenomena of a requirement reference can be the same as the phenomena of an interface between domains. Can the phenomena of one interface between domains be the same as the phenomena of another interface between the same – or different – domains?

No, they can't. Each set of shared phenomena must be shown in just one interface in the diagram, and each interface must connect all the domains that share those phenomena. So if you have three domains A, B and C, there can be at most four interfaces between them:

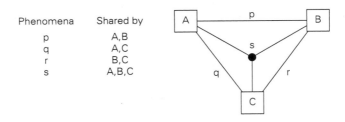

Phenomena	Shared by
p	A,B
q	A,C
r	B,C
s	A,B,C

All the interfaces of three domains

If the particular set *p* of phenomena is shared just by domain A and domain B, it belongs to the interface between those two domains and not to any other interface. The sets of phenomena *p, q, r* and *s* must be disjoint.

So there can never be two interfaces between the same pair or the same triple of domains?

That's right.

So if an interface is marked 'a', is it allowable to refer to it as 'the interface a'?

Yes, it is. There can't be another interface in the same diagram marked 'a'. But remember that there can be a requirement reference marked 'a'.

3.1.2 Another simple problem

Here's another little problem.

Odometer display problem

A microchip computer is required to control a digital electronic speedometer and odometer in a car. They look like this:

$$\boxed{36.5 \text{ km/h}}$$

$$\boxed{50436.9 \text{ kilometres}}$$

Speedometer and odometer displays

One of the car's rear wheels generates pulses as it rotates. The computer can detect these pulses and must use them to set the current speed and total number of miles travelled in the two visible counters on the car fascia. The underlying registers of the counters are shared by the computer and the visible display.

Here's the problem diagram:

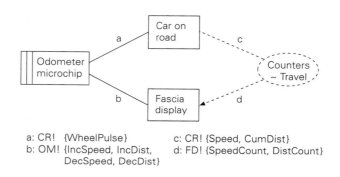

a: CR! {WheelPulse}   c: CR! {Speed, CumDist}
b: OM! {IncSpeed, IncDist,   d: FD! {SpeedCount, DistCount}
        DecSpeed, DecDist}

Odometer display: problem diagram

The car on the road (CR) controls the *WheelPulse* events, which are the phenomena *a* shared with the machine (the odometer microchip). The machine (OM) controls the *b* events *IncrementSpeed, IncrementDistance, DecrementSpeed* and *DecrementDistance*, which it shares with the fascia display device. The fascia display device (FD) contains the speed and distance counters, and changes their values *SpeedCount* and *DistCount* in response to the corresponding increment and decrement events.

Requirement reference and constraint

The requirement is called Counters~Travel. We'll often use the symbol '~' to suggest some kind of *correspondence* between two domains. So this is an appropriate name because the fascia counter values must correspond to the speed and distance travelled by the car. The requirement refers to the *Speed* and *CumulativeDistance* phenomena *c* controlled by the car on the road, and to the phenomena *d* which are the values of the *SpeedCount* and *DistanceCount* controlled by the fascia display and displayed on the fascia. It stipulates that the speed and distance values should be the current speed of the car, in kilometres per hour, and the cumulative distance it has travelled, in kilometres.

The requirement reference to phenomena *d* has an arrowhead, but the reference to *c* has none. As we saw before, the arrowhead indicates that the requirement doesn't just *refer* to the phenomena but *constrains* them. The requirement here constrains the behaviour of the fascia display, but it places no constraint on the behaviour of the car on the road. That means that you can't solve the problem by setting both counters to zero and permanently immobilising the car. The car can do what it likes, subject to its domain properties; the fascia counter values must correspond to whatever the car does.

Any questions?

It seems clear that the behaviour of the car on the road domain can't be constrained by the requirement. The annotations show that all its interface phenomena are controlled by the domain itself, so there is no causal chain by which the machine could possibly affect it. Is that right?

Yes. Absolutely right.

I notice that the control markings in the connection annotations all use two-letter abbreviations for the domain names. Is that a universal rule?

It's a handy convention. We'll always try to give each domain a name that has a natural two-letter abbreviation, different from all the other domains in the diagram.

Dashed lines seem to mean 'intangible' and solid lines 'physical'. Is that right?

Yes.

3.1.3 Simple problems

It wasn't hard to draw the problem diagrams for the one-way traffic lights problem and the odometer display problem because they are very simple. Here are the most important aspects of their simplicity:

- their requirements are simple: they correspond to intuitively recognisable purposes. The general sense of each requirement is easily captured in words. The traffic lights requirement is to make the light units behave in a certain way; the odometer requirement is to use the fascia display to present information about the movement of the car on the road;

- the interfaces are simple, too: it's easy to characterise the way the parts interact at each interface. At one interface in the traffic lights problem the lights controller controls the light units by causing pulse events; at the other – if you think of the requirement reference as an interface – the customer watches the Stop and Go lights. At one interface in the odometer problem the machine detects WheelPulses, and at another it drives the fascia display. At one requirement reference the customer is watching the behaviour of the car on the road; and at the other, checking that the fascia display numbers correspond correctly;

■ the *roles* played by the domains are also simple. The light units' behaviour is subject to control by the machine. The behaviour of the car on the road is subject to no control, but must be monitored by the machine; the fascia display is used to present information.

We'll see in later chapters that even simple problems can need very careful analysis. They can raise many concerns and difficulties that offer plenty of opportunity for going wrong. The idea of problem frames is to classify and analyse the common types of simple problem so that you can hope to recognise them when you meet them, to anticipate their concerns and difficulties, and to apply familiar and effective techniques to their solution.

3.1.4 Problem analysis and the problem diagram

The problem diagram provides a basis for problem analysis because it shows you what you are concerned with, and what you must describe and reason about if you are going to analyse the problem completely. The essential topics of your descriptions will be:

■ the *requirement* that the machine must be built to satisfy. The requirement is what your customer *would like* to be true in the problem domain. Its description is *optative* (it describes the *option* that the customer has chosen). Sometimes you already have an exact description of the requirement, sometimes not. The requirement for the one-way traffic lights – the description of the repeated cycle of four phases given in the problem introduction – is probably exact enough. Perhaps you just need to make it a little more formal. The requirement for the odometer display is not exact enough. If the car is travelling in reverse, what speed value should be shown? How should reverse travel affect the cumulative distance? Is reverse travel detectable? How should very low speeds be treated? What precision is required?

■ the *domain properties*. You need to investigate and describe the relevant properties of each problem domain. These descriptions are *indicative* – they indicate the objective truth about the domains, what's true regardless of the machine's behaviour. For the odometer display you'll need to investigate and describe both the car – how the WheelPulses are related, through the turning of the wheels, to the car's motion – and the fascia display – what numbers the counters can display, and how the fascia device changes them in response to increment and decrement events. For the light units, you'll need to investigate and describe how the Go and Stop lights respond to RPulses and GPulses;

■ the machine *specification*. Like the requirement, this is an *optative* description: it describes the machine's *desired* behaviour at its interfaces with the problem domains. For the lights controller this just means describing the timed sequence of RPulse[i] and GPulse[i] events it must produce. For the odometer microchip it means describing how it causes increment and decrement events in response to whatever WheelPulses it detects.

The importance of domain properties

The indicative domain properties are at the heart of your analysis. You are relying on the domain properties to bridge the gap between the *specification phenomena* that the machine can directly sense and cause, and the *requirement phenomena* that your customer is interested in. That's why it's so important to bring the domains and the requirement together in a problem diagram. Never believe that you know the domain properties because they are 'obvious'. Are you inclined to assume, in the one-way traffic lights problem, that a GPulse turns on the green light and an RPulse the red light? And that green is Go and red is Stop? If you make those assumptions, you're just guessing. You need to examine the light units, to talk to their designers, to read their technical manual.

At the end, you'll need to argue that your work has been successfully completed. That means showing that if the programmers build a machine that behaves according to your specification, the domain properties you have found and described will ensure that the customer's requirement is satisfied.

Of course, these are only general principles. They do hold for every kind of problem that we are considering in this book, but to be really useful they must be specialised for different kinds of problem. The work of analysis will vary with the kind of problem you're dealing with. We'll go into a lot more detail about requirements, domain properties and machine specifications in the next few chapters.

Any questions?

Where do the terms 'optative' and 'indicative' come from?

They are grammatical terms. Grammar is not very fashionable nowadays, so you may be more comfortable with the terms that Ben Kovitz suggests: *prescriptive* and *descriptive*.

Why not just use the term 'shall' that is commonly used in requirements?

Three reasons. First, because what's indicative or optative is a complete description, not just one sentence. It's a very bad idea to mix indicative and optative statements in the same description. Second, because you can't write 'shall' in a state-transition diagram or in any kind of graphical or tabular description. And third, because you often need to treat the same description as indicative in one subproblem and optative in another subproblem. You can't do that if you have written the distinction between them into the text of the description itself.

The traffic lights problem is ridiculously simple. Why are we bothering with such simple problems?

Because simple problems provide the best illustration of many important principles. Simple problems are often not quite as simple as they seem at first sight – and that's an important lesson in its own right. And because we want to structure realistically complex problems into simple problems. So it's a good idea to understand what a simple problem looks like.

So what are the domain properties of the traffic light units?

We'll describe them in the next chapter.

3.2   Realistic problems

Realistic problems are rarely simple. They are usually large and complicated. That makes them hard to understand, analyse and solve. If you try to draw a problem diagram for the patient monitoring problem, leaving out the annotations, it will look something like this:

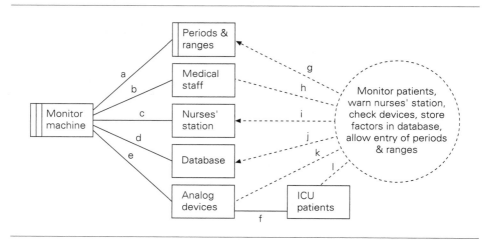

Patient monitoring: all-in-one problem diagram

Complexity of a realistic problem
This is not the problem diagram of a simple problem. The requirement is complex. It has several parts and aspects, and you certainly can't boil it down to any simple sentence that suggests its general content in a few words.

The references between the requirement and the problem domains are also complex. For example, look at the requirement reference g. It represents the requirement constraint that the periods & ranges data must be set according to the editing instructions h of the medical staff. That is why it has an arrowhead. But the same dashed line also represents the requirement reference indicating that the periods & ranges data must govern the monitoring of patients' vital factor phenomena l. This second requirement reference isn't a constraint on the periods & ranges data g, so from that point of view the reference g should have no arrowhead. The two requirement references are in conflict.

The complexity of the interfaces and references makes it hard to see the required relationships among the problem domains. Are the values j of the database domain required to correspond to the behaviour of the analog devices phenomena k? No: they are required to correspond only to the behaviour of the ICU patients phenomena l, monitored at the periods given in the periods & ranges domain. Are the values of the periods & ranges required to correspond to the behaviour of the ICU patients? No, they are not. Must the behaviour of the nurses' station phenomena i, where dangerous conditions are to be notified, be determined by the behaviour of the medical staff? No: it must be determined only by the analog devices – their failures are the phenomena k – and by the vital factors l of the ICU patients.

3.2.1 Decomposition

The key to mastering problem size and complexity is, of course, decomposition. You break down a given large and complex problem into a number of smaller and simpler *subproblems*. A good decomposition helps you not only to solve the problem but also to capture it, to describe it, to understand it, and to analyse it. But there's a catch. How can you choose a good decomposition? How can you know that the subproblems you identify are really any easier than the problem you started with? And, even if the subproblems are easier, how can you know that they will fit together smoothly and add up to the problem you started with?

Top-down functional decomposition

Of the many approaches to problem decomposition this is one of the oldest and worst. The basic idea is to arrange the functions in a hierarchy of several levels. At each level each function is decomposed into a number of functions at the next level, until a level is reached at which the functions are regarded as elementary.

This approach is bad because it takes no explicit account of the problem to be decomposed. If you're not already familiar with the problem, you're unlikely to achieve a good decomposition. Here's a small example of a bad decomposition. Suppose that you have to structure the problem:

Printing prime numbers
Print the prime numbers up to 1,000,000 in ascending order.

Here's the decomposition, in the form of a little program:

```
{ p := 2;
  while (p ≤ 1000000) {
  print p; p := nextPrime(p)
}}
```

What makes this decomposition very bad is that the subproblem of calculating *nextPrime(p)* – the next prime number after a given prime number *p* – is not only not easier than the original given problem, it's actually harder. The decomposition has made the job more difficult.

Use case decomposition
This is a fashionable approach. The basic idea is that the whole problem can be seen as one of building a machine to support a set of use cases. In each use case an *actor* interacts with the system and obtains an observable result of value. For example, some of the use cases for a banking system might be: draw cash, open new account, order new chequebook, and so on.

The use case view can work quite well when it makes sense to think of the machine as a facility offering discrete services that are used in clearly delimited episodes. Users obtain the services in short bouts of intensive interaction that constitute the use cases. The more independent the use cases are from each other, the better it works. Traditional telephone systems, where the idea of use cases originated, are like that. Each telephone call is a clearly defined short bout of interaction between the user and the system, and it's almost completely independent of every other telephone call.

But in many problems most of the requirement simply doesn't consist of use cases at all. The requirement is for a continuing interaction between the machine and the problem domains. What are the use cases in the patient monitoring problem? In the one-way traffic lights problem? In the home heating control problem? In the odometer display problem? Even if you can find some use cases here, they cover only a small part of the requirement.

3.2.2 Problem structuring

We're going to take the approach of decomposing the problem, along with the machine and problem domains, into subproblems of recognisable and familiar classes. The key to this approach is prior knowledge: knowledge of the problem classes; knowledge of what's involved in solving them; and knowledge of the concerns and difficulties that can arise for each problem class.

The ideal kind of prior knowledge is a deep knowledge of problems in the application area. You are best equipped to solve the library administration problem if you know all about libraries and have solved ten similar problems already in your career. To solve the patient monitoring problem, you need ideally to know all about medical monitoring. Then the problem facing you will be almost exactly like one you have solved before. You'll be able to say confidently: this is just another patient monitoring problem, with just another collection of analog device failures to be diagnosed and reported. I know how to do this. There are no significant new difficulties here.

But much software development must be done with more limited knowledge of the application and of earlier systems. Then you need a more general knowledge of the subproblem classes that occur frequently in almost every application area. You can decompose the patient monitoring problem with some confidence into subproblems that are familiar to you at this more general level. You'll be able to say: I didn't know about patient monitoring before, but having studied and analysed it I can now see that it's made up of these seven subproblems. Each of the seven is an instance, in the patient monitoring world, of a subproblem class that I have seen many times before in other contexts. If you know how to count apples, it's not such a big leap to solving a problem of counting oranges.

Subproblems

The familiar subproblem classes that we'll rely on in decomposition are defined by *problem frames*. Until we have established some frames and their characteristics it will be hard to say anything very specific about problem decomposition, so the next few chapters are devoted to problem frames. Then, in Chapter 10, Decomposition revisited, we will return to exploring the process of problem decomposition and show its application to a realistic example.

But even before we start our discussion of problem frames, we can make some general points here: about the nature of the decompositions; about some characteristics of the subproblems defined by frames; and about the problem structures that result.

■ *Subproblems are complete*. Regard each subproblem as a complete problem in its own right. It has its own problem diagram, with a machine, one or more problem domains, and a requirement. When you analyse each subproblem, assume that the other subproblems are solved. This helps you to avoid confusing each subproblem by considerations imported from other subproblems. Regarding the other subproblems as solved is the essential basis of any effective separation of concerns.

■ *Parallel structure*. Think of the subproblems as fitting primarily into a *parallel*, rather than a *hierarchical*, structure. The structure of subproblems isn't like the engineering bill of materials, in which products are composed of assemblies, assemblies of subassemblies, subassemblies of parts, parts of lower-level parts, and so on. It's much more like the colour separation familiar from printing. There's a cyan separation, a magenta separation, a yellow separation and a black separation. The four are superimposed to give the full picture.

To use a different, mathematical, metaphor familiar from database technology, each subproblem is a *projection* of the full problem. Its requirement is a projection of the full requirement; its machine is a projection of the full machine; its problem domains are projections of the full problem domains; and its interfaces are projections of the full interfaces.

■ *Concurrency*. Because of the parallel structure you must pay conscious attention to the relationships among subproblems and the ways in which they may interact. Often, you can understand this interaction as arising from the concurrent execution of two or more subproblem machines, with the problem domains acting as shared variables. But there are other forms of interaction too. You must give them all explicit consideration.

■ *Composite problem frames*. Because subproblem interactions are important, some of the problem frames we'll be discussing are composite frames. A composite frame defines a familiar problem class that has a familiar standard decomposition into elementary subproblems. The decomposition and the proper treatment of the resulting interactions are an integral part of the problem frame.

Composite problems are familiar from some everyday products that solve them. Ben Kovitz gives the nice example of the clock radio. It solves two problems: it turns a selected radio transmission into sound; it also continuously displays the current time and notifies you when a preset alarm time is reached. There's also an area of interaction: the clock alarm can be used to time the radio.

Coffee addicts can buy a gadget that combines a clock with a kettle and coffee pot. Before the preset alarm time is reached it boils the kettle and decants the water into the pot. Then, when the alarm goes off, your coffee is ready when you wake up. A tow truck combines some of the functions of a lifting crane with those of a truck. An answering machine combines functions of a telephone with those of an audio cassette recorder.

Any questions?

Where is the clock radio example discussed?

In Ben Kovitz, *Practical Software Requirements*, Manning, 1998. Kovitz also gives the example of the answering machine.

Isn't this approach very like design patterns?

Yes and no. Yes, because the patterns approach is also based on the idea of working in terms of things you are familiar with. No, because the patterns approach has been chiefly applied to object-oriented solutions rather than to problems.

But isn't there a lot about problem patterns in Martin Fowler's book?

You must mean Martin Fowler, *Analysis Patterns*, Addison-Wesley, 1996. It's a great book. And there's certainly a lot about problems in it. But there's also a strong focus on 'object modelling', by which Fowler means something that is more solution-oriented than most of its practitioners recognise. The term 'object modelling' can also be used in a more problem-oriented sense. For example, in some interesting work that you can read about in Daniel Jackson and Martin Rinard, *The Future of Software Analysis,* in *The Future of Software Engineering*, Anthony Finkelstein (ed), ACM Press, 2000.

Why not just model the problem domains and then fit the system function into the model?

By 'model the problem domains' here you presumably mean 'make a model in terms of objects that will be part of the software'. Chapter 1 explained why that's not at all the same thing as describing the problem domains. We'll come back to the subject of models and other problem domains in Chapter 7.

There's another difficulty, too. Making just one 'model' – or description – to serve all the requirements is very hard. It would have to be simultaneously all the models – or descriptions – you need for all the different subproblems. By choosing to do that you're effectively deciding not to decompose the problem at all.

If you assume, in dealing with one subproblem, that all the other subproblems are solved, does that mean that you're treating their optative descriptions as indicative?

Yes, definitely. That's a very good observation. Aren't you glad now that you didn't write those optative descriptions in terms of 'shall'?

3.3 Subproblem examples

In the rest of this chapter we'll sketch a few examples of subproblems. We'll identify them as parts of some of the larger problems we have already begun to consider. We'll show how the subproblems are represented in diagrams, and briefly discuss how you can see them as projections of the full problem – that is, of the larger problem being decomposed. We'll also pay a little attention to some potential interactions with other subproblems in the same decomposition.

We won't go into the subproblem requirements in any detail, but leave them mostly to the imagination. We'll also rely for now on the very vague and intuitive kind of subproblem familiarity with which we started this chapter. In the next chapter we'll begin to make these intuitions more precise by defining the basic familiar problem classes in problem frames.

3.3.1 Heating display

This is a subproblem from the home heating controller problem. The introductory description of the full problem included the sentence:

> *'There is a control panel at which the furnace can be turned on or off manually; the panel also provides a display that indicates the system state and any malfunction.'*

The subproblem will be to satisfy the requirement of driving the control panel display, indicating the system state and any malfunction. Intuitively, this seems to be a reasonably self-contained aspect of the full problem. It's some kind of reporting or information function. It doesn't interfere with the main business of controlling the heating equipment in the rooms and the furnace; it just requires a subproblem machine that looks to see what's going on and displays suitable indications on the control panel.

To picture the subproblem you have identified, you draw its problem diagram. Here's the problem diagram for the heating display subproblem:

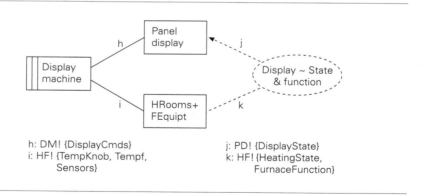

h: DM! {DisplayCmds}
i: HF! {TempKnob, Tempf, Sensors}

j: PD! {DisplayState}
k: HF! {HeatingState, FurnaceFunction}

Heating display: problem diagram

The subproblem machine is called the display machine. The subproblem domains are the panel display domain and the HRooms+FEquipt domain. The panel display domain is just the display part of the control panel domain from the full problem.

The HRooms+FEquipt domain is a combination of the heated rooms and furnace equipment domains from the full problem. For purposes of this subproblem there is no good reason to keep the heated rooms and the furnace equipment as two separate domains.

The subproblem requirement is named Display ~ State & function, giving a rough indication of its content. The requirement is to ensure that the display on the control panel corresponds in a stipulated way to the state and function of the HRooms+FEquipt domain. The requirement constrains the state and behaviour of the panel display domain: the control panel must show certain information – the *DisplayState* phenomena *i* – correctly related to the state phenomena *k* of the heated rooms (the *HeatingState*) and the furnace equipment (the *FurnaceFunction*). It doesn't constrain the *HeatingState* and *FurnaceFunction*: so far as the requirement of this subproblem is concerned, they can be anything whatsoever, subject to their domain properties.

A subproblem as a problem projection

When you decompose a problem into several subproblems you are creating several *projections* – which later on you will capture in descriptions – of the original problem and its machine and domains. The use of the word 'projection' here is the same as in relational databases: a projection of a relational table contains just the columns needed for some particular purpose. In the same way, the parts of each subproblem – the requirement, machine and problem domains – are projections of the parts of the full problem, and concern only the phenomena that are relevant to the subproblem.

Here's how the requirement, domains and interfaces of the subproblem are projections of those in the full problem. The projections, roughly stated, are:

- *requirement.* The full problem requirement includes monitoring room occupancy, controlling the furnace and room radiators, responding to manual commands entered at the control panel, and displaying the system state and functioning. The requirement in this subproblem is only the display aspect;

- *control panel.* The subproblem is concerned only with the *DisplayCmds* events and the *DisplayState*. The *Command* events, by which the heating controller can be commanded manually to turn the furnace on and off, are of no interest in the subproblem. So the projection of the control panel has been named 'panel display';

- *heated rooms and furnace equipment.* The subproblem is concerned only with sensing and interpreting the states of the rooms and the furnace, not with the commands by which the heating controller can operate the radiator valves and the furnace equipment. The two domains of the full problem have been combined to give the *union domain* HRooms+FEquipt in the subproblem. For purposes of the subproblem, the interactions between them are not of interest. It's more useful to treat them as a single domain about which information is needed;

■ *machine.* The display machine in the subproblem is a projection of the heating controller machine in the full problem. It displays the information required, but it does nothing else. It doesn't act on *Command* events; it doesn't shut down or start the furnace; it doesn't operate the valves and motors; it doesn't try to anticipate room usage. In a later stage of dealing with this subproblem you'll need to describe the behaviour of the display machine. That description will describe a projection of the behaviour of the heating controller machine.

Projection and partition

Thinking about subproblem domains as *projections* of the domains of the full problem is important because it's different from thinking of them as *partitions*. You can see the difference in this diagram:

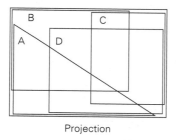

Projection

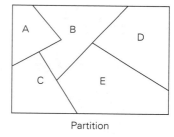

Partition

Projection and partition

On the left, the rectangular area is covered by four projections A, B, C and D. The projections overlap, so elements of the area can appear in more than one projection. When the rectangular area is partitioned, as on the right, each element of the area appears in exactly one partition.

When you decompose into projections, you will find that some of the domains and some of their phenomena will also appear in other subproblems. For example, the heating display subproblem machine detects the temp states – the room temperatures – because it must display them. The same states must be detected by the machine that controls the room heating. This overlapping of projections means that the information about one domain, and even one event class, is often distributed over several subproblems. In a partitioning, each phenomenon would appear in only one partition.

Any questions?

Are colour separations projections?

Yes. The cyan colour separation is a projection of the whole picture that includes only the parts that have cyan in their colouring.

Is the subproblem requirement really a projection of the full requirement? Isn't the full requirement really decomposed into partitions?

Well, you could look at it like that. In some ways the decomposition of the requirement itself is more like a partition than a projection: an optative description stated in one subproblem requirement wouldn't be stated again in another. But remember that requirement references in the subproblems can overlap: the same phenomena can appear in requirement references of different subproblems. They certainly don't form partitions.

3.3.2   Entering periods & ranges

Here's a second subproblem example, from the patient monitoring problem. The original full problem sketch was:

Patient monitoring problem

A patient-monitoring program is required for the intensive care unit (JCU) in a hospital. Each patient is monitored by an analog device which measures factors such as pulse, temperature, blood pressure, and skin resistance. The program reads these factors on a periodic basis (specified for each patient) and stores the factors in a database. For each patient, safe ranges for each factor are also specified by medical staff. If a factor falls outside a patient's safe range, or if an analog device fails, the nurses' station is notified.

The problem requires the medical staff to enter the periods and ranges for the patients. You can see that this is a reasonably self-contained aspect of the full problem. It's a familiar kind of data entry problem. The monitoring of the patients will eventually be affected by the values that the medical staff enter, but you don't need to consider those effects here. The problem diagram will be like this:

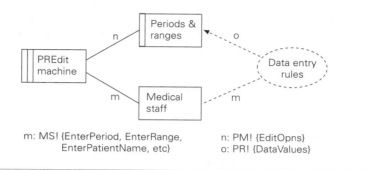

m: MS! {EnterPeriod, EnterRange,
    EnterPatientName, etc}

n: PM! {EditOpns}
o: PR! {DataValues}

Entering periods & ranges: subproblem diagram

We have called the subproblem machine the *PREdit machine*. The periods & ranges domain and the medical staff domain are as shown in the full problem context diagram. The other domains shown in the full context diagram – the patients, the analog devices, the nurses' station and the database – are all irrelevant to this subproblem, and do not appear here.

The medical staff control a set of events *m* – *EnterPeriod, EnterRange, EnterPatientName, etc* – in which they enter values of periods, ranges and patient names. The *etc* is a reminder that there will surely be other events for navigating around data already entered. The PREdit machine controls the *EditOpns* phenomena *n*. These are events, shared by the designed periods & ranges domain, which cause values of periods and ranges to be created and changed.

The subproblem requirement is named *data entry rules*. It stipulates what *Data Values*, the phenomena *o*, must result from any possible sequence of data entry events *m* that the medical staff may perform. Notice that the requirement refers directly to the phenomena *m* at the interface between the machine and the medical staff, but not directly to the phenomena *n* at the interface between the machine and the periods & ranges. The requirement constrains only the *DataValues* of the periods & ranges domain. From the point of view of the requirement, data entry by the medical staff is not constrained; the requirement stipulates only what the results must be.

Projections
The projection in this subproblem of the medical staff domain is an *identity* projection. An identity projection is a projection in which everything is included, so the result of the projection is identical to the original domain. The medical staff domain won't appear in any other subproblem because the medical staff play no part in the system except to specify the periods and ranges for monitoring. So everything to do with the medical staff domain is included here. That's not particularly uncommon. It happens whenever a domain appears in only one subproblem.

The periods & ranges domain projection is not an identity projection. Periods & ranges appears in two subproblems. It appears in this subproblem, where it is created and updated. It also appears in whatever other subproblem may use it for the monitoring itself. This problem needs both the *EditOpns*, which the PREdit machine controls in response to the activities of the medical staff, and the *DataValues*, which are referred to by the requirement because they are the required result of the editing. But the projection in the other subproblem, which uses the periods & ranges, is concerned only with accessing the *DataValues* to read and use them. So it doesn't need the *EditOpns* by which the values can be created and changed.

A subproblem interaction

There's a clear danger of undesirable interaction between the machine in this data entry subproblem and the machine in the subproblem that performs the monitoring. Think of the two machines as two concurrently running processes. Then the periods & ranges domain is a *shared variable*: one of the processes reads it and the other writes it. There is a possibility that the reading process may read one part of a piece of information before it has been updated and another part of the same piece of information after it has been updated. The two *processes* may combine to give nonsense, with disastrous results.

Do you have to do something about this interaction now, while you are considering the data entry subproblem? No, you don't. In any problem decomposition you must consider how the subproblems fit together, and how their solutions are to be combined to give a solution to the full problem. But for several reasons it's good to separate these concerns about subproblem interactions from the analysis of the individual subproblems. First, you want to see each subproblem as clearly as possible, without the complications that other subproblems may add. Second, you won't be able to see the interaction concern clearly until you have a good idea what the interacting subproblems are. And third, there are usually many ways of dealing with this and other kinds of subproblem interaction: you don't want to pick one prematurely before you can see the whole set of possibilities.

It's worth adding that separating the interaction concern from the analysis of the potentially interacting subproblems makes especially good sense because you are dealing with problems rather than with solutions. If the outcome of your work is a representation of software objects in some design notation, it's natural to think of it as a program that must be complete to be correct. Programs are not projections, and you can't add to a program – at least, not in most programming languages – by adding another projection. So if you have left out a mechanism to deal with the interaction concern, your program is to that extent just wrong. But subproblems are about projections, and adding another projection is the usual way of proceeding.

Any questions?

Could we use a shrink-wrapped component to do the editing of periods & ranges?

Yes, perhaps. You will need to connect it to other parts of the solution later on, and the component must provide for those connections.

Why are two of the lines in the entering periods & ranges subproblem diagram marked with the same letter m?

Because they are an interface and a requirement reference that have the same phenomena. It saves writing the same annotation twice. Remember that all the identifiers on lines identify sets of phenomena.

3.3.3 Membership reports

Here's the third subproblem. It's taken from the library administration problem introduced in Chapter 1. Here again is the introductory sketch of the full problem:

Library administration problem

A system is needed to administer a lending library. Membership is required for borrowing books, but not for reading them in the library premises. Books may be ordered and can be obtained from associated libraries. Overdue books incur fines. Various management reports are required.

The context diagram for the full problem, a little simplified, looks like this:

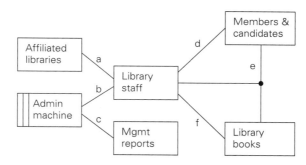

a: InterLibraryBorrow, Lend
b: StaffDataEntry etc
c: WriteReportData

d: Enrol, Resign, Pay
e: BorrowBook, ReturnBook, RenewBook
f: Acquire, Catalogue, Dispose

Library administration: context diagram

The members & candidates domain is all those people who are members, or might become members by enrolling. Enrolled members borrow and return books by taking them to the desk, where the library staff deal with the transaction using the computer. The *BorrowBook, ReturnBook* and *RenewBook* events are shared by the members, the books and the staff. The staff interaction with the computer is by the phenomena *b*. Membership transactions – phenomena *d* for enrolment, resignation and payment of membership fees and book fines – are also conducted with the help of library staff. Some of the work of the staff involves books but not members, for example, dealing with the acquisition, cataloguing and disposal of books.

The subproblem requirement is to produce weekly membership reports, showing the membership changes that have taken place during the past week because of enrolments and resignations. This seems to be a reasonable subproblem because, rather like the heating display subproblem, it produces information without affecting the parts of the world about which the information is needed. It's self-contained and doesn't intrude on other subproblems.

The subproblem diagram

The problem diagram for the subproblem is straightforward:

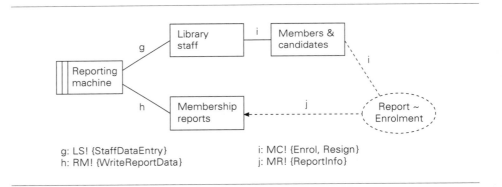

g: LS! {StaffDataEntry}   i: MC! {Enrol, Resign}
h: RM! {WriteReportData}   j: MR! {ReportInfo}

Membership reports: subproblem diagram

The affiliated libraries domain and the library books domain aren't relevant to this subproblem. So they don't appear here. They have, in effect, null projections. The domains and interfaces that do appear are, of course, projections of the domains in the context diagram:

■   the members & candidates in the subproblem domain have nothing to do with payments or with books. They engage only in *Enrol* and *Resign* events, which they control, and the interface phenomena set *i* contains only those events;

- the library staff in the subproblem domain perform only the *StaffDataEntry* events g that are associated with *Enrol* and *Resign* events. We haven't shown these in detail.

- the membership reports domain is a projection of the full problem's mgmt reports domain. It contains only the reports of membership changes, and only data for those reports – the phenomena set h – is written by the reporting machine. The result of the data written by the phenomena h is the report information phenomena j in the requirement reference;

- the requirement is called Report~Enrolment. It stipulates only how the report information in the membership reports must be related to the occurrences of *Enrol* and *Resign* events in the phenomena set i.

The fact that the library staff are interposed between the members and the reporting machine is potentially a very significant feature of the subproblem. It raises the possibility of an important class of malfunction or misoperation. Someone might come into the library to enrol, give the necessary personal details to one of the staff, pay the membership fee and leave. The staff member may then fail to enter the enrolment into the machine, perhaps because of a data entry error, or because the machine power has been cut off. The resulting situation is that the *Enrol* event has happened at the interface marked i, but the corresponding data entry event has not happened at the interface marked g. To deal properly with this subproblem you'll need to consider this, and similar situations, with care.

Where's the database?

It's pretty obvious that any eventual solution to the full problem will make use of some kind of database. It's also obvious that the solution to this subproblem will need the database too. So shouldn't the database appear in your subproblem diagram?

No, it shouldn't. The subproblem requirement doesn't say anything about a database. It just says that certain reports must be produced containing certain information about the enrolments and resignations that have taken place in the previous week. If there is going to be a database it will be a part of the solution, not a part of the problem. So you don't want to introduce it yet, even if you are sure that you will introduce it eventually.

Any questions?

Why is the members' domain called 'members & candidates' and not just 'members'?

It's not called 'members' because the scope of the problem includes enrolling new members. A person applying for membership must be in the domain, but is not yet a member.

Why is the library staff domain necessary? The staff are there only to connect the members & candidates to the machine, aren't they?

Well, yes: the library staff is a connection domain. If you leave it out you can't take account of the possible connection failures in any sensible and coherent way. Malfunction and misoperation by the library staff is very significant.

Remember: if a connection domain is not completely reliable, you must include it in the problem context diagram. And the same rule applies, of course, to a problem diagram.

Hasn't something been left out of the library administration context diagram? If a member loses or destroys a book, isn't that an interaction between members and books in which the library staff do not (presumably) participate?

Yes. Absolutely right. And, of course, the machine doesn't participate either. You can't analyse a problem properly if you confine yourself to what happens when the problem world is interacting with the machine. The context diagram should have another interface for phenomena shared by members and books but not by staff.

Should the requirement really be about the Enrol and Resign events shared with the staff? Is it not really about events that are deeper into the world?

That's a good question. Your instincts are absolutely right. But in this case it's hard to see what those deeper events could be. Even the library managers don't expect reports telling them when a member has *decided* to resign: *deciding* doesn't count; it's *telling* the library staff that counts.

Why is there a distinction between WriteReportData in interface h, and ReportInfo in interface j?

Because the requirement is about what information appears in the report, and the machine can only write data in the packets that are acceptable to the printer. Suppose that the report must contain some table with data arranged in rows and columns. The requirement might stipulate a condition on columns, but the machine can write only in rows.

If there's eventually going to be a database, won't its design have to take account of lots of subproblems like this one? If so, does it really make sense to consider this subproblem, and others like it, in isolation?

Yes, it does make sense. You can consider the subproblems initially in isolation, and then later in combination when you come to the design of the database. We'll return to this point when we talk about models in Chapter 7.

3.3.4 Furnace operation

The full home heating problem is quite complex. We identified the problem of displaying the system state and function, and briefly sketched it out above. The controller must respond appropriately to commands from the control panel. There is a non-trivial control problem of capturing the pattern of room occupancy and using it for more economical heating of unoccupied rooms. There is a control problem of managing the water circulation and furnace to keep the rooms within the desired temperature range. The furnace equipment itself is elaborate, and must be operated correctly and safely.

We'll take the correct and safe furnace operation as our fourth subproblem. Here's the relevant part of the initial problem sketch from the home heating control problem:

> '. . . Water is heated by an oil-burning furnace. Oil admitted through a valve is blown into the combustion chamber and ignited. There is a flame sensor, a fuel-flow sensor, a blower motor speed sensor, and a water temperature sensor. A pump circulates the water through the system. There is a control panel at which the controller can be commanded manually to turn the furnace on or off . . .'

The subproblem is just about turning the furnace on and off, effectively and safely.

The home heating controller must turn the furnace on and off, sometimes in response to a command at the control panel, sometimes as a means to increasing or decreasing the temperature of the water circulating in the room radiators. To turn the furnace on successfully it's necessary to operate the fuel blower, oil valve and ignition device in the right order. It's also important to follow an appropriate operational procedure in turning the furnace off. The most important concern is safety. For example, it's essential to avoid any danger of building up a large mass of unburned oil vapour in the combustion chamber that might be suddenly ignited, either by the ignition device or by accidental exposure to a flame or a spark.

The subproblem diagram

Here is a condensed form of the subproblem diagram:

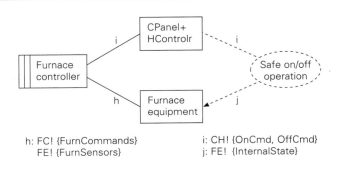

h: FC! {FurnCommands}   i: CH! {OnCmd, OffCmd}
FE! {FurnSensors}   j: FE! {InternalState}

Furnace operation: condensed subproblem diagram

The domain CPanel+HControlr is a union domain, like the domain HRooms + FEquipt. It's the combination of the control panel and the heating controller machine. It issues commands to turn the furnace on and off by causing *OnCmd* and *OffCmd* events in its shared phenomena set *i* with the furnace controller machine. The display part of the control panel is not relevant to this subproblem.

The furnace equipment domain is a projection of the domain in the context diagram. It doesn't include the water and water pump because they are not involved in the operation of the furnace itself. The phenomena set *h* which it shares with the furnace controller machine contains only the commands and sensors that belong to the furnace, not those that belong to the water and the water pump.

The requirement is called safe on/off operation. It stipulates that in response to *OnCmd* and *OffCmd* events, the *InternalState* of the furnace should change in a way that satisfies certain conditions: an *OnCmd* should place the furnace in its burning state, and an *OffCmd* should place it in its shutdown state, subject to some overriding safety constraints. For example, the flame must not be lit if there is oil or oil vapour in the combustion chamber. To satisfy this requirement it will be necessary to follow a strict, timed procedure for starting and shutting down. For example, after shutting down, time must be allowed for any residual oil vapour left in the combustion chamber to disperse before the ignition is turned on again.

Any questions?

Where did the rules for furnace operation come from?

If you are asking about the writing of this book, they came from the problem state-ment given by Grady Booch in *Object Oriented Design with Applications*, Benjamin/Cummings, 1991. But if you are asking about sound software develop-ment practice, they must come from a meticulous investigation into the furnace properties, from assiduous interviews with the furnace design engineers, and from the furnace equipment operating manual.

Why draw a separate problem diagram for each subproblem? Why not just add lots of requirement ovals to the full context diagram?

That's definitely a possibility. Sometimes it works out quite well, when there are not many domains and only two or three subproblems. Then you can get all their requirement ovals and all their requirement reference connections on to the same diagram, along with all the domains.

But it's still not perfect. One reason is that you can't show the domain projections at the interfaces: the annotation of each interface of shared phenomena must show all the shared phenomena for all the subproblems, although some phenom-ena are irrelevant to some subproblems. Another reason is that you sometimes need to distinguish the role of a domain in one subproblem from its role in another subproblem. That needs different symbols for the same domain, as we'll see in later chapters. Obviously, you can't do that in a single diagram.

If there are several domains and many subproblems you certainly won't be able to show the subproblems in one diagram. It will just turn into a nasty, ghastly, beastly mess. Like trying to analyse the whole problem without structuring it into subproblems, wouldn't you say?

CHAPTER 4

Basic problem classes and frames

A problem frame is a kind of pattern. It defines an intuitively identifiable problem class in terms of its context and the characteristics of its domains, interfaces and requirement. Domain and interface characteristics are based on a classification of phenomena. In this chapter, five basic frames are briefly described, and for each one the fit between the frame and a problem of the defined class is illustrated.

4.1 Problem classes

Are all software development problems essentially the same? Of course not. Patient monitoring, home heating control, library administration and one-way traffic lights are very different problems, with very different difficulties and concerns. But different problems may have similar subproblems that fall into the same few classes. Perhaps entering periods & ranges in patient monitoring is a subproblem of the same class as cataloguing books in library administration. Perhaps detecting and reporting failure of analog devices in patient monitoring belongs to the same class as detecting and reporting malfunction in home heating control. Perhaps heating display is in the same class as odometer display, or furnace control is in the same class as one-way traffic lights.

4.1.2 Problem frames

The subproblems identified in a good decomposition are much simpler than complete realistic problems. That's why you can hope to classify them into a reasonably small number of recognisable problem classes that occur over and over again. That's what problem frames aim to do. A problem frame is a kind of pattern that captures and defines a commonly found class of simple subproblem.

In this chapter we'll discuss five basic problem frames. The five are far from a complete or definitive set. But they are enough to illustrate the idea and to show how it can help you to structure and decompose realistic problems and to address the subproblems that you have identified.

All basic problem frames are unrealistically simple. Even a carefully identified sub-problem will rarely fit a basic frame perfectly. Usually something is left over that the frame doesn't provide for, or some domain or interface doesn't quite fit perfectly. So each of the basic frames has several different *flavours* and *variants* that can accommodate some realistic variations. In this chapter we'll look only at the vanilla flavour of each frame, and ignore any variants. The frame concern and some related concerns for each basic frame are discussed in the next chapter. In Chapter 6 we'll deal with frame flavours and some of their consequences. In Chapter 7 we'll look at one of the most important variants – information problems with model domains. After that, in Chapter 8, we'll look at some other variants.

4.1.2 Five basic frames

The five basic frames that we'll look at in this chapter are required behaviour, commanded behaviour, information display, simple workpieces, and transformation. Each basic frame corresponds to an intuitive idea of a problem class.

- *Required behaviour:* there is some part of the physical world whose behaviour is to be controlled so that it satisfies certain conditions. The problem is to build a machine that will impose that control.

- *Commanded behaviour:* there is some part of the physical world whose behaviour is to be controlled in accordance with commands issued by an operator. The problem is to build a machine that will accept the operator's commands and impose the control accordingly.

- *Information display:* there is some part of the physical world about whose states and behaviour certain information is continually needed. The problem is to build a machine that will obtain this information from the world and present it at the required place in the required form.

- *Simple workpieces*: a tool is needed to allow a user to create and edit a certain class of computer-processable text or graphic objects, or similar structures, so that they can be subsequently copied, printed, analysed or used in other ways. The problem is to build a machine that can act as this tool.

- *Transformation:* there are some given computer-readable input files whose data must be transformed to give certain required output files. The output data must be in a particular format, and it must be derived from the input data according to certain rules. The problem is to build a machine that will produce the required outputs from the inputs.

4.1.3 How problem frames differ

Even these very roughly stated intuitive ideas suggest important differences between the problem classes.

First, their r*equirements* are different. The customer for a transformation problem will check whether the data and structure of the output files are correctly related to the input files. The customer for a required behaviour problem will just look at the controlled part of the world to see how it behaves under the machine's control. The customer for a workpieces problem will check whether a sequence of editing commands has produced the right results in the text being edited.

Second, their problem domains have different *domain characteristics*. The important properties of the input and output files in a transformation problem are their data values and structures. The important properties of the physical world to be controlled in a required behaviour problem are its internal causal connections. The user in a workpieces problem is a human being, with all that this implies.

Third, the domains in each problem frame have different *involvements* in the problem. The part of the physical world about which information is required in an information display problem is involved only to the extent that it's monitored by the machine. It's just monitored, not changed or affected in any way. But the physical world in a required behaviour problem is involved by being controlled by the machine. The user in a workpieces problem is involved as an active source of commands to be obeyed.

Fourth, each problem frame has its own distinctive *frame concern* to be addressed in the problem analysis. You must make appropriate descriptions of the requirements and the machine and problem domains, and fit them together into a convincing argument. The argument must convince you – and your customer – that the machine you are developing will ensure that the requirement is satisfied. The differences between the requirements, domain characteristics, and domain involvements of the frames lead to important differences in their frame concerns.

4.2 About phenomena and domains

Our subject is problems, not solutions. Problems are in the world. So being more precise about problem frames and their domains means being more precise about the world and its phenomena. Before we describe the frames themselves we must clarify some notions about domains and their phenomena.

Unlike a computer, the world doesn't come with a programming manual. So we must choose and understand appropriate abstractions of phenomena. This is necessary both at the very general level of talking about differences between problem frames, and at the specific level of individual problems and domains. We'll only be scratching here at the surface of a deep and difficult topic. But the notions we'll discuss briefly are enough for the distinctions we'll need to talk about problem frames. We'll discuss some refinements when we come to examples that need them.

We'll distinguish six kinds of phenomena: the first three are kinds of individuals, the second three are kinds of relations among individuals. Then we'll distinguish two larger categories of phenomena. And finally, on the basis of what we've said about phenomena, we'll distinguish three different kinds of domain.

4.2.1 Individuals

An individual is something that can be named and reliably distinguished from other individuals. There are three kinds of individual.

- *Events*. An event is an individual happening, taking place at some particular point in time. Each event is *indivisible* and *instantaneous* – the event itself has no internal structure and takes no time to happen. So you can talk about 'before the event' and 'after the event', but you can't talk about 'during the event'.

    We'll assume that no two events can occur simultaneously. So if *e* and *f* are distinct events, either *e* occurs before *f*, or *f* occurs before *e*.

    A *GPulse* or *RPulse* in the one-way traffic lights problem is an event. An *OnCmd* in the furnace operation subproblem is an event. When a zoo visitor inserts a coin into the coin acceptor, that's an event. As usual, you must distinguish individual events from classes of events – the insertion of one penny by Jill at 2.15pm on July 14 must be distinguished from the class of all *CoinInsert* events.

- *Entities*. An entity is an individual that persists over time and can change its properties and states from one point in time to another. Some entities may initiate events; some may cause spontaneous changes to their own states; some may be passive.

    A *patient* in the patient monitoring problem is an entity. A library *book* or *member* is an entity. A *room* in the home heating problem is an entity. They belong to entity classes of *patients*, *books*, *members* and *rooms*. The *fuel blower* and the *ignition device* are entities, too. They belong to entity classes *fuel blower* and *ignition device*: each of these classes has only one entity.

- *Values*. A value is an intangible individual that exists outside time and space, and is not subject to change. The values we are interested in are such things as numbers and characters, represented by symbols.

In the patient monitoring problem, a *period* is a number of minutes – the maximum between successive checks – and is therefore a value. A *range* is a pair of values. The number shown as the *DistanceCount* in the odometer display problem is a value. Examples of value classes are *integers, characters, strings*, and so on.

4.2.2 Relations

A relation is a set of associations among individuals. If you like to think in concrete terms, you can think of a relation as it is represented by a table in a relational database. A relation consists of some number of *tuples*, just as a database table consists of some number of rows. Each tuple involves one or more individuals. Every tuple of a relation involves the same number of individuals, just as every row in a database table has the same number of attribute values – one for each column of the table. There are three kinds of relation.

- *States*. A state is a relation among individual entities and values; it can change over time. In the patient monitoring problem, *Failed(AnalogDevice123)* is a tuple of the state *Failed(x)*; and in the home heating control problem, *Temperature(Kitchen,72.5)* is a tuple of the state *Temperature(x,y)*, and *BlowerSpeed(1450)* is a tuple of the state *BlowerSpeed(x)*.

  Where there's no danger of confusion we'll often use 'state' in place of 'tuple'. We'll say that a state holds (is true) or doesn't hold (is false): '*BlowerSpeed(1450)*' holds exactly when the blower speed is 1450, and so on.

- *Truths*. A truth is a relation among individuals that cannot possibly change over time. The individuals are always values, and the truth expresses mathematical facts, such as *LengthOf("ABCDE",5)* or *GreaterThan(5,3)*.

- *Roles*. A role is a relation between an event and individuals that participate in it in a particular way. Each role expresses what you might otherwise think of as one of the 'arguments' of the event. For example, if you are interested in White's 17th move in a chess game, you might ask: Which piece was moved? The queen. Which square of the board was it moved to? c5. Instead of writing *Move(W17,Queen,c5)*, you separate out the two roles of the event:

  PieceMoved(W17,Queen) and *TargetSquare(W17,c5)*.

It's useful to do this for two reasons. First, because it often happens that an event class is shared between two domains but some of its participants are not shared. For example, when a computer reads from a sequential file on an external tape drive, the input buffer in the computer participates in the *read* event, but the buffer is private to the computer, and is not shared with the tape drive.

Second, the control of a role is sometimes divorced from the control of the event itself: the computer controls the occurrence of the *read* event, but the tape drive determines which record is read.

In the one-way traffic lights problem, the role *UnitPulsed(Pulse,Unit)* expresses which light unit receives a particular pulse. In this case, the lights controller machine chooses when the event should happen, and also which light unit should participate, so it controls both the event and the role.

Any questions?

Surely two events can occur simultaneously? When you leave out the Post Office in the postal chess problem, doesn't that mean that the SendPostcard and ReceivePostcard events occur simultaneously?

No. It means that you have chosen to regard the sending and receiving as one shared event. You could say that this shared event is called *SendPostcard* in your description of one domain and *ReceivePostcard* in the other, but it's still just one event, not two.

Are relations the same as predicates?

Close enough, for our purposes.

What if a state has no individuals, for example the state 'Locked' in the zoo turnstile problem?

That's not a problem. Just write *Locked()*. If you prefer, you can think of it as having one implicit individual: the state is *Locked(EntryBarrier)*. But you're not forced to. We'll be rather casual about how we write states, sometimes writing *Locked()* and sometimes just *Locked*.

Is a state the same as an association in UML?

There's a lot in common. But states are simpler than UML associations. Also, unlike associations, they include relations between entities and values. In UML those would be regarded as object attributes.

Do roles change over time, like states, or are they fixed, like truths?

They are fixed. If White moves the White Queen on the 17th move, then *PieceMoved(W17,Queen)* is true for ever and *PieceMoved(W17,Knight)* is false for ever. Of course, *PieceMoved(W18,Knight)* may be true, but *W18* is a different move, so that's a different tuple of the *PieceMoved* role.

The word 'state' seems to mean many different things. I'm confused.

Sorry. Here are the meanings we'll use, and some other common meanings.

(a) A state phenomenon of the kind discussed earlier – a relation (or predicate). For example, *Temperature(x,y)*. We'll use this a lot.

(b) A particular tuple of a state relation. For example, *Temperature(Kitchen,72.5)*. We'll use this, too.

(c) The set of all state phenomena of interest in a particular problem or domain. For example, {*the blower speed, whether the ignition is on, the temperatures of all rooms, the fuel flow, the settings of all room temperature control knobs, . . .*}. We won't use this at all.

(d) A particular set of tuples of (c). For example, {*BlowerSpeed(1450), Ignited(), Temperature(Kitchen,72.5), Temperature(Bedroom,68.0), . . .*}. We won't use this at all.

(e) A situation denoted by a state symbol in a state-machine description. For example, the state '1:' in the diagram:

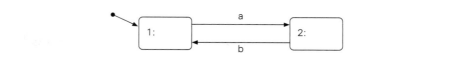

A state-transition diagram

We'll use this when we talk about state-transition diagrams and other state-machine descriptions.

There are yet more meanings, but we won't use them.

You said that the lights controller controls both the pulse event and the role. But you didn't say whether the role UnitPulsed(Pulse,Unit) was shared. Why not?

That's a very good question. For two domains to share a role they must share both the event and the participant in the event. Are the units shared with the machine? We'll come back to this issue when we discuss the *identities concern* in Chapter 9.

4.2.3 Causal and symbolic phenomena

We'll also recognise two larger categories of phenomena:

- *causal* phenomena are events, or roles, or states relating entities. These are causal phenomena because they are directly caused or controlled by some domain, and because they can cause other phenomena in turn. For example, a pulse event in a light unit may cause a state change in the Stop and Go lights;

- *symbolic* phenomena are values, and truths and states relating only values. They are called symbolic because they are used to symbolise other phenomena and relationships among them. A symbolic state that relates values – for example, the data content of a disk record – can be changed by external causation, but we don't think of it as causal because it can neither change itself nor cause change elsewhere.

4.2.4 Domain types

Often, one kind of problem is distinguished from another by different domain types. To a large extent these distinctions arise naturally out of the domain phenomena. But it's also useful to make a broad classification into three main types.

- *Causal* domains. A causal domain is one whose properties include predictable causal relationships among its causal phenomena. For example, the mechanical and electrical equipment of a lift are a causal domain: if the lift motor is switched on it will start turning; if the lift car is at floor 2 in the concrete shaft, it must arrive at floor 3 before it can arrive at floor 4; if the motor starts turning, the lift car will rise. These causal relationships allow you to calculate the effect of the machine behaviour at an interface with the domain.

    The coin acceptor domain in the zoo turnstile problem is a causal domain. A coin that participates in an *AcceptCoin* event is retained inside the acceptor and can't be retrieved by the visitor. The nurses' station in the patient monitoring problem is a causal domain: if the monitor machine causes a *Notify* event, the notification will appear on the screen.

    A causal domain may control some or all or none of the shared phenomena at an interface with another domain. Books in the library are a causal domain. Books control no phenomena, but if a book is at a member's house, it cannot simultaneously be in the library shelves.

- *Biddable* domains. A biddable domain usually consists of people. The most important characteristic of a biddable domain is that it's physical but lacks positive predictable internal causality. That is, in most situations it's impossible to compel a person to initiate an event: the most that can be done is to issue instructions to be followed. An overdrawn bank customer can't be compelled to repay the loan. A library member can't be compelled to return an overdue borrowed book. A zoo visitor who has caused an *InsertCoin* event can't be compelled to *Push* on the entry barrier.

But in many situations, and these examples are among them, it still makes sense to describe a procedure to be followed, and to regard any departure from the procedure as an undesirable deviation. The extent to which a human domain is biddable in this way varies from the user of an ATM – who may be entirely ignorant of its operation, and from ignorance or malice may perform any physically possible action at any time – to the driver of a train, who is trained to follow stipulated procedures and can be expected to do so.

■ *Lexical* domains. A lexical domain is a physical representation of data – that is, of symbolic phenomena. It combines causal and symbolic phenomena in a special way. The causal properties allow the data to be written and read. For example, the sectors of a disk are areas of magnetic material: a *write* operation involving a particular character string causes them to be magnetised in a particular way. This is just like a GPulse or RPulse causing the light unit to set its Stop light on or off. But for a lexical domain, the significance of its physical states is that they provide representations for values and truths. The magnetisation represents the character string that was written, and the same string can be retrieved by a *read* operation.

So you can always look at a lexical domain from two points of view. You can regard it just as a structure of symbolic phenomena, perhaps records, fields and values. Or you can regard it as a causal domain, in which *write* and *read* events cause state changes. In most problems that have lexical domains you need both points of view. Often, the requirement is expressed in terms of symbolic phenomena, but the machine must interact with the domain in terms of its causal phenomena.

The periods & ranges domain in the patient monitoring problem is a lexical domain.

We will explore the properties of the three main domain types a little more deeply as we encounter them in this chapter. They will also play an important part when we come to consider different flavours and variants of problem frames in later chapters.

Any questions?

Where does the word 'lexical' come from?

In natural language, a 'lexical unit' is a word or a meaningful part of a word. It's an important concept in G M Nijssen's NIAM method (sometimes known as Object Role Modelling). NIAM is described in:

G M Nijssen, *A Framework for Advanced Mass-Storage Applications* in Medinfo 1980, Proceedings of the Third World Conference on Medical Informatics, North-Holland, 1980.

G M A Verheijen and J Van Bekkum, *NIAM: An Information Analysis Method* in Information System Design Methodologies: A Comparative Review, T W Olle, H G Sol and A A Verrijn-Stuart (eds), pages 537–589; North-Holland, 1982.

G M Nijssen and T A Halpin, *Conceptual Schema and Relational Database Design, a fact oriented approach*, Prentice Hall, 1989.

NIAM distinguishes lexical and non-lexical objects: lexical objects are 'strings that can be uttered and which refer to an object'; non-lexical objects are 'real or abstract things in the object system which are non-utterable'. If you read French you could also consult these accounts:

Henri Habrias, *Le Modé Relationnel Binaire: Méthode I.A. (NIAM)*, Paris, Editions Eyrolles, 1988.

Henri Habrias, *Introduction a la Spécification*, Masson, Paris, 1993.

Where does the word 'biddable' come from?

It means 'ready to do what is bidden'. We're taking an optimistic view of biddable domains.

Aren't causal and symbolic phenomena often mixed up together? For example, reading a record is an event, so presumably it's a causal phenomenon, but a record value is presumably symbolic.

Yes, they are mixed up together. The causal phenomena provide the physical representation of the symbolic phenomena. That's why you must make abstractions that focus on what's important in each particular situation, even within one simple problem.

4.3   Problem frames

The core of a problem frame is the *frame diagram*. In this section we'll look at the frame diagrams for our five problem classes, and see how some small examples fit the frames. Then, in the next chapter, we'll move on to the frame concerns and the descriptions needed for problem analysis.

4.3.1   Required behaviour

The intuitive notion of a required behaviour problem is:

> *'There is some part of the physical world whose behaviour is to be controlled so that it satisfies certain conditions. The problem is to build a machine that will impose that control.'*

Here is the frame diagram for the required behaviour problem frame:

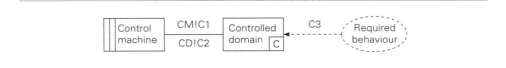

Required behaviour: problem frame diagram

As you see, a frame diagram is just a slightly fancier generic problem diagram. It's different from an ordinary problem diagram in these ways:

- the names of the parts – here they are required behaviour, control machine and controlled domain – are chosen to suggest their involvements in the general form of the problem;

- the sets of interface and reference phenomena are denoted by short stylised names – here the names are C1, C2 and C3. The names indicate what kind of phenomena they are: C indicates causal phenomena. The names on interface connections also include the usual control prefixes – here they are CM! and CD! – that indicate which domain controls each set of phenomena. Because these names are short they can be written on the connection lines instead of being given in separate annotations;

- each problem domain is marked in its lower right corner by a single-letter code that indicates what kind of domain it is – here the controlled domain is marked by C, indicating that it is a causal domain. The machine in a problem frame is always a causal domain, so it's unnecessary to indicate this explicitly.

The control machine is the machine to be built. The controlled domain is the part of the world to be controlled. The requirement, giving the condition to be satisfied by the behaviour of the controlled domain, is called the required behaviour.

The controlled domain is a causal domain, as the C in the bottom right corner of its rectangle indicates. Its interface with the machine consists of two sets of causal phenomena: C1, controlled by the machine, and C2, controlled by the controlled domain. The machine affects the behaviour of the controlled domain by the phenomena C1; the phenomena C2 provide feedback. Phenomena shared by a problem domain and the machine are called *specification phenomena*.

The requirement is expressed in terms of a set C3 of causal phenomena of the controlled domain. These are the *requirement phenomena*. In general, C3 will be different from C1 and C2. This gap must be bridged by the indicative domain properties of the controlled domain.

Two little examples

We have already seen one example of a required behaviour problem: the one-way traffic lights. You can show how the problem fits the frame by marking the frame part names on the problem diagram, like this:

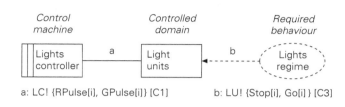

One-way traffic lights: fitted to required behaviour frame

The lights controller is the control machine, the light units are the controlled domain, and the lights regime is the required behaviour. The RPulse and GPulse events are C1; and the Stop and Go states are C3. The parts fit correctly: the pulses are events and are therefore causal phenomena (as C1 and C3 must be), and the light units is a causal domain (as the controlled domain must be). The set C2 of phenomena is empty, so it's not shown: in this very simple problem there is no feedback from the controlled domain to the control machine.

The gap between the C3 requirement phenomena – the Stop and Go states – and the C1 specification phenomena – the RPulses and GPulses – must be bridged by the domain properties of the light units.

Here is another example. This time the set of phenomena C2 is not empty.

Sluice gate control

A small sluice, with a rising and falling gate, is used in a simple irrigation system. A computer system is needed to control the sluice gate: the requirement is that the gate should be held in the fully open position for ten minutes in every three hours and otherwise kept in the fully closed position.

The gate is opened and closed by rotating vertical screws. The screws are driven by a small motor, which can be controlled by clockwise, anticlockwise, on and off pulses. There are sensors at the top and bottom of the gate travel; at the top it's fully open, at the bottom it's fully shut. The connection to the computer consists of four pulse lines for motor control and two status lines for the gate sensors.

Here is the problem diagram fitted to the required behaviour frame:

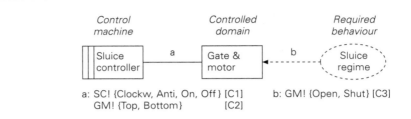

Sluice gate control: fitted to required behaviour frame

The sluice controller is the control machine, the gate & motor is the controlled domain, and the sluice regime is the required behaviour. The *Clockw, Anti, On* and *Off* pulses are C1, and the *Top* and *Bottom* sensor states are C2. The sluice controller machine exercises control over the gate & motor by causing the C1 pulses; it receives some feedback in the C2 sensor states which indicate the gate position when it's at the limits of its travel.

The requirement phenomena C3 are the *Open* and *Shut* states. Again, the specification phenomena are causal, and the problem domain is causal, as they must be to fit the frame.

Any questions?

How are the sets of phenomena named in the frame diagram – C1, C2, C3 and so on?

The letters denote the kind of phenomena; numbers are just assigned from 1 upwards. If two sets have the same name they are exactly the same phenomena. This can happen only when the set in a requirement reference is the same as the set in a domain interface. But two sets with different names might be the same phenomena in a particular problem. For example, you might have a required behaviour problem in which the C3 phenomena are the C2 phenomena.

In the sluice gate control problem, are the Open and Shut states C3 not the same as the Top and Bottom states C2?

No. *Open* and *Shut* are positions of the gate; *Top* and *Bottom* are sensor settings. The difference will matter a lot if sensor reliability is called into question.

Doesn't it make a lot of difference whether C2 is empty? A control problem with feedback is very different from one without.

Yes, it makes a huge difference. We'll discuss this in Chapter 6 when we look at different domain and problem frame flavours.

Why are requirement phenomena so called?

Because they are referred to in the requirement.

Why are specification phenomena so called?

Because they can be referred to in the specification of the machine behaviour. In the last chapter we said that a specification is a description of the machine's desired behaviour at its interfaces with the problem domains. So the specification phenomena of a problem are the phenomena that the machine shares with other domains.

4.3.2 Commanded behaviour frame

The commanded behaviour problem frame differs from the required behaviour problem frame because it has an operator domain and a different emphasis in its requirement. This is the intuitive idea that the frame is intended to capture:

> *'There is some part of the physical world whose behaviour is to be controlled in accordance with commands issued by an operator. The problem is to build a machine that will accept the operator's commands and impose the control accordingly.'*

Here is the problem frame:

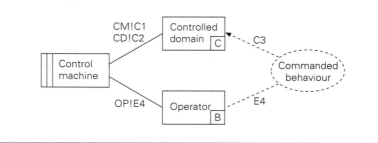

Commanded behaviour: problem frame diagram

The control machine and controlled domain, and their phenomena C1, C2 and C3, are the same as in the required behaviour frame. But now there is also an operator, assumed to be a biddable domain, as shown by the B marking in the lower right of the rectangle. The operator issues *commands*, which appear in the diagram as events E4, shared with the machine and controlled by the operator.

The requirement is called the commanded behaviour. It constrains the behaviour of the controlled domain by describing general rules for its behaviour and specific rules for how it must be controlled in response to the operator's commands E4. The requirement phenomena of the operator domain are the E4 events, which are also *specification* phenomena – that is, they are shared with the machine. So for the operator domain there is no gap to be bridged between the requirement and the specification phenomena.

The operator is *autonomously active*, that is, the operator spontaneously causes E4 events with no external stimulus. Nothing in the problem frame affects the operator's behaviour. It may be that in fact the operator can see the controlled domain, and takes account of its state, but we have chosen to ignore that fact here, and it will play no part in the problem analysis. The operator's E4 commands are separate and distinct from the C1 phenomena by which the machine controls the controlled domain. An important part of the problem analysis is to determine how and when the machine should – or should not – cause C1 phenomena in response to E4 commands.

As in the required behaviour frame, the domain properties of the causal controlled domain bridge the gap between the requirement phenomena C3 and the specification phenomena C1 and C2 at the machine interface.

An example

As an example of a commanded behaviour problem we'll take a modified version of the sluice gate control problem. Here's the sketch, with the modifications in italics.

Occasional sluice gate control

A small sluice, with a rising and falling gate, is used in a simple irrigation system. *A computer system is needed to raise and lower the sluice gate in response to the commands of an operator.*

The gate is opened and closed by rotating vertical screws. The screws are driven by a small motor, which can be controlled by clockwise, anticlockwise, on and off pulses. There are sensors at the top and bottom of the gate travel; at the top it's fully open, at the bottom it's fully shut. The connection to the computer consists of four pulse lines for motor control, two status lines for the gate sensors, *and a status line for each class of operator command.*

Here is the problem diagram fitted to the commanded behaviour frame:

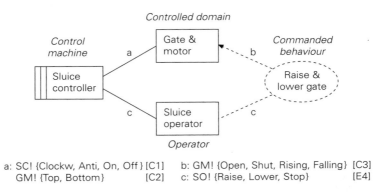

a: SC! {Clockw, Anti, On, Off } [C1]   b: GM! {Open, Shut, Rising, Falling} [C3]
GM! {Top, Bottom}   [C2]   c: SO! {Raise, Lower, Stop}   [E4]

Occasional sluice gate: fitted to commanded behaviour frame

The sluice controller is the control machine, the gate & motor is the controlled domain, the sluice operator is the operator, and the *Raise*, *Lower* and *Stop* commands issued by the sluice operator are the phenomena E4.

The required behaviour is called raise & lower gate. The general idea is that the operator can position the gate as desired by issuing *Raise*, *Lower* and *Stop* commands: the machine should respond to a *Raise* by putting the gate & motor into a *Rising* state, and so on.

Rising and *Falling* are defined in terms of the vertical position of the gate and whether and how it changes over time. The vertical position of the gate is a private state phenomenon of the gate & motor domain, that is, it is not shared with the sluice controller. The *Rising* and *Falling* states are mutually exclusive, they cannot hold simultaneously.

Introduction of the operator raises a number of fresh concerns. In particular, it may be impossible or inappropriate for the machine to obey a particular command. For instance, it should obviously not try to obey a *Raise* command when the gate is already at the top of its travel. And if the operator issues two *Stop* commands in succession, the machine can't act on both of them.

Any questions?

Why does the operator cause only events? Could the interface not be, for example, a lever that the operator holds in one position or another, in which case it would be a state?

Well, yes. But an operator state interface of the kind you describe would probably be best abstracted as events corresponding to the state changes. The fluid interplay between state and event phenomena is one of the reasons for identifying causal phenomena as a more general class. We have chosen here to treat the operator commands as events. Perhaps that's a little arbitrary.

Surely Rising and Falling states aren't really needed in the occasional sluice gate problem. They just correspond to Motor set Upwards and On, and Motor set Downwards and On, don't they?

No, they don't. They are distinct phenomena in their own right. The motor states you mention may not correspond to *Rising* and *Falling* because the mechanism may be broken. In this kind of problem that an important concern. We'll discuss it in Chapter 9.

Why not just treat the operator as a part of the controlled domain? Then the commands E4 would belong to the set of feedback phenomena C2.

Because the operator is not a part of the controlled domain. There is no causal connection between the operator and the controlled domain. Making that connection through the machine is an important aspect of the requirement. As a rough rule of thumb, all the phenomena in a causal domain should be causally connected. There's one exception. The exception is a domain containing isolated entities of the same class. The light units domain contains two isolated light unit entities that are not causally connected.

But isn't the operator probably watching the controlled domain and reacting to its states?

Perhaps. But we are not taking account of that in this problem frame.

4.3.3 Information display frame

The information display frame is intended to capture this intuitive idea:

> *'There is some part of the physical world about whose states and behaviour certain information is continually needed. The problem is to build a machine that will obtain this information from the world and present it at the required place in the required form.'*

Here is the problem frame diagram:

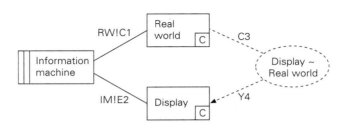

Information display: problem frame diagram

The part of the world about which information is required is called the real world. The display is the part of the world where the information is to be presented. The machine to be built is called the information machine. The requirement is called display~Real world, suggesting that it stipulates a correspondence between the symbolic requirement phenomena Y4 of the display domain and the causal requirement phenomena C3 – events or states – of the real world. What shows on the display, interpreted as information about the real world, must be true.

Both the real world and the display are causal domains, as indicated by the Cs in the bottom right corners of their rectangles. The real world is *active* and entirely *autonomous*. It causes spontaneous events and state changes, it controls all the shared phenomena at its interface with the machine, and the requirement places no constraint on it. Nothing in the problem context can affect the behaviour of the real world: it has its own internal causal relationships, but subject to those it behaves with complete freedom.

The machine must satisfy the requirement constraint by diagnosing real world requirement phenomena C3 from the C1 phenomena at its interface. The gap between C1 and C3 must be bridged by the causal domain properties of the real world. To produce the information, the machine must cause changes in the symbolic values and states Y4 of the display domain by causing events E2 at its interface with the display.

Two little examples
The odometer display problem introduced in the previous chapter is a very simple example of an information display problem. We won't repeat the problem statement. Here is its problem diagram fitted to the information display frame:

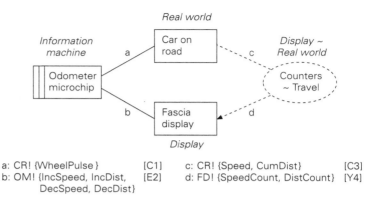

Real world

Information machine   a   Car on road   c   *Display ~ Real world*

Odometer microchip   Counters ~ Travel

b   Fascia display   d

Display

a: CR! {WheelPulse}   [C1]   c: CR! {Speed, CumDist}   [C3]
b: OM! {IncSpeed, IncDist,   [E2]   d: FD! {SpeedCount, DistCount} [Y4]
     DecSpeed, DecDist}

Odometer display: fitted to information display frame

The requirement stipulates a correspondence between the counter values in the fascia display and the *Speed* and *Cumulative Distance* of the car on the road. The machine's interface with the car gives it access to the *WheelPulses* generated by rotation of the wheels; its interface with the fascia display allows it to cause events that increment and decrement the counters.

The indicative domain properties for the car on the road are very simple. Essentially, they govern how the *WheelPulses* are produced and how far the car travels between successive *WheelPulses*, to bridge the gap between the requirement phenomena *Speed* and *Distance* on one side and the *WheelPulses* that the machine can detect on the other. The domain properties for the fascia display will govern how the *Speed* and *Cumulative Distance* counters change when increment and decrement events occur.

Here is another little example.

Local traffic monitoring

The traffic in a narrow, one-way residential street is to be monitored. Four sensor tubes are positioned across the road in a pattern like adjacent equal signs '=='. When a car passes along the street, it crosses the sensors in the pattern '=↑=': first its front wheels activate the two lower sensors, then they activate the two upper sensors, then its rear wheels activate the two lower sensors and finally its rear wheels activate the two upper sensors. A motorbike will activate only one lower sensor and one upper sensor.

The sensors are connected to a computer equipped with a time-of-day clock. There is also a small printer, on which the computer must produce a monitoring report on a continuous paper strip. The report has a line for each passing vehicle, showing the date and time, and the vehicle type; it also has a cumulative total for each type, printed hourly. The vehicle types to be distinguished are motorbikes, cars and commercial delivery vehicles with three or more axles.

Here is the problem diagram fitted to the information display frame:

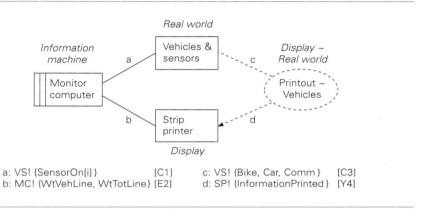

a: VS! {SensorOn[i] }   [C1]   c: VS! {Bike, Car, Comm }   [C3]
b: MC! {WtVehLine, WtTotLine} [E2]   d: SP! {InformationPrinted }   [Y4]

Local traffic monitoring: fitted to information display frame

The monitor computer is the information machine. The vehicles & sensors domain and the strip printer domain are causal domains, as they must be to fit the frame. The requirement stipulates a correspondence between the state of the strip printer, as manifested in its printed output, and the *Bike, Car* and *Commercial Vehicle* events of the real world.

We have been a little casual about the strip printer's requirement phenomena Y4 – which we have shown rather vaguely in the diagram as *InformationPrinted* – and its specification phenomena shared by the machine and the strip printer – which we have shown only as *WtVehLine* and *WtTotLine*. This vagueness about the strip printer is justified if you are sure that it is a very simple device displaying information of simple structure and content.

Any questions?

Isn't controlling the display domain really a required behaviour problem?

In principle, yes. But in an information display problem you are assuming that controlling the display is very simple, and doesn't deserve to be treated as a sub-problem in its own right. As a required behaviour problem it's just *vestigial*: you can easily absorb it into the main problem in hand. But if controlling the display is a significant problem in its own right, you would separate it out and treat it as a required behaviour subproblem.

Surely the real world isn't really completely autonomous. For example, isn't the car on the road controlled by its driver, by traffic lights, by road conditions, and so on?

That's true. But the problem diagram shows that we have decided to ignore that. The real world is autonomously active from the point of view of the subproblem that fits the information display frame. Everything about domains and interfaces in a subproblem is seen from the subproblem point of view.

4.3.4 Simple workpieces frame

This is the intuitive idea captured by the simple workpieces problem frame:

> *'A tool is needed to allow a user to create and edit a certain class of computer-processable text or graphic objects, or similar structures, so that they can be subsequently copied, printed, analysed or used in other ways. The problem is to build a machine that can act as this tool.'*

A *workpiece* is the piece of material worked on by a tool or machine: a wood block being turned in a lathe, or a metal casting being drilled in a pillar drill or ground in a centreless grinder, is a workpiece. The same term applies naturally when the tool is a computer being used for creating or editing a text or graphic object. The document you edit in a word processor, or the diagram you make in a drawing package, is a workpiece.

Here is the problem frame diagram:

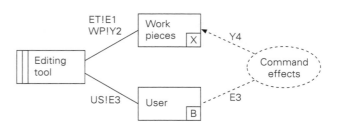

Simple workpieces: problem frame diagram

The machine is called the editing tool. There is a user, who is a person and therefore a biddable domain, as indicated by the B in the lower right corner of its rectangle. The user is *autonomous*, spontaneously causing E3 events without external stimulation.

The workpieces domain is a lexical domain, as indicated by the X in the lower right corner of its rectangle. It shares an interface with the machine, at which the machine controls the event phenomena E1. These events E1 are the *operations* on the workpieces, by which they can be caused to change their symbolic values and states; the symbolic phenomena Y2 accessible to the machine at the same interface allow the machine to examine current states and values of the workpieces.

The workpieces domain is *inert*: it may change its state in response to an externally controlled event, but it initiates no state changes and no events.

The user shares an interface of event phenomena E3 with the editing tool machine. The events E3 are controlled by the user: they are the *commands* issued by the user to the tool. Some of these commands will not be obeyed, for reasons of the kinds we discussed earlier in the commanded behaviour frame.

The requirement is called command effects: it stipulates what effects the commands E3 issued by the user to the editing tool should have on the symbolic values and states Y4 of the workpieces. The set of phenomena Y4 may have nothing in common with the set Y2, or may overlap it in any way at all. But, of course, both Y2 and Y4 are symbolic phenomena of the workpieces domain.

The simple workpieces frame doesn't include any provision for printing or displaying the workpieces, or using them as machine-processable inputs in other problems. That's part of another problem.

The symbolic phenomena Y4 will often have some meaning to the human user or to other people, that is, they will symbolise or describe some state of affairs of some other domain. For example, a text being edited may be a list of the last month's daily visitor numbers for the zoo turnstile. But this meaning is not significant within the simple workpieces problem itself. It can't be, because the symbolised or described domain – here, it would be the turnstile entry barrier – isn't included in the frame. So it won't be considered in the problem analysis.

An example
Here's an example of a simple workpieces problem.

Party plan editing

Lucy and John need a system to keep track of the many parties they give and the many guests they invite to them. They want a simple editor to maintain the information, which they call their party plan. Essentially, the party plan is just a list of parties, a list of guests, and a note of who's invited to each party. The editor will accept command-line text input, in a very old-fashioned DOS or Unix style. To begin with, at least, we are not concerned with presenting or printing the information, just with creating and editing it.

Here's the problem diagram – with very sketchy interface annotations – fitted to the simple workpieces frame:

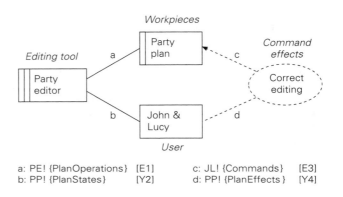

a: PE! {PlanOperations} [E1]   c: JL! {Commands}   [E3]
b: PP! {PlanStates}   [Y2]   d: PP! {PlanEffects } [Y4]

Party plan editing: fitted to simple workpieces frame

The machine is called the party editor; the requirement is called correct editing. The party plan domain is to be designed, following the class diagram provided by Lucy and John. The interface annotations are sketchy because we need to find out more about the interfaces John and Lucy have in mind before we make them more exact. We'll look at this in more detail in the next chapter.

Any questions?

Why is the workpieces domain lexical, while the display domain in an information problem is not?

Because a lexical domain is one that stores symbolic phenomena and allows later retrieval. The display domain merely displays them, but doesn't store them. The displayed phenomena are symbolic, of course.

There is no provision for the user to see the workpieces during editing. Isn't that completely unrealistic?

Yes, it's unrealistic, although it's possible to construct convincing small examples, and even to find some real ones, in which it's true. Later we'll discuss more realistic versions of the workpieces frame as a composite frame in Chapter 11.

Shouldn't the parties and guests appear as domains in the party plan editing problem?

Well, perhaps they should. You need to talk that over with John and Lucy. But if they should, then it isn't a workpieces problem. If what's needed is a repository of data that accurately records the state of Lucy and John's parties and guests, you should see this as an information problem of some kind. The party plan would probably be a model domain.

The commanded behaviour frame and the workpieces frame look very similar to me. What's the difference?

First, the workpieces domain is lexical and formal, but the controlled domain is causal and informal. For example, you don't have to worry about approximation in the workpieces domain. This is the most important difference.

Second, the workpieces domain is always inert: it never initiates any event or state change. The controlled domain in the commanded behaviour frame is not, in general, inert, although it may be inert in some particular problem, for example, in the one-way traffic lights problem.

Third, the requirement in the workpieces frame relates the workpiece symbolic states only to the user's commands. In the commanded behaviour frame the requirement stipulates the response to the operator's commands, and also other conditions on the controlled domain behaviour that are not guaranteed by the domain itself, for example, that the gate is not driven beyond the limits of its vertical travel.

4.3.5 Transformation frame

Here is the intuitive idea of a transformation problem:

> *'There are some given computer-readable input files whose data must be transformed to give certain required output files. The output data must be in a particular format, and it must be derived from the input data according to certain rules. The problem is to build a machine that will produce the required outputs from the inputs.'*

Here's the problem frame:

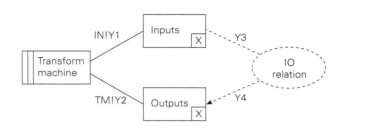

Transformation: problem frame diagram

The inputs and the outputs domains are both lexical, as indicated by the X in the bottom right corner of their rectangles. The inputs are given; the outputs are to be made by the machine. The requirement is called IO relation, an abbreviation of input-output relation. It stipulates a relationship between the symbolic phenomena Y3 – values and truths and states that relate them – of the inputs domain and the symbolic phenomena Y4 of the outputs domain. The relationship must be established by making the outputs appropriately; the inputs are given and cannot be changed.

The machine is called the transform machine. It has access to the symbolic phenomena Y1 of the inputs domain, and can determine the symbolic phenomena Y2 of the outputs domain. Y1 may or may not be the same phenomena as Y3, and Y2 may or may not be the same as Y4. As a general rule they are likely to be different. The machine must deal in more elementary phenomena, such as characters, while the requirement refers to larger phenomena, such as records and fields.

The transform machine, being a computer, necessarily works by doing things over time. Repeatedly, it reads some data from the inputs, processes it in some way, and writes processed data to the outputs. But this dynamic behaviour is an aspect of the specification, not of the problem requirement. The IO relation stipulates only the static result: that the outputs eventually produced should bear a certain relation to the given inputs. So although the inputs and outputs domains must have some basis in physical devices – such as a disk drive or a CD drive or a printer – and those devices must have dynamic properties, the requirement is concerned only with their static properties.

An example

Here's an example of a transformation problem.

Mailfiles analysis

Fred has decided to write a program to analyse some patterns in his email. He is interested in the average number of messages he receives and sends in a week, the average and maximum message length, and similar things. After some thought he has worked out that he wants a report that looks like this:

Name	Days	#In	Max.Lth	Avg.Lth	#Out	Max.Lth	Avg.Lth
Albert	124	19	52136	6027	17	21941	2123
Anna	92	31	13249	1736	37	34763	2918
....	...	...	....	.....	...	....	....

Fred's mailfiles analysis report

The report contains a line for each of his correspondents. The line shows the correspondent's name, how many days the report covers, the number of messages received from the correspondent and their maximum and average lengths, and the same information for the messages sent to the correspondent by Fred.

The problem diagram, fitted to the frame, looks something like this:

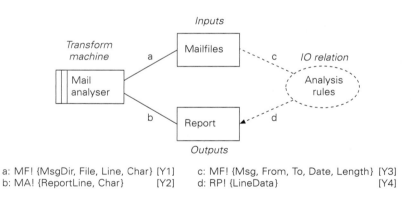

a: MF! {MsgDir, File, Line, Char} [Y1]   c: MF! {Msg, From, To, Date, Length} [Y3]
b: MA! {ReportLine, Char}   [Y2]   d: RP! {LineData}   [Y4]

Mailfiles analysis: fitted to transformation frame

At the interface marked *a*, the mail analyser machine has access to the directory of files in the mailfiles domain, and to the lines and characters in each file. The files contain email messages constructed by email clients and modified by internet nodes during routing. For example, an email message has a header containing *From* and *To* and *Date* lines.

At the interface marked *b*, the machine determines the lines and characters of the report domain. The analysis rules requirement describes how the messages in the mailfiles, and their various header line field values, must be related to the data in the lines of the report.

4.3.6 The transformation restriction

The transformation frame imposes a restriction that we have already seen imposed in the workpieces problem. The symbolic phenomena Y3 and Y4 must have some meaning to someone: there must be something they symbolise. But when you choose the transformation frame you are choosing to exclude that meaning from the problem. The lexical inputs and outputs domains are the only problem domains: there is no room in the frame for any other domain that they might describe, or that their meanings might refer to.

Many problems can happily accept this restriction, and fit the transformation frame without distortion. For example, these could be transformation problems:

■ reformatting an address book held in one personal computer application to import it into another application;

■ generating a family tree from a genealogical database;

■ reconciling a bank account statement with a list of cheques issued and a list of authorised recurring payments;

■ generating HTML for a Web page from a server database and a query.

All of these problems are concerned to manipulate data. The requirement gives the rules by stipulating how the outputs must correspond to the inputs.

So in the mailfiles analysis problem there is no mention of the domains or phenomena symbolised by the data in the mailfiles. Nothing is said about the friends with whom Fred is corresponding by email, and nothing about the routing of messages through the nodes of the Internet.

Any questions?

Surely the transformation frame, and perhaps the workpieces frame also, should be forbidden. Don't they break the rule about the requirement being not at the machine interface but deeper into the world?

Your instincts are very admirable! Technically, these frames don't break the rule because they recognise inputs and outputs and workpieces as explicit domains that have their own properties. We'll see that in more detail in the next chapter.

But that's not what you meant, is it? You can think of any problem as being somewhere on a progression towards the machine, like this:

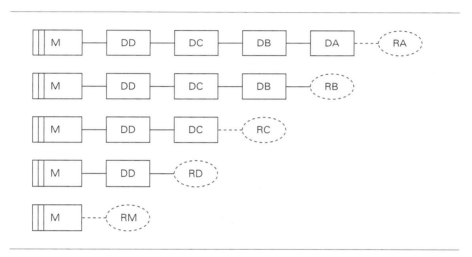

A progression of problems

The top problem is deepest into the world. Its requirement RA refers to domain DA. By analysis of the requirement RA and the domain DA, a requirement RB can be found that refers only to domain DB, and guarantees satisfaction of RA. This is the requirement of the next problem down. Eventually, at the bottom, is a pure programming problem whose requirement refers just to the machine and completely ignores all problem domains.

A transformation or workpieces problem has a requirement like RD: it's just one step down from the non-transformation problem RC and one step up from the machine problem RM. When you frame a problem as a transformation or workpieces problem RD, you are assuming that either:

(a) the RC problem has already been properly analysed, and satisfying RD guarantees satisfaction of RC; or

(b) your customer doesn't care about RC and DC, but, only about RD.

So in the mailfiles analysis problem you are making one of these assumptions:

(a) Fred's information requirement about his friends' email behaviour has been properly investigated. The investigation has included the way email files are created by email clients, and how they are modified by routing nodes. All the results of the investigation are embodied in the analysis rules requirement;

(b) Fred doesn't really care what his email files mean, he just wants to analyse them as data objects.

Of course, for many problems neither assumption holds. Then your problem doesn't fit the transformation frame, and treating it as a transformation problem would be a bad mistake: if you ignore the RC and deeper domains, you are ignoring essential parts of the problem.

I think I have understood this, I'm not sure. Give me an example of moving from one level of the progression to the next one down.

In the zoo turnstile problem from Chapter 2, take the coin acceptor and entry barrier as DD and the zoo visitors as DC. The requirement is RC; let's call it 'happy paying visitors'. Analyse the visitors' behaviour very carefully, and express it all in terms of desirable sequences of *InsertCoin* and *Push* and *Enter* events.

Now you could drop the zoo visitors domain from the problem, and take these sequences as the requirement 'proper acceptor and turnstile behaviour'. That would be the RD requirement.

Wouldn't that be a good idea?

It's fine. It's good because you have taken a step from the original 'happy paying visitors' requirement towards your goal of a machine specification to satisfy that requirement.

What would not be so good is to decide that the zoo visitors are no longer a part of the problem, and to throw away all the analysis you did about their behaviour. Now you will have some difficulty when your 'proper acceptor and turnstile behaviour' requirement is questioned. Or when the area around the turnstile is rearranged and the zoo visitors start behaving a little differently.

So what is the right judgement about the mailfiles analysis?

You'll have to ask Fred.

CHAPTER 5

Frame concerns and development descriptions

Each frame has a frame concern that must be addressed in any problem of the class. The frame concern identifies the descriptions you must make and how you must fit them together in a correctness argument. In conjunction with the characteristics of the problem domains, the frame concern gives rise to other particular concerns that distinguish the problem class. If you try to fit a problem into an inappropriate class, the resulting development will certainly be awkward and probably unsuccessful.

5.1 The frame concern

Your goal in any problem frame is to propose a machine by describing its behaviour in a specification. To do this properly, you must address the *frame concern*. That is, you must make descriptions and fit them together into a correctness argument. Your argument must convince yourself and your customer that your proposed machine will ensure that the requirement is satisfied in the problem domain.

Your central task in addressing the frame concern is always to investigate and describe the problem domain properties. But there is more to it than that. The frame concern is different for each different frame. In this chapter we'll look at the frame concerns for the five basic frames already introduced.

5.2 Required behaviour frame concern

Let's start by looking at the frame concern as it applies to the one-way traffic lights problem. Here is the problem diagram again:

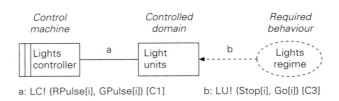

a: LC! {RPulse[i], GPulse[i]} [C1]   b: LU! {Stop[i], Go[i]} [C3]

One-way traffic lights: fitted to required behaviour frame

As in any non-trivial problem, there is a gap between the *requirement phenomena*, in terms of which the requirement is expressed, and the *machine-interface phenomena*, which are those that the machine directly monitors and controls at its interface with the problem domains. Here the requirement phenomena are the *Stop* and *Go* states of each light, and the machine-interface phenomena are the *GPulses* and *RPulses*.

5.2.1 The frame concern

Obviously, the task of problem analysis here is finding a machine behaviour that will make the lights do what is required. The frame concern captures this task in terms of the descriptions you must make.

Addressing the frame concern adequately means making *requirement, specification* and *domain* descriptions that fit together properly. For the one-way traffic lights problem your descriptions must support the argument shown in this diagram:

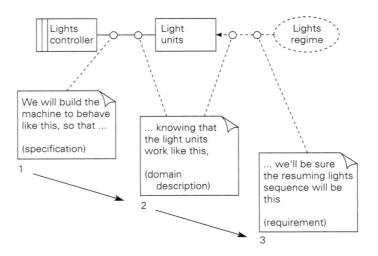

Frame concern in required behaviour frame

This is the argument you must eventually give to convince your customer that you have mastered the problem. The specified machine behaviour (1), combined with the given domain properties (2), will achieve the required behaviour (3).

Reversing the direction of the argument suggests a sequence of thinking that can sometimes help you to devise the machine specification. Start by capturing the requirement (3), then investigate and describe the light units domain, identifying causal properties that will allow the machine to control the lights as the requirement demands (2), then devise a machine behaviour that exerts that control (1).

Of course, the one-way traffic lights problem is very simple. Even the sluice gate control problem is a little harder because there the machine can and must use the feedback provided by the sensor states. We'll come back to these and other flavours of required behaviour problems in the next chapter. For now we'll look at the three descriptions for the one-way traffic lights.

5.2.2 Three descriptions

Just to fix the idea of these three descriptions, here they are, roughly sketched out, for the traffic lights problem.

- The *requirement* is completely straightforward. Let's suppose that you write it like this:

    ```
    forever {
        show only Stop(1) and Stop(2) for 50 seconds;
        show only Stop(1) and Go(2) for 120 seconds;
        show only Stop(1) and Stop(2) for 50 seconds;
        show only Go(1) and Stop(2) for 120 seconds;
    }
    ```

- The *domain* description shows how the light units change their Stop and Go states in response to pulses. The two light units are identical. Your investigation shows that each one behaves independently. You describe its behaviour in a state-machine diagram like this:

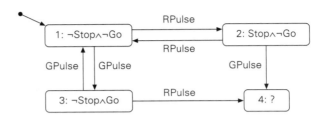

Behaviour of one traffic light unit

The symbols '¬' and '∧' are used in logic: '¬' means 'not' and '∧' means 'and'. Initially, in state 1 neither light is showing: 'not (¬) Stop and (∧) not (¬) Go'; a GPulse in state 1 causes a transition to state 3, in which Go is showing, but not Stop; and so on. The effect of an RPulse in state 3 or a GPulse in state 2 is not described. You expected they would cause a transition to a 'Stop∧Go' state, with both lights showing, but you were unable to confirm this in your investigation. The gap in your knowledge is indicated by showing these events as transitions to a single *unknown* state 4. In this state, Stop, or Go, or both, or neither, may be showing; or the light unit may be broken.

■ The *specification* shows how you want the machine to behave at its interface with the light units. You have chosen to use a program-like notation. The comments, written following '//', suggest the intended effects, but they are not formally a part of the description:

```
{ RPulse(1); RPulse(2);              // set Stop(1) Stop(2) only
   forever {
      wait 50 seconds; RPulse(2); GPulse(2);    // change Stop(2) to Go(2)
      wait 120 seconds; GPulse(2); RPulse(2);   // change Go(2) to Stop(2)
      wait 50 seconds; RPulse(1); GPulse(1);    // change Stop(1) to Go(1)
      wait 120 seconds; GPulse(1); RPulse(1);   // change Go(1) to Stop(1)
} }
```

If you're an energetic kind of reader who doesn't skip the detailed bits, you should convince yourself that these descriptions really do allow you to make the argument shown in the picture. It's worth doing because it will give you a much better feel for why the three descriptions are different and why they are all needed to complete the analysis up to the programming stage. Don't worry – we won't do this for every problem frame. We'll start leaving out some of the descriptions. Then you'll be glad you looked carefully at this little example.

5.2.3 Why one description is not enough

Three descriptions may seem two too many for as problem as simple as this. What a lot of people do in practice is to skip the domain description and the requirement and go straight to a 'system model' that is essentially the program specification with some added decorations.

A 'system model' is just a single description of the machine and the problem domain together. To make the description a little shorter to write, let's assume that only one light shows in each unit at any one time, so if Stop1 is true, Go1 must be false, and so on. Then the single description might be something like this:

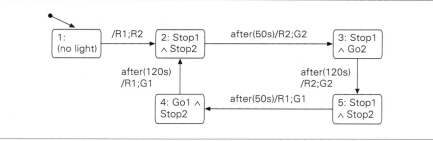

Trying to combine the specification, domain properties, and requirement

The annotations on the transitions are roughly as in a UML state chart. For example: 'after(50s)/R2;G2' means that after 50 seconds in state 2 the machine causes an R2 pulse followed by a G2, and takes the transition to state 3. The '/R1;R2' transition from state 1 to state 2, with its accompanying pulses, is taken without any delay.

For a very small and simple problem, combining the three descriptions like this may not be completely disastrous because you can probably tease out most of what was in the three underlying descriptions from it.

- When you talk to your customer, you treat the description as a requirement. You ignore the actions that cause the pulses, and focus just on the timing events and the states. 'To begin with,' you say, 'both units should show Stop; then, after 50 seconds, the second unit should switch to Go;' and so on.

- When you talk to the programmer, you treat it as a specification of the machine. You look only at the transitions with the timing events and the pulses. 'First the machine must cause an RPulse[1] and an RPulse[2],' you tell the programmer, 'then, after 50 seconds, an RPulse[2] and a GPulse[2];' and so on. The Stop and Go states have no significance to the programmer because they aren't visible to the machine; at best they are enlightening comments explaining why the pulses are to be caused.

■   When you want to check your understanding of the domain properties, you focus just on the pulses and the way they affect the states. 'An initial RPulse for each unit puts them both in the Stop state; then an RPulse followed by a GPulse for the second unit puts it in the Go state,' and so on.

Although this multiple use of one description may seem alluringly economical, it's not good practice, for four reasons. First, it won't work on any realistic problem. If the problem and the description were just a little more complex, it could become very hard to tease out its three aspects.

Second, a single description like this can be confusing because it combines a description of what you *want to achieve* – the *optative* properties described in the requirement and specification – with a description of the domain properties that you're *relying on* – the *indicative* properties described in the domain description.

Third, the combined description is inadequate in an important way. Because it's essentially a description of the machine behaviour, it can't accommodate a description of what would happen if the machine were to behave differently. So there is no way to tell from the combined description that the order of the RPulse and GPulse actions in the pairs 'R1;G1' and 'R2;G2' must not be reversed – that 'G1;R1' and 'G2;R2' will put the light units into the unknown state 4 of our earlier domain description. The unknown state – precisely because the machine correctly avoids it – can't appear in the description.

Fourth, the combined description isn't really re-usable. Because the embodied domain description, in particular, is only a partial description, and is also merged with the requirement and the specification, you won't be able to re-use it in another problem that deals differently with the same problem domain.

In short, the three descriptions really do say different things. If you combine them into one description you may find that it doesn't hurt much, but you may find that the confusion and inadequacy of the combined description cause you a lot of trouble. The disasters of software development come from too little care in the early stages, not from too much.

Any questions?

Why is it such a big deal to have three descriptions? We had 37 in my last project.

The big deal is to separate the two optative domain descriptions and the indicative domain description. You can write 37 descriptions and still not do that. Perhaps you should have had 111 descriptions.

Do the two state-machine descriptions use standard UML state chart notation?

Not quite. The states are labelled in a different way. We have used a number to identify each state, and added an annotation showing what state phenomena hold in that state.

Isn't the combined description wrong just because it doesn't have an object class model of the light units?

No. In this problem you don't need a *model* of the light units; it would only get in the way. You need an explicit *description* of their properties. We'll have more to say about the difference in Chapter 7, where we discuss model domains.

What are the properties of the unknown state? For example, what happens if a further pulse arrives in the unknown state?

The unknown state is just that: unknown. You don't know what states hold, or what the effects of events might be. In a word, all bets are off.

Might the unknown state actually be the same as another state in the diagram?

No. It might show the same Stop and Go configuration, and it might make the same outgoing transition on the next event. Or it might not. The point is that you don't know. In the other state you do.

Why did you say 'Lets assume that only one light shows in each unit at any one time'? It's obviously true.

Go to the bottom of the class. You must never, ever, treat a domain property as 'obviously true'. And anyway, this one is certainly not true for some traffic lights: it's common practice to use simultaneous *Stop* and *Go* lights to indicate 'Stop, but be prepared to Go'.

Is state 1 in the combined description the same as state 1 in the light unit behaviour description?

No. The identifiers written in state symbols are local to the diagram. The identifiers in different diagrams are completely independent.

Could the frame concern argument be stated more formally?

Formal treatment of the general frame concern argument is discussed in Carl A Gunter, Elsa L Gunter, Michael Jackson and Pamela Zave, *A Reference Model for Requirements and Specifications*, IEEE Software, Volume 17, Number 3, pages 37–43, May/June 2000.

5.3 Commanded behaviour frame concern

Here's the problem diagram for the occasional sluice gate problem:

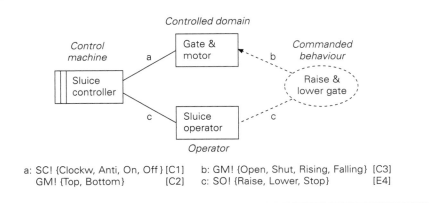

a: SC! {Clockw, Anti, On, Off } [C1]   b: GM! {Open, Shut, Rising, Falling} [C3]
   GM! {Top, Bottom}   [C2]   c: SO! {Raise, Lower, Stop}   [E4]

Occasional sluice gate: fitted to commanded behaviour frame

The added complication in the commanded behaviour frame is the operator. Remember that the operator is autonomous, issuing *Raise*, *Lower* and *Stop* commands at will.

5.3.1 Disobedience

You can't assume that the operator will adhere perfectly to any particular discipline in issuing commands. Of course, you will provide operating instructions containing such statements as 'After a *Raise* command, be sure to press the *Stop* button before entering a *Lower* command,' and 'Never press the same button twice in succession'. But because the operator is a biddable domain, you absolutely must not rely on these instructions being followed perfectly on all occasions.

As a result, the control machine can't be required to obey every command issued by the operator. We'll consider two main reasons for disobedience:

■ some commands aren't *sensible* – they make no sense in the context of preceding commands;

■ some commands are not *viable* – they are inappropriate or impermissible in the current state of the controlled domain.

There's at least one more reason, which we won't discuss here. The operator may issue successive commands too quickly for the machine to react immediately. We'll leave this one aside until Chapter 9, where we'll treat it as a particular concern – the *overrun* concern – that arises in several kinds of problem.

5.3.2 The frame concern

In addition to concerns like those of the required behaviour frame, analysis of a commanded behaviour problem must address these concerns about obedience to commands.

To address the frame concern adequately for a commanded behaviour problem you must be able to make the argument shown in this diagram:

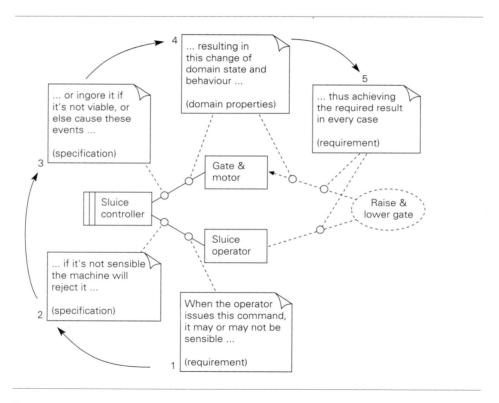

Frame concern in commanded behaviour frame

The requirement (1) says which commands are sensible, and (5) what effects they should bring about in the controlled domain if they are viable, that is, if those effects are permissible and achievable in the current domain state.

The specification says how the machine reacts to all commands that occur, including those that are:

■ not sensible (2);

■ not viable because of the current state of the domain (3);

■ both sensible and viable, and therefore to be obeyed (3).

The domain properties description (4) says how the domain state and behaviour are affected by what the machine does at their shared interface. You have to show that the domain state and behaviour resulting from all of this are what is required (5).

Because of the interplay of the operator's behaviour, the reasons for disobeying commands, and the given and required properties of the domain, there is a more subtle relationship among the descriptions in a commanded behaviour problem than in a required behaviour problem. You may need to be a little more careful in recognising what is in the optative requirement and what is in the indicative domain properties.

5.3.3 The sensible commands requirement

Some commands make no sense in the context of the preceding commands. For example, in the sequence *<Raise,Stop,Stop>*, the third command makes no sense, regardless of the state of the controlled domain. It must be rejected.

You will need to describe carefully which commands must be rejected for this reason. Let's suppose that you decide that a sequence of sensible commands is a repetition of any number of *movement orders*, where a *movement order* is a *Raise* or a *Lower*, followed by a *Stop*. Any command that doesn't fit in isn't sensible and should be rejected.

You can describe all this conveniently in three stages. First, draw a state machine for sensible commands only. Then add transitions for all the commands that have been left out – these added transitions represent senseless commands. Of course, you don't allow these added transitions to change the state; if you did, you would be allowing them to affect the definition of the sensible command sequences. Finally, write definitions saying which commands of each class are sensible.

The three stages look like this:

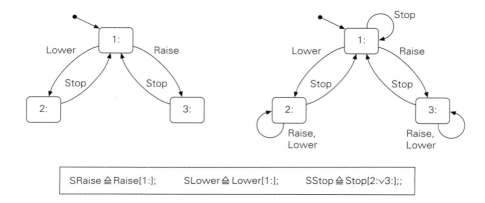

$$SRaise \triangleq Raise[1:]; \qquad SLower \triangleq Lower[1:]; \qquad SStop \triangleq Stop[2:\vee3:];;$$

Defining sensible commands

The added transitions are for *Stop* in state 1, and for *Raise* or *Lower* in states 2 and 3. Adding them ensures an outgoing transition on every command in every state, so the diagram accommodates every sequence of commands the operator could possibly issue. The definitions use the definition symbol '$\triangleq$'. They mean 'SRaise is a Raise occurring in state 1:', 'SLower is a Lower occurring in state 1:', and 'SStop is a Stop occurring in state 2: or state 3:'.

At first sight this may look like a domain description of the operator. But it's not. It's really a part of the requirement. Its only purpose is to define the sensible commands. In fact, it doesn't even say that the machine must reject the commands that aren't sensible – we'll have to say that separately.

5.3.4 The viable commands requirement

The requirement also stipulates which of the sensible commands are viable, and what the results of obeying sensible viable commands must be. The requirement is, broadly, to obey sensible commands without ever running the gate beyond its *Open* and *Shut* limits. We need to make it more precise.

This requirement is expressed in terms of the operator commands, and of the gate & motor state phenomena *Open*, *Shut*, *Rising* and *Falling*. Before you can express it you need to define the meanings of *Rising* and *Falling*.

These must be defined in terms of the gate's vertical position *Posn(p)*:

> Posn(p) holds when the gate is at a position p inches above the bottom of its vertical travel:
>
> Rising $\triangleq$ Posn(p) holds for p increasing with time
> Falling $\triangleq$ Posn(p) holds for p decreasing with time

These definitions guarantee that *Rising* and *Falling* can never be true at the same time.

We have already defined the sensible commands *SRaise*, *SLower* and *SStop*. Now you could write the requirement like this:

1. Regardless of commands, the gate must stop at the top and bottom of its travel:
    1.1 If Open becomes true while Rising is true, then Rising must immediately become false and Falling must remain false.
    1.2 If Shut becomes true while Falling is true, then Falling must immediately become false and Rising must remain false.

2. Other than as required in 1, the gate must change its Rising and Falling state only in response to *SRaise*, *SLower* and *SStop* commands that are viable:
    2.1 If an *SRaise* command occurs when neither Rising nor Falling is true, and Open is not true, then Rising must immediately become true.
    2.2 If an *SLower* command occurs when neither Rising nor Falling is true, and Shut is not true, then Falling must immediately become true.
    2.3 If an *SStop* command occurs when Rising is true, then Rising must immediately become false and Falling must remain false.
    2.4 If an *SStop* command occurs when Falling is true, then Falling must immediately become false and Rising must remain false.
    2.5 Other than as required in 1 or in 2.1 to 2.4, the Rising and Falling states must remain constant.

This seems rather verbose. You can express the same requirement more compactly in a state machine description:

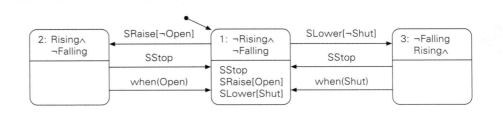

Requirement: obeying or ignoring sensible commands *SRaise, SLower* and *SStop*

(Remember that the state identifiers 1, 2 and 3 are local: they have nothing to do with the state identifiers in the diagrams for defining sensible commands.) In the starting state 1, in which the gate is neither Rising nor Falling, an *SStop* command must be ignored; so must an *SRaise* command if *Open* is true, and an *SLower* command if *Shut* is true. These three ignored commands appear in the lower section of the state symbol, indicating that they must cause no state transition.

A transition to state 2, in which the gate is Rising, must be taken on an *SRaise* command, but only if *Open* is false; a transition to state 3, in which the gate is Falling, must be taken on an *SLower* command, but only if *Shut* is false. From state 2 a transition must be taken to state 1 on an *SStop* command, or when *Open* becomes true. The requirement for state 3 is similar.

Notice that an *SRaise* or an *SLower* can't occur in state 2 because a *Raise* or *Lower* command immediately following an *SRaise* would not be sensible. Similarly, an *SRaise* or *SLower* can't occur in state 3.

5.3.5 Gate & motor domain properties

The gate & motor domain is more complex than the light units, but it's not hard to describe. The motor and gate have these observable state phenomena:

- MOn means that current is being applied to the motor;

- DCl means that the direction of rotation is set to clockwise; if DCl is false, the direction of rotation is set to anticlockwise;

- Posn(p) means that the gate is at a position p inches above the bottom of its vertical travel;

- Top means that the top sensor is activated;

- Bottom means that the bottom sensor is activated;

- Open means that the gate is open and water can flow;

- Shut means that the gate is shut and no water can flow.

As we saw earlier, *Rising* and *Falling* are defined in terms of *Posn(p)* like this:

Rising $\triangleq$ Posn(p) holds for p increasing with time
Falling $\triangleq$ Posn(p) holds for p decreasing with time

The total vertical travel is 48 inches. When the gate is within 0.5 inches of the top, it is in the *Open* state and the sensor state *Top* holds; *Shut* and *Bottom* hold when it's within 0.5 inches of the bottom. These are domain properties. You can describe them like this:

$$(\text{Open} \wedge \text{Top}) \leftrightarrow \text{Posn(p)} \wedge (47.5 \le p \le 48)$$
$$(\text{Shut} \wedge \text{Bottom}) \leftrightarrow \text{Posn(p)} \wedge (0 \le p \le 0.5)$$

'$\leftrightarrow$' means 'if and only if'. *Open* and *Top* are true if and only if ($\leftrightarrow$) *Posn(p)* is true and *p* is between 47.5 and 48. *Shut* and *Bottom* are true if and only if ($\leftrightarrow$) *Posn(p)* is true and *p* is between 0 and 0.5.

Now you can investigate and describe how the states of the domain are affected by the *Clockw, Anti, On* and *Off* pulses. Here's what you find, expressed in a state-transition diagram:

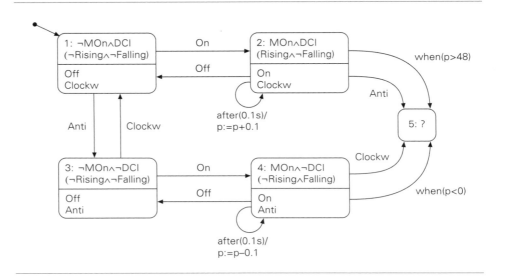

Sluice gate: further domain properties

When the motor is on, the gate moves at 0.1 inch per 0.1 second. Clockwise rotation moves the gate up, increasing *p*; anticlockwise moves it down. The motor is unaffected by an *On* pulse when it's already in the *MOn* state, by a *Clockw* pulse when its direction is already set clockwise, and so on. However, the motor must be stopped to change direction: the domain will enter the unknown state 5 if a *Clockw* or *Anti* pulse occurs while the *MOn* state holds. It will also enter the unknown state if the position *p* is allowed to increase beyond 48 or to decrease beyond 0.

Of course, these domain properties apply to the gate & motor domain for both problem versions, with and without the sluice operator.

5.3.6 The machine specification

The machine specification must describe a machine whose behaviour will ensure that the requirement is satisfied. This machine will:

- detect *Raise*, *Lower* and *Stop* commands issued by the sluice gate operator;

- reject commands that aren't sensible according to the sensible commands requirement.

- ignore those sensible commands that are not viable and cannot be obeyed in the current state of the gate & motor according to the obeyed commands requirement;

- exploit the gate & motor domain properties to achieve the required Rising and Falling states in response to the sensible viable commands, according to the obeyed commands requirement.

Any questions?

We seem to be assuming that when an Off event occurs, the motor and sluice gate stop instantaneously. Is this realistic?

It's an approximation that's close enough to the truth. The gate mechanism and the motor have very little momentum. We'll discuss other problems in the next chapter in which this approximation isn't good enough.

Why do you say that the states Rising and Falling are defined, when the others are observable?

Because the states *Rising* and *Falling* aren't separately observable as phenomena in their own right. If you observe *Posn(p)*, for a few moments, you already know everything you need to know about *Rising* and *Falling*.

Should we not have described the domain properties before writing the requirement?

Yes, probably. In most problems it's hard or even impossible to state the requirement without some knowledge of the domain. But the relationship between requirement and domain properties is circular. You need the domain properties to state the requirement, and you need the requirement to tell you which domain properties are significant in your problem.

Should we consider the possibility that the gate & motor don't in fact behave according to the domain description, for example, because something is broken?

Yes, definitely. We'll come to this as a particular concern in Chapter 9.

Would it be a good idea for the machine to sound an audible beep whenever it rejects or ignores an operator command?

Yes. But remember, we're not trying to make the problem frames, or these examples, realistic. We're trying to keep them as simple as possible, and sometimes a little simpler than that.

Why is each state in the diagram defining sensible commands marked only by a number?

Because there is nothing to say about them. Their state phenomena are, at most, psychological states of the operator. The identifying numbers '1:' and so on are there to allow us to mention the diagram states in discussion, that's all.

Isn't there a tricky interaction between rejecting commands that aren't sensible and ignoring commands that aren't viable?

Yes, there is. For example, if an *SRaise* is rejected as non-viable because the gate is already open, the operator must still issue the matching *SStop*.

Effectively the operator's commands are interleaved with commands issued by the machine – for example, to stop the gate at the end of its travel – that the operator didn't issue and may be unaware of. There's a significant concern here in the design of an appropriate HCI (human-computer interface). A badly designed machine behaviour will be hard and confusing to use.

5.4 Information display frame concern

Here's the problem diagram for the local traffic monitoring problem:

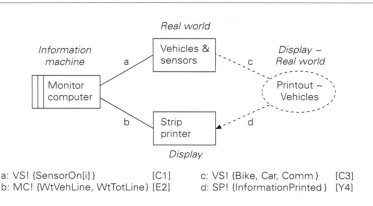

a: VS! {SensorOn[i]}   [C1]   c: VS! {Bike, Car, Comm}   [C3]
b: MC! {WtVehLine, WtTotLine} [E2]   d: SP! {InformationPrinted} [Y4]

Local traffic monitoring: fitted to information display frame

Like a behaviour problem, an information problem usually presents a significant gap between the requirement phenomena and the machine-interface phenomena. That gap is in the real world domain, between the C3 phenomena and the C1 phenomena. The machine is required to distinguish and report the passage of different kinds of vehicles – cars, motorbikes and commercial delivery vehicles with three or more axles. But it has direct access only to the *SensorOn[i]* states of the four sensor tubes positioned across the road. As usual, the gap must be filled by properties of the domain. Here that means properties of the vehicles & sensors domain.

5.4.1 The frame concern

To address the frame concern adequately for an information display problem, you must have descriptions of the requirement, the domain properties, and the machine specification that support the argument shown in this diagram:

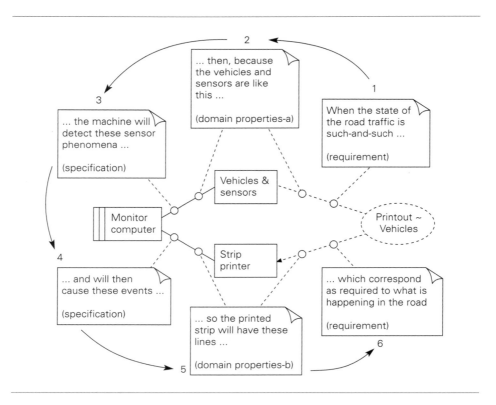

Frame concern in information display frame

The requirement (1) refers to some states of the real world, and stipulates the corresponding information to be displayed (6). The argument connecting the two requirement parts passes through the domain description of the real world (2), where it describes how the phenomena referred to in the requirement (1) give rise to phenomena that can be directly detected by the machine (3). The machine must respond as described in its specification (4), and the domain properties of the display domain (5) will guarantee the required information outputs (6).

As in all problem frames, the domain description is of central importance. And the most important domain description in this frame is the description of the vehicles & sensors domain. The real world is the focal domain in any information problem because it's the domain that your customer needs information about.

The display domain in an information display problem is usually easy to deal with. Often it has been designed specifically for ease of operation: this will certainly be true of the strip printer. If the display domain in an information problem is not easy to operate, then driving it should be seen as a separate behaviour subproblem to be dealt with in its own right. In the information problem itself you really need only assure yourself that the display domain won't raise difficulties. The strip printer won't raise any difficulties. That's why we allowed ourselves to be a little casual in our treatment of its interfaces in the problem diagram.

The real world domain – here, the vehicles & sensors – may be much harder to deal with. The core of your task is to bridge the gap between the requirement phenomena, which are the passage of various vehicles along the road, and the phenomena at the machine interface, which are the sensor states. The machine behaviour must embody the rules needed to infer the passage of each particular type of vehicle from the sensor state sequences it causes.

5.4.2 Vehicles & sensors domain properties

Each sensor is *On* when compressed and *¬On* when not compressed; when a vehicle wheel passes over the sensor tube, the sensor state changes from *¬On* to *On* and then back to *¬On*.

The two pairs of sensor tubes are placed 36 inches apart. So, for example, if a car with a 84 inch wheelbase is travelling at 30mph, its front axle will compress the further sensors approximately 3/44 second after the nearer sensors, and its rear axle will compress each sensor approximately 7/44 seconds after the front axle.

To classify and count the vehicles it's necessary to distinguish between successive axles belonging to the same vehicle and axles belonging to different vehicles. This can probably be done accurately enough by detecting the pattern of sensor compressions over time, and taking proper account of several factors:

- the possible ranges of vehicle speeds on the road;

- the possible ranges of spatial separation between successive vehicles at given speeds;

- the commonly occurring axle patterns, including the distances between successive axles of the same vehicle (for a two-axle vehicle this is the wheelbase).

Making a good enough description of this domain to allow you to address the frame concern properly isn't a particularly easy job. Two factors contribute to the difficulty. First, the real world domain description in an information problem must be *total*. Second, the vehicles & sensors domain is highly *informal*.

Partial and total descriptions

In the one-way traffic lights problem, this was our domain description of the light units:

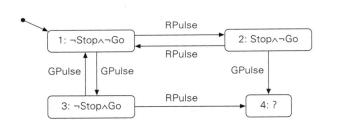

Behaviour of one traffic light unit

The role of this description in the behaviour frame concern was to show how sequences of *RPulses* and *GPulses* affect the *Stop* and *Go* light states. For example, for the sequence <*RPulse,RPulse,GPulse,GPulse*> it shows that the *Stop* light goes on, then it goes off, then the *Go* light goes on, then it goes off. But the description is only *partial*: it only describes the effect of some of the pulse sequences. For the sequence <*RPulse,GPulse,...*> it says that first the *Stop* light goes on, and after that the effect is unknown: the light unit enters its unknown state 4, and nothing more is said about what happens on subsequent pulses.

In the behaviour frame, a partial domain description like this is often enough. The lights controller never causes any of the pulse sequences <*...,RPulse,GPulse,...*> or <*...,GPulse,RPulse,...*> that lead to the unknown state. So the partial description need not say what their effects would be.

But in an information problem, the description of the real world domain must be *total*. That means that you must describe, within the bounds of some chosen abstraction, everything that can happen in terms of the requirement phenomena, and all the effects that can be observed in terms of the phenomena at the machine interface.

For the traffic monitoring problem, this means that you must describe:

- total vehicle behaviour – everything that can happen by way of the passage of bikes, cars and commercial vehicles, including tailgating, overtaking, breakdowns, and all kinds of things like that;

- total sensor behaviour – every possible pattern of sensor states that the machine can encounter;

- the complete relationship between the two.

Omit some vehicle behaviour and you won't be able to account for all the vehicles. Omit some sensor behaviour and the machine you specify may break down on an unanticipated state sequence. Omit any part of the relationship between the two and you won't be able to specify the machine behaviour in all circumstances.

Informal domains

To describe domain properties usefully it's necessary to draw a neat boundary around the phenomena that are relevant. For the light units, only pulse events and Go and Stop states are relevant. The states change only on pulses, and the pulses cause only the state changes; the description shows how they are related. In the vehicles & sensors domain we would like sensor states to change only on vehicle passage, vehicle passage to cause sensor state changes, and the relationship to be easily described.

But all physical domains are somewhat informal. There are always phenomena lurking outside the boundary, ready to invalidate your description. For the light units, these phenomena include light bulb failure, a spike on the power line, lightning, and power supply failure. We ignored them because – implicitly – we thought them very unlikely. For the vehicle & sensors domain, ignoring the phenomena outside the boundary is less easily justified because they are more likely. People hitch trailers to their cars; skilful motorbike riders ride with the front wheel lifted off the ground; two motorbikes cross the sensor tubes side by side; a car crosses the tubes at a sharp angle; a vehicle comes to rest straddling the tubes; a sensor tube is struck by a log falling from a vehicle, or by the hooves of a horse; a stretch limo passes by. For any rule you make about recognisable patterns of sensor changes, there will be some unusual case that frustrates your intention.

We'll return in the next chapter to the treatment of informal domains. In a moment we'll move on to the workpieces frame. But first ...

Any questions?

The local traffic monitoring problem seems dreadfully hard. Is it really so difficult?

You could decompose it into two subproblems. In one you solve the problem as given, assuming that the traffic and sensors are very well behaved – just standard-size vehicles spaced well apart. In the other you check whether this assumption has broken down. If so, monitoring is suspended until order and sanity are restored. We'll look at this kind of decomposition in a later chapter.

Would the problem be easier if you introduced a model of the vehicles?

If you mean an explicit model domain to act as an analogic model of the vehicles (and perhaps of other agents that can set the sensors), then yes, certainly. We'll look properly at model domains in Chapter 7.

5.5 Simple workpieces frame concern

Here's the problem diagram for John and Lucy's party plan editing problem:

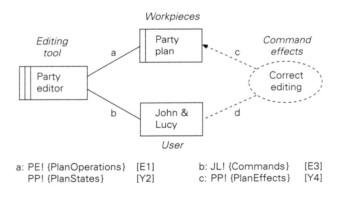

a: PE! {PlanOperations}   [E1]   b: JL! {Commands}   [E3]
   PP! {PlanStates}   [Y2]   c: PP! {PlanEffects}   [Y4]

Party plan editing: fitted to simple workpieces frame

The user in a workpieces problem is, as you would expect, somewhat similar to the operator in a commanded behaviour problem, and some of the same concerns arise. In particular, the machine must consider the context in which the user issues each command, and may reject some of them.

The only domain gap to be filled in a simple workpieces problem is in the workpieces domain itself. In this problem that's the party plan, which is a lexical domain. In response to user *Commands* E3, the party editor machine causes *PlanOperation* events E1. By the properties of the party plan domain, these events cause changes to the symbolic *PlanEffects* phenomena Y4, which are the party plan data values. Unlike the controlled domain in a behaviour problem, the workpieces domain is always passive. It never initiates any action or change. In response to a *PlanOperation* event it merely changes state and waits passively for the next event.

This greatly simplified behaviour shifts more emphasis to another part of the frame concern. The user's *Commands* E3 are completely distinct from the *PlanOperations* E1. An important aspect of the machine behaviour is interpreting the user *Commands* and generating *PlanOperations* that will have the desired effect.

5.5.1   Simple workpieces frame concern

Here's a diagram, in the usual style, of the simple workpieces frame concern:

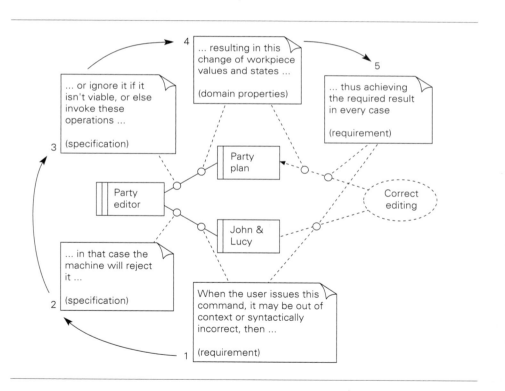

Frame concern in workpieces frame

As you might expect, it bears a strong resemblance to the frame concern for the commanded behaviour frame because the user has a role and characteristics very similar to the operator in a commanded behaviour problem.

The chief difference is in the characteristics of the central domain. Although the workpieces domain has a causal aspect supporting its operations and their effects, its main significance is lexical. Also, it's usually a designed domain.

The party plan domain has a data structure that can hold values and relationships among the values, and operations that can cause changes in the values and relationships held in the data structure. If you want to think of it in purely programming terms, and jump straight to an object-oriented description, you can think of the data values and relationships as being accessible only by invoking object methods. But there's some value in deferring the choice of access methods until you know what you need to access.

There's also the usual question about the order in which you should consider the domain properties and the requirement. Broadly, you can start by describing the party plan domain and then go on to consider the user *Commands*; or you can describe the user *Commands* and their required effects, and then describe the party plan domain and its *PlanOperations*. Either way, you must develop the machine behaviour afterwards.

5.5.2 Party plan domain description

Here's the structure of the party plan in a little class diagram:

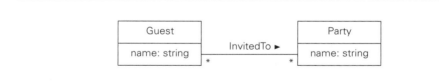

Party plan: class diagram

The party plan has any number of named guests and any number of named parties. Any number (*) of guests may be invitedTo each party, and each guest may be invitedTo any number (*) of parties. The resulting symbolic values and states Y4 are therefore:

IsG(gname): a state that holds if and only if there is a guest named gname;

IsP(pname): a state that holds if and only if there is a party named pname;

Invited(gname,pname): a state that holds if and only if there is an invitedTo association between a guest named gname and a party named pname.

Party plan operations

Here is a possible set of operations for the party plan domain:

- AddG(gname)   // add a guest object named gname;

- RmvG(gname)   // remove the guest object named gname;

- AddP(pname)   // add a party object named pname;

- RmvP(pname)   // remove the party object named pname;

- AddInv(gname,pname)   // add an invitedTo association between the guest named gname and the party named pname;

- RmvInv (gname,pname)   // remove the invitedTo association between the guest named gname and the party named pname.

These are the *PlanOperations* E1, controlled by the party editor. The party editor also controls the roles, that is, the choice of names to participate in each event. The general intention of each operation is clear from the comment, but the effect of each operation, including erroneous operations, must be stated in the domain behavioural description.

Party plan behaviour

The party plan symbolic values are *IsG*, *IsP* and *Invited*. Its operation events are *AddG*, *RmvG*, *AddP*, *RmvP*, *AddInv* and *RmvInv*. If you are designing the domain yourself, the domain description is your specification for implementing it. If it has been designed by someone else, you will need to investigate it just as you needed to investigate the light units domain in the one-way traffic lights problem. Either way, there are three main choices in the party plan domain design. They are:

- what is the domain behaviour if an operation occurs in response to which no state change is possible: for example, an *AddG* operation that purports to add an already existing guest, or a *RmvP* or *RmvInv* operation that purports to delete a non-existent party or invitedTo association?

- if an *AddInv(gname,pname)* operation occurs when there is no guest *gname* or no party *pname*, should the missing guest or party be automatically created, or should the operation leave the state unchanged?

■ if an *RmvG* or *RmvP* operation occurs for a guest or party for which there are invitedTo associations in existence, should those associations be automatically deleted, or should the operation leave the state unchanged?

The crucial thing to understand about these choices is that they are not choices about the interface that John and Lucy will see. The *PlanOperations* are not user *Commands*. But they will certainly affect the machine specification because they will affect the translation of user *Commands* into *PlanOperations*.

5.5.3 User commands

John and Lucy want the individual user *Commands* to be as short as possible. So they will be context-sensitive and have very short command names. They are entered at the machine's keyboard, each command terminated by the enter key. They are:

- ■ 'G gname'   // add a guest named gname to the plan or to a particular party;

- ■ 'XG gname'   // remove the guest named gname from the plan or from a particular party;

- ■ 'P pname'   // add a party named pname to the plan or to the set of parties to which a particular guest is invited;

- ■ 'XP pname'   // remove the party named pname from the plan or from the set of parties to which a particular guest is invited;

- ■ 'EG gname'   // refer the following commands to the context of the guest named gname;

- ■ 'EP pname'   // refer the following commands to the context of the party named pname;

- ■ 'E'   // refer the following commands to the context of the party plan.

The context-sensitivity allows the sequence of commands:

    <EP Birthday, G Anne, G Fred, G Bill, G Judy. ...>

to mean that Anne, Fred, Bill and Judy are all invited to the birthday party, and so on.

We'll have to give a full account of the effects of commands when we describe the requirement. How those effects are to be achieved by *PlanOperations* will be part of the machine specification.

5.5.4 The requirement

The requirement has three aspects:

- stipulating which commands are syntactically incorrect and must be rejected;

- defining the command context in terms of the EG, EP and E commands;

- stipulating the effects of other commands according to their command contexts and the current party plan state.

Incorrect syntax

A command is syntactically incorrect if it has an unrecognised command code (for example, 'H name') or contains superfluous characters (for example, 'E Fred') or a required name is absent (for example, 'G').

Command context

Four contexts are defined for the interpretation of syntactically correct commands. The context is set by E, EG and EP commands, as shown in this state-machine description:

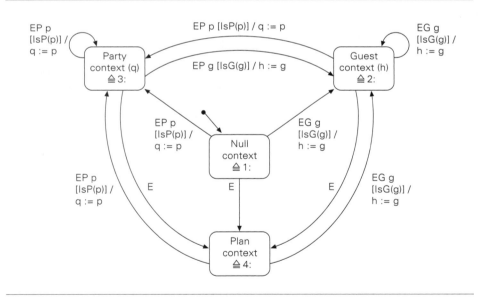

Party plan requirement: defining contexts

Initially, in state 1, the context is null. In any state, an E command selects the plan context, an EG g command where there is a guest named g selects the guest h context with h = g, and an EP p command where there is a party named p selects the party q context with q = p. All other commands leave the context unchanged.

The context is not an independently observable phenomenon. So this description, like the description of the sensible commands in the occasional sluice gate problem, is only *defining* some new terms on the basis of observable phenomena. The '$\triangleq$' in the state markings shows that the markings are definitions. For example, 'guest context(h)' is defined to mean 'in state 2 in this diagram'; the value of h is given by the event causing the transition into the state.

Command effects

The required effects of syntactically correct user commands G, XG, P and XP in the different contexts are:

- in the null context all commands are ignored;

- in the plan context all commands are ignored except:
    - G g [$\neg$ IsG(g)]: IsG(g) becomes true;
    - XG g [IsG(g)]: IsG(g) becomes false and Invited(g,p) becomes false for all p;
    - P p [$\neg$ IsP(p)]: IsP(p) becomes true;
    - XP p [IsP(p)]: IsP(p) becomes false and Invited(g,p) becomes false for all g;

- in the guest g context all commands are ignored except:
    - P p [$\neg$ Invited(g,p) $\wedge$ IsP(p)]: Invited(g,p) becomes true;
    - XP p [Invited(g,p) $\wedge$ IsP(p)]: Invited(g,p) becomes false;

- in the party p context all commands are ignored except:
    - G g [$\neg$ Invited(g,p) $\wedge$ IsG(g)]: Invited(g,p) becomes true;
    - XG g [Invited(g,p) $\wedge$ IsG(g)]: Invited(g,p) becomes false.

The requirement, of course, is about the effects of user *Commands*. The effects of *PlanOperations* are the subject of the party plan domain description.

5.5.5 Party plan editing specification

The machine specification describes the machine behaviour necessary to satisfy the requirement. That means:

- recognising and rejecting commands that are syntactically incorrect;

- providing an implementation of the command context and maintaining it in accordance with the sequence of syntactically correct commands;

- causing party plan operations that will ensure production of the required effects by exploiting the known properties of the party plan domain.

Any questions?

How is the simple workpieces frame related to the object-oriented model-view-controller (MVC) pattern?

MVC is usually thought of as something larger than a pattern. There is quite a lot about it in the 'Gang of Four' book: Erich Gamma, Richard Helms, Ralph Johnson and John Vlissides, *Design Patterns: Elements of Reusable Object-Oriented Software*, Addison-Wesley, 1995.

There MVC is discussed as a 'triad of classes' that contains a number of patterns: observer, composite and strategy. MVC is treated as an 'architectural pattern' in Frank Buschmann, Regine Meunier, Hans Rohnert, Peter Sommerlad and Michael Stahl, *Pattern-Oriented Software Architecture: A System of Patterns*, John Wiley, 1996.

The triad of classes in MVC is the *model*, the *view* and the *controller*. You can think of the workpieces domain as roughly corresponding to the MVC *model*. It contains the data that is being edited in this problem and will persist for use in other problems. The editing tool in the simple workpieces frame is roughly the MVC *controller*. In the simple workpieces problem there is nothing corresponding to the MVC *view*. That's why it's so – unrealistically – simple.

Why do you stress that the contexts are defined and aren't separately observable?

In the traffic light units the Stop and Go states are separately observable from the pulses that cause them to change, so the domain description relating states and pulses makes assertions that can be true or false. A definition isn't true or false: it's just a decision to use a term in a certain way. So writing 'Guest Context (h) $\triangleq$ 2:' is equivalent to say 'when I say "guest context (h)" I just mean that some sequence of commands has occurred that in this diagram leads to state 2'. There is nothing to observe separately from that sequence of commands.

Is the party plan of John and Lucy's parties and guests and invitations?

No. If it were, then the parties and guests and invitations would be included as domains in this problem. We'll look at the problem of making a model of a real world in Chapter 7.

Is the party plan a model of the users John and Lucy?

No. It's not a model of anything. It's a lexical domain for which no interpretation is needed or given in this problem.

Wouldn't the party plan problem be a lot easier if you just used MVC?

It might be easier to build a good system for John and Lucy, but it would be harder to explain the underlying principles. MVC is a solution, not a problem, pattern. And it's much more complicated than the workpieces frame.

Doesn't the party plan domain need some operation to produce a list of the guests, or of the parties?

Yes: in a problem that uses the party plan information, it probably does. But not in this problem, so we have left it out.

Why are you making such a big thing out of such a small problem?

Well, you can always ask that question about problem frames. Small problems let you distinguish concerns that might otherwise be thrown together in a confusing jumble. In a problem like this it's easy to confuse the workpieces domain with the machine, and the workpieces operations with the user commands. Clarity in small problems leads to clarity in larger problems.

5.6 Transformation frame concern

We're going to stick to the mailfiles analysis problem. You'll remember that Fred needs to analyse his email files to produce a report with a line for each of his correspondents. For each correspondent he wants to show the correspondent's name, how many days the report covers, the number of messages received from the correspondent and their maximum and average lengths, and the same information for the messages sent to the correspondent by Fred.

Here's the problem diagram:

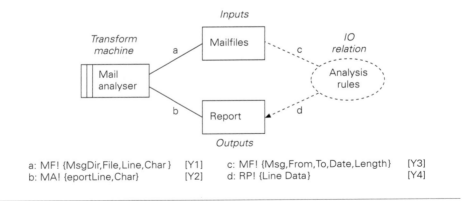

a: MF! {MsgDir,File,Line,Char }   [Y1]   c: MF! {Msg,From,To,Date,Length}   [Y3]
b: MA! {eportLine,Char}   [Y2]   d: RP! {Line Data}   [Y4]

Mailfiles analysis: fitted to transformation frame

The two problem domains – the inputs and the outputs – are both lexical. In each case the domain's requirement phenomena are different from its specification phenomena at the machine interface. In a transformation problem, the relationship between the requirement phenomena and the specification phenomena of each domain is an important concern.

Another aspect of the same concern is the relationship between the purely symbolic view of the inputs and outputs as lexical domains, and the causal view that you need to understand how their data can be accessed by the transform machine. The machine must *traverse* (travel over) the inputs and outputs domains to satisfy the requirement.

We need to see what this concern means before we look at the transformation frame concern. So we'll start by looking at the domain properties and other descriptions, leaving the frame concern until a little later.

5.6.1 Inputs domain properties

Fred's email client is very simple, and he has been very systematic in using it. All the files are in one directory. There is one file for each correspondent, and the file name is the correspondent's name. So he has a file named 'Albert', a file named 'Anna', and so on. The file for each correspondent contains all messages received from or sent to that person. So this is the large-scale structure of the inputs domain:

Mailfiles directory: partial domain description

Each individual mailfile has a sequential structure. It consists of a sequence of lines, where a line is a sequence of no more than 127 printable characters followed by a CRLF (carriage return, line feed).

The lines of a mailfile form a sequence of messages. Each message begins with a prefix line containing the local message id allocated by Fred's email client. This prefix is followed by the message header, which is a sequence of non-blank lines indicating, among other things, the message origin, destination, routing and date and time sent. The message header is followed by one blank line, which is followed by the text of the message.

The ordering of lines is a central property of the mail file structure. You can't conveniently describe it in a class diagram like the description of the directory structure because class diagrams don't allow you to describe the ordering of the constituent parts of an aggregation. You might use a tree diagram, like this:

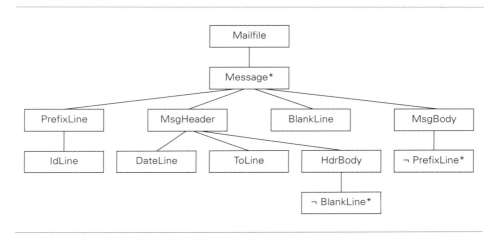

One mailfile: partial domain description

The diagram says that a mailfile consists of zero or more (*) messages, one after the other. Each message is a sequence of four parts: PrefixLine, MsgHeader, BlankLine and MsgBody, in that order. The MsgHeader consists of a DateLine, followed by a ToLine, followed by the HdrBody, which consists of zero or more non-blank lines. The MsgBody consists of zero or more non-prefix lines – lines that do not have the form of a PrefixLine.

These are the line formats:

■ a blank line is a line containing no characters except spaces (' ') and the terminating CRLF;

■ an IdLine looks like this:

'MsgId: 87632794'

where the numeric id is assigned by Fred's email client;

■ a DateLine looks like this:

'Date: Mon Mar 02 1999 14:16:58'

■ a ToLine line looks like this:

'To: someone@ispmail.com'

For a message received by Fred, the address is 'Fred@supermail.com'. For a message sent by Fred, the address is a different email address belonging to one of his correspondents.

5.6.2 Outputs domain properties

The report is a sequence of lines. Its structure is:

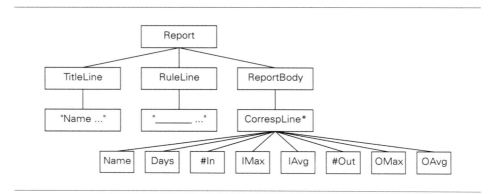

Mail analysis report: domain secription

The first line is the TitleLine, the second is the RuleLine under the TitleLine, then the ReportBody consists of zero or more CorrespLines. The data fields of each correspondent line are the correspondent name followed by seven integers, as shown in the picture of the analysis report given in the previous chapter. The values of these fields, and how they must be related to the content of the mailfiles, are stipulated in the requirement.

5.6.3 The requirement

The requirement is straightforward. Somewhat roughly stated, it is this:

- the ReportBody has one CorrespLine for each mailfile:
  - The CorrespLines must be in ascending order by name;

- the values in the eight fields of the CorrespLine are derived from the data in messages of the associated mailfile like this:
  - Name is the MFName from the mailfile DirectoryEntry;
  - Days is one more than the difference between the earliest and latest days in the DateLines of messages in the mailfile;
  - #In is the count of received messages in the mailfile (these are messages whose ToLine is 'To: fred@supermail.com');

- IMax is the length of the longest received message (the length of a message is the number of characters in the MsgBody including the CRLF characters);
- IAvg is the average length of received messages;
- #Out is the count of messages that are not received messages;
- OMax is the length of the longest message that is not a received message;
- OAvg is the average length of messages that are not received messages.

5.6.4 Traversals

The properties of the mailfiles and report domains we have described so far are all symbolic properties of lexical domains. The orderings shown by the tree descriptions are static sequences, like the sequences of stations on the different lines in a railway map, or the sequence of poems in an anthology. It's a fixed ordering, and does not change over time. In the same way, the requirement is concerned only with static sequencing – the sequence of the lines in the report and of the fields in each line.

But a specification is concerned with the behaviour of the machine, that is, with its behaviour in terms of events occurring over time. The machine must traverse the inputs domain, accessing the data values it needs by visiting the places in the domain where they are to be found. In the same way it must traverse the outputs domain, creating data values one after another by depositing them at the places where they are required. For simplicity and efficiency, you want the two traversals to be simultaneous, that is, to be neatly interleaved so that the inputs data are always visited just before they are needed for the outputs.

This idea of a *traversal* applies most obviously when the domains are inherently sequential, like a DOS file on disk, or a printed report, or a magnetic tape file on a backup device. Then execution of a *read* operation moves on in the domain so that the next *read* operation will retrieve the next record. But the idea also applies to domains that are not inherently sequential, such as a relational database or an object structure. Then the machine performs its traversals by following pointers or selecting tuples or computing data addresses: the traversal operations are less obviously physical, but they are still there.

5.6.5 The frame concern

Now we're ready to look at the frame concern. The frame concern for the transformation frame has a rather different shape from the others. Its main burden is to show that the effect of the chosen traversal will satisfy the requirement. You must show that as the machine traverses the inputs and outputs domains simultaneously, it correctly calculates the values to be written to the outputs domain from the values encountered in the inputs domain.

Here's the frame concern, pictured in our usual style:

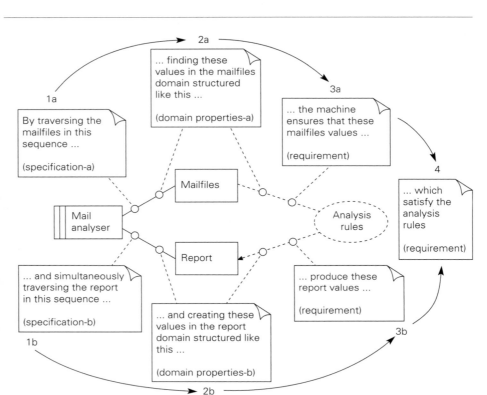

Frame concern in basic transformation frame

The argument, like the machine behaviour, follows two paths simultaneously. The double traversal, and its embedded operations to retrieve and deposit symbolic values, must correspond correctly to the structure and content of the two domains, and ensure that the IO relation given in the requirement is satisfied.

5.6.6 Efficiency of a transform machine

Traversal of a lexical domain by a machine involves causal phenomena, by which the machine makes progress in its traversal. In traversing a magnetic tape the machine causes the tape device to advance the physical position of the tape under the read/write head. In traversing a database the machine causes the disk heads to move to physically different parts of the database.

These physical interactions often raise concerns of efficiency. Once the requirement and domain properties have been understood and described, the central task in devising a machine behaviour to solve a transformation problem is often to find an efficient traversal of the inputs and outputs domains. The ideally efficient traversal is a simple copying of inputs to outputs. A practical efficient traversal avoids:

- multiple visits to the same data;

- unnecessary visits to irrelevant data;

- having to save a large amount of data in transit between input and output.

An efficient traversal

The mailfiles analysis problem has an obvious efficient traversal, provided that:

- the directory entries can be visited in sequence, as if the directory were a sequential file;

- the sequence is in ascending order by file name (and thus by the name of the correspondent whose messages are contained in the file).

Then the obvious efficient interleaved traversal has a structure that you can describe in another tree diagram like this:

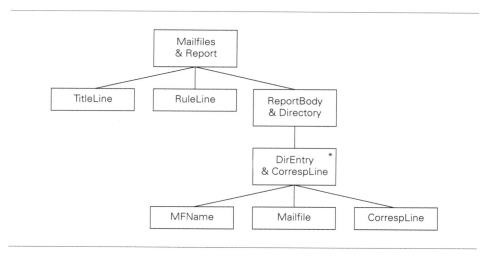

Mailfiles analysis: traversal specification

First the mail analyser machine produces the TitleLine and RuleLine of the report. Then it traverses the ReportBody and Directory simultaneously, producing a CorrespLine from each directory entry. First it retrieves the MFName from the directory entry, then it traverses the mailfile of that name, collecting the data for the CorrespLine. Finally it produces the CorrespLine.

Any questions?

Why do you say that a class diagram can't show ordering? What about the notation ordered *in UML?*

That notation just lets you say that a set of objects is ordered, it doesn't let you show each one individually and say where it is in the order.

How can you be sure that the MsgBody of a message in a mailfile doesn't include a PrefixLine?

That's a good question. It has three different, incompatible answers. First, any sequence of lines that contains a PrefixLine is not, by definition, a MsgBody. Second, any line included in a MsgBody is not, by definition, a PrefixLine. Third, if a MsgBody contains a PrefixLine then something has gone wrong with the mailfile. We'll come back to this topic in the next chapter.

5.7   Two comments

There's a lot more to say about problem frames, and we'll be saying some of it in the chapters that follow. At this stage it's appropriate to make two general comments.

5.7.1   Problem frames and development methods

The mailfile analysis problem illustrates an aspect of problem frame use that is, regrettably, far more uncommon than it should be. The efficient traversal that we used for the machine specification can be arrived at by a systematic method. The method makes it easy to see whether a straightforward interleaving of the inputs and outputs traversals is possible. If so, it helps you to find it easily. If not, it shows clearly what you have to do to overcome the difficulty – usually, to introduce an intermediate data structure of some kind.

Ideally, each problem frame would be associated with a systematic method that is known to be effective for analysing and solving any problem that fits the frame. It's not sensible to look for a general-purpose method that addresses all development problems. It's sensible to seek several specific methods that address problems of very specific classes. As a rule of thumb, the more specific the problem class, the more sharply focused, and therefore the more effective, the method can be.

We're a very long way indeed from that goal. But a necessary first step towards it is surely to identify different problem classes, by describing their frames, and to begin to map out the concerns that are important in each frame. The frame concerns that we have described in this chapter show how the different frames raise different concerns and therefore need different methods. Each frame concern indicates what development descriptions you must make, and provides a structure into which you must fit them.

5.7.2 Frame misfits

If you pick up the wrong frame for the problem you're dealing with, you'll find that its frame concern demands some description that doesn't seem to make much sense, and leaves out some other description that is obviously necessary.

Sluice gate as information display

Suppose, for example, that you're mistakenly trying to force the occasional sluice gate control problem into the information display frame. You'll have to treat the sluice operator as the real world, and the gate & motor as the display domain. The frame concern will demand a major emphasis on the domain properties of the real world: there must be an indicative description showing how the requirement phenomena are causally related to the phenomena at the machine interface. But the requirement phenomena of the sluice operator are the *Raise, Lower* and *Stop* commands, and these are also shared with the machine. Not much causal relationship there. On the other hand, you'll be wanting to say that some of the commands are rejected or ignored. But there's no provision in the information display frame for rejecting or ignoring real world phenomena: the indicative domain description must be total. It won't be any better assigning the domains the other way around. You've got the wrong frame.

Sluice gate as workpieces

Here's another example. Suppose that you're now trying to force the occasional sluice gate control problem into the simple workpieces frame. The sluice operator, is, presumably, the user, and the gate & motor is the workpieces domain. Now you're in trouble with the gate & motor domain. The workpieces are lexical and inert: their only behaviour is to change state immediately on the stimulus of an externally controlled event. That's why it's possible and convenient to describe them in terms of operations on a data structure. But the gate & motor aren't like that. Once the motor has been started, the gate is moving and the domain state is changing continuously; eventually it will reach one end of its travel, and the top or bottom sensor will close. You won't be able to describe the gate & motor as an instance of an abstract data type, or as a passive object. This is definitely not a simple workpieces problem.

Furnace operation as information display

One last example. You're trying to use the information display frame for the furnace operation problem. You're forced to think of the furnace sensor states and the *OnCmd* and *OffCmd* events as the real world because they provide the input to the machine. And you're forced to treat the furnace commands to the oil valve, fuel blower and ignition device as the events shared by the machine and the display domain because they are the output from the machine. Now you're in very serious trouble with the furnace equipment domain, which you have split into two domains. You really do need to describe how the furnace commands alter the internal state of the furnace, and how they cause changes in the furnace sensor states. There's nowhere in the information display frame to put this description. It can't be in the requirement because any requirement is purely optative, and this is an indicative description. It can't be in the domain description of the real world because you have excluded the furnace commands from the real world. It can't be in the domain description of the display domain because you have excluded the furnace sensors from the display domain. You have nowhere to turn. Try another problem frame.

It comes to this. Different frames capture different problem classes that need different development descriptions. If your problem doesn't fit your chosen frame, you'll be unable to analyse it in a coherent and systematic way.

Any questions?

What method for transformation problems are you referring to?

One that I worked on many years ago. You can read about it in:

M A Jackson, *Principles of Program Design*, Academic Press, 1975.

John Cameron, *JSP & JSD: The Jackson Approach to Software Development*, IEEE CS Press, 2nd Edition, 1989.

The IEEE tutorial by John Cameron includes a summary of the method that originally appeared in M A Jackson, *Constructive Methods of Program Design* in Proceedings of the 1st ECI Conference 1976, pp 236–262, Springer Verlag LNCS 44, Heidelberg, 1976.

Doesn't the possibility of frame misfits suggest that I would be better off without problem frames at all? They seem to have made things harder, not easier.

No. They reveal concerns and difficulties early in development that might otherwise have lain unrecognised until much later – perhaps too late. Ignoring a difficulty doesn't make it go away.

CHAPTER 6

Frame flavours and development descriptions

Problem analysis descriptions are about problem domain phenomena. Problem frames use coarse classifications of domains – biddable, causal or lexical – and phenomena – causal or symbolic. More finely classified domain properties give different domain flavours, and hence different problem flavours within a frame. These flavours, in static, dynamic and control domains, and in informal and conceptual domains, demand different descriptive languages and notations, and give rise to different development concerns.

6.1 Frames and flavours

Each problem frame has a frame concern that says what descriptions you must make and how they must fit together. Your descriptions, whether indicative or optative, are always about the phenomena of problem domains: even the machine specification is strictly about the machine's behaviour in terms of phenomena shared with the problem domains. The frame also defines the broad classification – biddable, causal, or lexical – of each problem domain, and of the shared phenomena – causal or symbolic, states or truths, values or events – at its interfaces with the requirement and with other domains.

So each frame restricts both the content of your development descriptions and the argument structure they must fit into. But it does not restrict them very closely. There is still a lot of scope within the frame restrictions for variations in domain characteristics. There are many different structures commonly found in lexical domains: a sequence is very different from a tree. Causal domains can have different internal structures of causality, giving rise to important differences in the problem of imposing constraints on their behaviour. These variations in domain characteristics can have significant effects on the development descriptions you must make, on the choice of language for each description, and on the arguments necessary to address the frame concern. We'll call these variations within a frame different *flavours* of the frame and of its domains. The menu for your development work doesn't change its shape. But the courses taste different.

6.1.1 The scope of a domain description

Domain descriptions are concerned with the domain's interfaces with other domains and with its requirement references. Look at this abstract problem diagram:

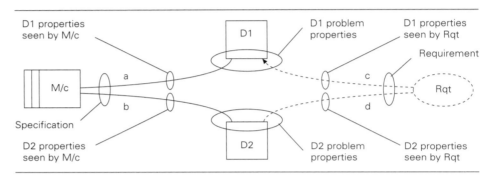

Domain properties at interfaces

In analysing the problem you may have to consider and describe each domain's properties from the point of view of several different interfaces and references.

- The requirement describes the required relationship between the two domains in terms of their phenomena sets *c* and *d*. You could say that the *scope* of the requirement is the phenomena {*c, d*}.

- Part of the requirement description may be concerned only with domain D1; the scope of that description is {*c*}.

- The specification describes the machine behaviour side of the domains' relationship in terms of their phenomena sets *a* and *b*: its scope is {*a, b*}.

- Part of the specification may be concerned only with domain D2; the scope of that description is {*b*}.

- You may need to make a separate description of the problem properties of D1 – its complete interface with the rest of the context and requirement; the scope for this description is {*a, c*}.

So it's too simple to think of a domain as having just one clearly well-bounded set of properties. You must think of its properties in relation to the requirement, to some other domain in the problem context, or to some description you need to make.

Sometimes to describe a domain property adequately you must refer to private phenomena that are neither shared with any other domain nor mentioned in the requirement. For example, in describing the properties of the sluice gate & motor domain, we need to describe how its *Open* and *Shut* states are affected by the pulses that turn the motor *On* and *Off* and set its direction *Clockwise* or *AntiClockwise*. For that, we need to refer to its state *Posn* – the position of the gate within its range of vertical travel. So the scope of this description is the phenomena {*On*, *Off*, *Clockwise*, *AntiClockwise*, *Open*, *Shut* and *Posn*}.

It's often necessary to make a description in two or more parts. The furnace operation subproblem is a part of the home heating control problem. We introduced it in Chapter 3. Its requirement falls naturally into two parts: one part describes the stipulations for safe operation in turning the furnace on and off; the other describes how the *OnCmd* and *OffCmd* events must be treated. The stipulations for safe furnace operation are essentially that the furnace must not be *ignited* while there is any oil *vapour* in the combustion chamber that has not yet *dispersed*. Its scope is the phenomena {*Vapour*, *Disperse*, *Ignited*}. Nothing about *OnCmd* or *OffCmd* events here.

6.1.2 Domain flavours

In short, you will probably need to make several descriptions of each domain in your development. The scope of each description is a set of phenomena of the domain; for each description you must consider the domain's characteristics as they appear filtered through the lens of that scope. So when we talk about domain flavours, we are always talking about the flavours seen from the point of view of a particular description with a particular scope.

Not a complete account
We won't try to give a complete account of all possible domain flavours. Instead we will look at some particular groups of flavours in particular contexts. Distinguished by a partly *ad hoc* terminology, they are:

- *static flavours*. These are structural flavours that are important both in lexical domains and in some causal domains;

- *dynamic flavours*. These are small-scale behavioural flavours that affect domain interactions in a relatively short-term, local way;

- *control flavours*. These are larger-scale behavioural flavours that characterise different levels of difficulty in behaviour problems;

- *informal flavours*. These are flavours of causal or biddable domains, or occasionally of lexical domains, that make reliable formal reasoning about domain behaviour and properties very difficult or even impossible;

- *conceptual flavours*. These are flavours of domains that are hard to talk about because they seem to consist largely of concepts and intellectual constructs that are inconveniently subjective.

The variety of domain flavours and the variety of descriptive notations and techniques necessary to deal with them faithfully is a substantial part of computer science and software engineering.

Any questions?

Why not just make one description of the properties of a domain, and use it everywhere the domain appears?

For at least two reasons. First, there can't be a universally valid description: any description must be made with some particular purpose in mind. This lesson was learned – or should have been learned – on a larger scale from the failure of the 'enterprise model' idea. The enterprise model was going to be a universally valid description of the enterprise. No one ever succeeded in making one.

Second, because some of your descriptions must be indicative and others optative. You need a clear separation between them.

6.2 Static flavours

A static domain is one that has no time dimension. It causes no events, and has no changeable states. Everything is fixed.

As always, domain properties are to be understood in some particular scope. The lexical domains of a transformation problem are static domains for purposes of the requirement. The requirement, in the form of an input/output relation, stipulates only the final result of each execution of the transform machine. It tells you how to check Fred's mailfiles against his analysis report. It says nothing about the dynamic process of traversal, in which the mail analyser machine steps its way through the directory and through each mailfile, and simultaneously through the analysis report, or about the status of the analysis report when it is half-complete.

6.2.1 Physical static domains

A physical domain may be static. It can have entities and states, and the entities may participate in externally controlled events. But when they do, nothing in the domain is affected. Of course, a physical static domain can't be the controlled domain in a behaviour problem. It has no behaviour, so its behaviour can't be controlled.

Consider a problem for which the context is, roughly, a Formula 1 motor race. The road layout for the race is a static physical domain. The road layout and all its properties are regarded as fixed, at least for the duration of the race. The layout certainly causes no events, but it can participate in events caused by the cars in the race. If a car crashes at a corner, it makes perfectly good sense to ask: Which corner of the layout participated in the crash event?

Here's another example of a static domain, taken from a problem that we'll look at more than once later in the book.

Package router control

A package router is a large mechanical device used by postal and delivery organisations to sort packages into bins according to their destinations.

The packages carry bar-coded labels. They move along a conveyor to a reading station where their package-ids and destinations are read. They then slide by gravity down pipes fitted with sensors at top and bottom. The pipes are connected by two-position switches that the computer can flip (when no package is present between the incoming and outgoing pipes). At the leaves of the tree of pipes are destination bins, corresponding to the bar-coded destinations.

A package cannot overtake another either in a pipe or in a switch. Also, the pipes are bent near the sensors so that the sensors are guaranteed to detect each package separately. However, packages slide at unpredictable speeds, and may get too close together to allow a switch to be set correctly. A misrouted package may be routed to any bin, an appropriate message being displayed. There are control buttons by which an operator can command the controlling computer to stop and start the conveyor.

The problem is to build the controlling computer to obey the operator's commands, to route packages to their destination bins by setting the switches appropriately, and to report misrouted packages.

The router equipment looks something like this:

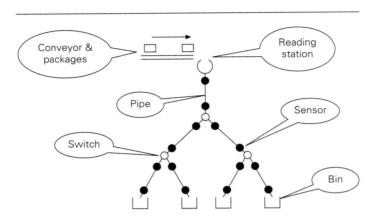

A schematic picture of the package router

One aspect of the problem is that the machine must identify the correct route to any particular bin from any point in the layout of pipes and switches. If this package is to be routed to bin 17, and it's now at switch sw3, should it go left or should it go right?

For this purpose, the layout of pipes, switches and bins forms a static domain. Like the Formula 1 road layout, this layout is fixed. For purposes of identifying the route to a particular bin, the settings of the switches are irrelevant. So you can just ignore the switch setting states. All that matters about a switch is that it has a certain pipe coming in and two other pipes going out.

Problem relativity

Of course, the layout is fixed only if you confine your attention to an operational period in the life of the package router in which it is running continuously. When the router is not in operation, the company that owns it may decide to alter its infrastructure configuration by adding pipes, switches and bins to accommodate new package destinations. If you are dealing with a problem of managing the router reconfiguration, the layout of pipes, switches and bins would be a dynamic domain. The characteristics and flavour of a domain don't depend only on the scope of your description but also on the problem that the domain appears in.

6.2.2 Structural flavours

The description of a static domain is often concerned with its *structural* properties. For example, the package router layout is a *tree*. The reading station is the *root* node, the switches are the *interior* nodes, the bins are the *leaf* nodes, and the pipes provide the *arcs* that connect each non-root node to its unique parent node. Because the switches are two-position switches, they have only two outgoing pipes, so the tree is a *binary tree*.

Structural properties are fundamental both to static physical domains and to lexical domains. In a lexical domain, the structural properties govern what traversals are meaningful and possible. The correctness of an argument is often determined by a structural property and its consequences.

Here's an example:

Family tree printing

A small genealogical database contains information about many members of an extended family. The information for each person includes name, mother, father and birthDate, except that mother and father are not given in every case. Because names are not unique, the information for each person includes an ID; a reference to a mother or father is the ID of a person in the database.

A program is needed that can print family trees showing up to six generations of the descendants of any specified person (called the *chosen ancestor*). The layout of the family tree in the printout is like this:

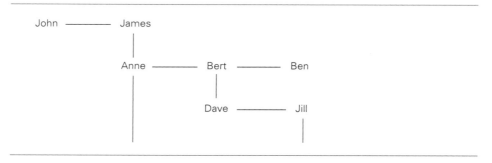

Family tree printout

In this example John is the chosen ancestor. His children are James, Anne and some more not shown in the diagram. Anne's children are Bert and Dave. Bert's only child is Ben. Ben has no children. And so on.

The structure of the database arises from the mother and father relationships. For the most efficient printing of the tree shown in the diagram the machine must make two simultaneous traversals:

- a traversal of the printed outputs domain that visits each line sequentially down the paper;

- a traversal of the database that visits each parent before visiting the parent's children.

The database traversal can be like this algorithm:

```
Traverse(root);
where Traverse(n) = { Visit(n);
                        forEach child c of n { Traverse(c) }
                      }
```

In analysing a problem containing a domain with a particular structural flavour, you must understand the structure properly. Structures of this kind are the subject of a large part of computer science. Did you understand the family tree properly? Here are two questions to help you to check your understanding.

- How many times does each person in the database appear in the printout?

- Why are mother and father not given in every case?

When a tree is not a tree

Here are the answers.

- A person in the database may appear as many as 16 times in one printout.

  This complication arises from the fact that the family tree isn't a tree in the accepted sense. A tree has only one path from the root to any other node. But if A's parents are cousins, they have a common grandparent. There are then two paths from A to the chosen ancestor at the root: one through A's mother and one through A's father. If the grandparent is the chosen ancestor, A will appear twice.

- Because the database must be of finite size.

  If everyone's mother and father are given, there's nowhere to stop in going back in the family generations.

Trees, of course, are only one particular structure. It's worth reading about the various static structures – sequences, trees, graphs – and about algorithms for traversal and for dynamic behaviour that may modify the structure.

Any questions?

Where can I read more about static structures?
An excellent book about structures, both static and dynamic, written from a pro-gramming point of view, is Robert Sedgewick, *Algorithms*, Addison-Wesley, 2nd Edition, 1988.

That is a little old-fashioned now. A newer and much larger book is Thomas H Cormen, Charles E Leiserson and Ronald L Rivest, *Introduction to Algorithms*, MIT Press and McGraw-Hill, 1990.

Why is 16 times the maximum number of occurrences of one person?
Here's why:

- each descendant of the chosen ancestor appears once for each time their mother appears, and once for each time their father appears;
- the children of the chosen ancestor appear only once (at level 1);
- assuming no incest, no person's mother and father are siblings. So grand-children of the chosen ancestor appear only once (at level 2);
- since cousins may marry, great-grandchildren of the chosen ancestor may appear twice (at level 3);
- the tree can show six generations of descendants, so it can extend to level 6.

Can't half-siblings marry?
No. See Leviticus xviii verse 9. The Code of Hammurabi contains laws forbidding incest, but is silent on this particular case. Perhaps we're straying a little outside our subject of software development.

Where does the package router control problem come from?
From a German research paper: G Hommel, 'Vergleich verschiedener Spezifikationsverfahren am Beispieleiner Paketverteilanlage', Kernforschungs zentrum Karlsruhe, Technical Report, August 1980.

It has also been used as an example problem in other research papers:

Daniel Jackson and Michael Jackson, *Problem Decomposition for Reuse*, Software Engineering Journal, Volume 11 Number 1, pages 19–30, January 1996.

Robert M Balzer, Neil M Goldman and David S Wile, *Operational Specification as the Basis for Rapid Prototyping*, ACM SIGSOFT Software Engineering Notes, Volume 7, Number 5, pages 3–16, December 1982. Reprinted in *New Paradigms for Software Development*, W W Agresti, IEEE Tutorial Text, IEEE Computer Society Press, 1986.

William Swartout and Robert Balzer, *On the Inevitable Intertwining of Specification and Implementation*, Communications of the ACM, Volume 25, Number 7, pages 438–440, July 1982.

Dynamic flavours

By 'dynamic flavours' we mean small-scale behavioural flavours that affect domain interactions in a relatively local way.

6.3.1 Tolerance in dynamic domains

An important characteristic of a dynamic causal domain is its capacity to tolerate externally controlled events of which only some cause changes in the domain state. Look at this description of the behaviour of the driver-controlled passenger door in a bus:

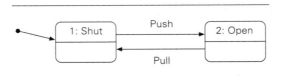

Door behaviour: incomplete description

The door has two states: it can be *Shut* or *Open*. Its movement is controlled by a control knob, which the driver can *Push* and *Pull*. The diagram shows – incompletely – how the door responds to these events.

What the diagram does not show is how the door behaves when a *Pull* event occurs while it is *Shut*, or when a *Push* occurs while it is *Open*. Its behaviour in relation to these events is its *tolerance* characteristic in respect of them. We can distinguish three cases: *robust, inhibiting* and *fragile*. They are shown in the three diagrams below:

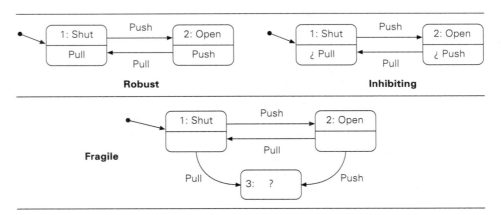

Robust, inhibiting and fragile behaviour

The *robust* behaviour in the upper left diagram allows the *Push* and *Pull* events in question to occur without causing any state change, as indicated by the undecorated event names in the lower section of the symbols for states 1 and 2. We saw this kind of tolerance behaviour in the sluice gate motor control in the previous chapter: an *On* pulse when the motor is already on is ignored, and similarly for *Off*, *Clockw* and *Anti* pulses when the motor is already off, set to clockwise or set to anticlockwise respectively.

The inhibiting behaviour in the upper right diagram *inhibits* the events in question, as indicated by the event names prefixed by '¿', in the lower sections of the state symbols. What the diagram shows is that *Pull* cannot occur in state 1, and *Push* cannot occur in state 2: not because the bus driver, who controls those events, will not try to make them occur, but because the domain we are describing prevents them from occurring. We saw this kind of behaviour in the zoo turnstile problem. In a *Push* event, a zoo visitor pushes on the entry barrier; the visitor causes the *Push* event, but the entry barrier may inhibit it if it is in the *Locked* state.

The *fragile* behaviour in the bottom diagram reacts to the events in question by entering an unknown state. This is state 3 in the diagram, indicated by the question mark. This behaviour is called fragile because we make the conservative assumption that in the unknown state the domain is broken. We saw this kind of behaviour in the light unit domain of the one-way traffic lights problem: an *RPulse* in the *Go* state, or a *GPulse* in the *Stop* state would break the unit.

6.3.2 Inhibition

Inhibiting behaviour is not at all uncommon, especially in devices that have two stable states. A typical domestic light switch participates in *FlipUp* and *FlipDown* events. These events are caused by users of the switch: it never flips itself spontaneously. But when the light switch is up, *FlipUp* events are inhibited by the mechanical properties of the switch, and *FlipDown* events are similarly inhibited when it is down. In the same kind of way, a car gearbox may be equipped with an interlock that prevents the user from engaging a low gear while travelling at more than 60mph. Only the user can cause the shift to a low gear, but the gearbox can inhibit it.

Event inhibition is sometimes an appropriate abstraction for more elaborate interactions. For example, the editing tool in a word-processing system may prevent the user from issuing certain commands in certain states by removing them from the menu, or by showing them only in a 'greyed-out' style. The user controls the command events, and the editing tool can inhibit them. Inhibition can also be used to avoid a more cumbersome description in terms of a request/permit protocol:

> 1: domain A requests permission to cause event E; then
> either 2a: { domain B refuses permission for event E;
>   domain A does not cause event E}
> or 2b: { domain B grants permission for event E;
>   domain A causes event E}.

More compactly, you can say that domain A controls the events, and domain B can inhibit them.

When you need to, you can show inhibition in the interface annotation of a problem diagram:

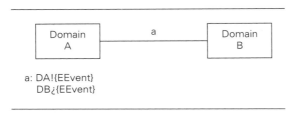

a: DA!{EEvent}
   DB¿{EEvent}

Showing inhibition in a problem diagram

Whether event inhibition is an appropriate abstraction depends, as always, on your purpose. If you are describing a large-scale bank accounting system, inhibition of cash withdrawal from ATMs is probably an appropriate abstraction: it is enough to say that customers control cash withdrawal events, but the machine can prevent them. But if you are developing the ATM software, inhibition is not appropriate. You must concern yourself with the full detail of the interactions in which the customer makes a withdrawal request and the ATM may refuse it.

As a general rule, you must treat inhibition with great care. Biddable domains – human beings – are able to play the role of domain A without disaster, adapting without much difficulty to the impossibility of an intended action. If at first you don't succeed, try something else or just give up. Causal domains can adapt only if the need for adaptation has been explicitly foreseen, and the adaptation has been explicitly programmed.

6.3.3 Discrete and continuous phenomena

In some causal domains the most important phenomena are *continuous* rather than *discrete*. Here's an example:

Airport shuttle control

An airport is equipped with a light monorail shuttle to move passengers from the gate area to the airport concourse. The shuttle moves on its own fixed track between the two areas. It is equipped with a bi-directional motor and a brake. The motor has an on/off state, a direction state, and five power levels; the brake has four braking levels. A sensor device detects the position of the shuttle on the track. The value of the sensor state is an integer in the range 0 – 9999. When the shuttle is at its rest position in the gate area, the sensor state value is 0; when it is at its rest position in the concourse area, the value is 9999; intermediate values represent positions equally spaced between the rest positions.

The control computer has direct access to the position sensor state, and can set the motor and brake states directly. It is required to control the shuttle by computer so that it moves continually backwards and forwards between the areas, stopping for 60 seconds in each area to allow passengers to embark and disembark. The journey should be as fast as possible, subject to certain limits on the speed, acceleration and deceleration. These limits are designed to give the passengers a comfortable ride and to avoid excessive wear on the motor and brakes.

The state of the position sensor is a *discrete* phenomenon. It has exactly 10,000 distinct integer values. Position 3456 is next to position 3457: there's nothing between them. But the exact location of the shuttle on the track is a *continuous* phenomenon with an unlimited number of distinct values. Whatever two distinct locations you choose on the track, there is a third location between them. In the shuttle problem you must deal with this situation carefully.

We have already seen a problem with discrete and continuous phenomena: the sluice gate control problem. Remember that in our fragmentary description of the sluice gate domain, we represented the movement of the gate when the motor is on in state 2 by an event expression describing discrete changes to the position p:

after(0.1s) / p:=p+0.1 .

That is, after 0.1 seconds in state 2 an event occurs in which the gate position is increased by 0.1 inches, and again after each further 0.1 seconds while the domain remains in state 2. This is a very crude discrete approximation to the continuous reality of smooth movement.

It's often convenient to use this kind of discrete approximation. It fits, more or less, into the expressive power of a state machine description. And, if you succumb to the constant temptation to look forward to the implementation, you can see that the implementation on a digital computer of the control machine in a behaviour problem will be forced to rely on sampling a continuous phenomenon at regular discrete intervals. So eventually you can't escape it.

Avoid premature approximations

However, you should be wary of rushing prematurely to a discrete approximation. Sometimes the earlier stages of your analysis must deal faithfully with the continuous phenomena, leaving the discrete approximation to later. The shuttle problem requirement refers not only to location but also to velocity and acceleration. These three states of the domain are related like this:

location = distance along track (from an arbitrarily chosen fixed point)
velocity = rate of change of position
acceleration = rate of change of velocity

Here we are assuming that the track is laid in a straight line. If it's not, then the matter is considerably more complicated. The computation of acceleration and deceleration must take the curvature of the track into account. You won't be able to deal properly with the requirement and the domain properties, including the track layout, if you have already migrated to a discrete approximation. Starting from a discrete representation of position, it's not too hard to represent velocity. But it's a lot harder to represent acceleration, and harder still to reason in terms of these representations. You really need a descriptive language in which you can state and manipulate expressions involving these phenomena in the most natural, continuous way. That's the kind of mathematical expressions you learned in your calculus classes.

When you're working with a discrete representation, and things are getting hard, ask yourself: Have I abandoned the continuous view too early?

6.4 Control flavours

In a behaviour problem, the difficulty of addressing the frame concern depends heavily on the characteristics of the controlled domain. You can understand these characteristics in terms of the different states in which the domain may be at any one time. In this section we'll look first at the states, and then at the domain characteristics.

6.4.1 Behavioural states

The simplest classification of states is into *active* and *passive* states.

- In an *active* state, the domain may cause shared events and shared state changes without the stimulus of externally caused events.

- In a *passive* state, the domain causes no shared events or shared state changes except possibly in response to the stimulus of externally caused events.

The difficulty of a behaviour problem depends very much on the relationship between the active and passive states of the controlled domain, and how transitions occur among them.

Some finer distinctions

Active states can be further classified into:

- *event-active* states, in which the domain may cause events without external stimulus;

- *state-active* states, in which the domain may cause state changes without external stimulus.

Passive states can be further classified into:

- *pure passive* states, in which the domain causes no events or state changes, even when an externally caused event occurs;

- *event-reactive* states, in which the domain may cause events in response to externally caused events;

- *state-reactive* states, in which the domain may cause state changes in response to externally caused events.

The different kinds of state are illustrated, in their purest forms, in this diagram:

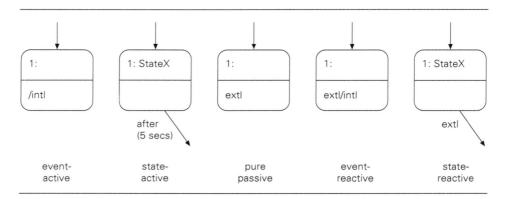

A classification of simple behaviour states

In the event-active state, the domain may spontaneously cause a shared event *intl*. In the state-active state it may cause a transition out of state 1, in which *StateX* holds, to another state in which, we will suppose, *StateX* does not hold. In the pure passive state, an externally caused event *extl* may occur, but the domain does not react in any way. In the event-reactive state, the domain reacts to an externally caused event *extl* by causing an event *intl*. In the state-reactive state, it reacts to an externally caused event *extl* by causing a transition out of state 1, in which the shared state *StateX* holds, to another state in which, we will suppose, *StateX* does not hold.

Here are some examples from problems we have already looked at.

- In the one-way traffic lights problem, the light units domain is pure passive at its interface with the lights controller. There is no shared state in this interface: when the lights controller has caused an *RPulse* or *GPulse*, it can detect no reaction by the light unit.

- In the one-way traffic lights problem, the light units domain is state-reactive for its domain description. For a scope that combines its interface with the lights controller and its requirement phenomena, the domain reacts to *RPulses* and *GPulses* by changing its *Stop* and *Go* states.

- In the party plan editing problem, the party plan domain is state-reactive at its interface with the party editor: it reacts to *PlanOperation* events by changing its *PlanStates*.

- In the patient monitoring problem, the patients domain is state-active for a scope of its requirement phenomena: the patients spontaneously change their *Pulse-rate, Temperature* and other physical states.

- In the library administration problem, the members & candidates domain is event-active at its interface with the library staff. It spontaneously causes *Enrol, Resign*, and *Pay* events.

- In the zoo turnstile problem, the entry barrier is event-reactive at its interface with the zoo visitors: when a visitor causes a *Push* event, the barrier reacts by causing an *Enter* event that completes the rotation of the barrier and guides the visitor into the zoo.

6.4.2   Behavioural domain characteristics

This pure classification of behavioural states is too simple for understanding the behavioural characteristics of most real domains. It's too simple for two reasons. First, because one domain state may combine the behaviour of two or more kinds of behavioural state. Here, for example, is one of the states of the sluice gate domain:

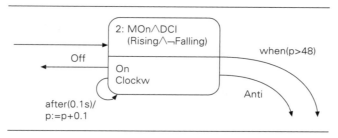

Sluice gate: one domain state

This state is pure passive with respect to *On* and *Clockw* events, but with respect to *Off* and *Anti* events it is state-reactive. In this state the domain also spontaneously changes its private state *Posn* – represented by the variable *p* – and makes a spontaneous transition when *p* exceeds 48, so it must also be regarded as state-active.

Second, most real domains have a variety of states, and make transitions between states of different classes. If we show two states of the sluice gate domain, we see:

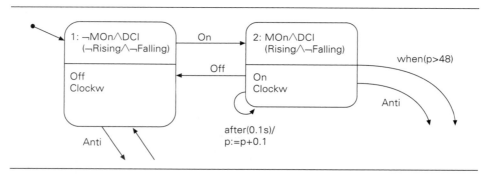

Sluice gate: further domain properties

In state 1, the sluice gate is at rest with the motor switched off. This state is pure passive with respect to *Off* and *Clockw* events, and state-reactive with respect to *On* and *Anti* events. But unlike state 2 it is not state-active: it makes no spontaneous transitions.

It makes sense to say that a state is active if it is active with respect to any of its phenomena, even if it is passive with respect to some other phenomena. Looking at the fragmentary domain description in the sluice gate diagram, you can then see that in state 1 the sluice gate is passive, but in state 2 it is active. You can also see that in its active state 2, the sluice gate can be made to transition immediately, by an externally caused *Off* event, to state 1. If the motor is switched off, the gate stops moving. We'll say that State 2 is *stoppable active*: it's active, but the activity can be stopped by a forced immediate transition to a passive state.

The classification of states into passive, stoppable active and unstoppable active underlies a classification of causal domains that is important for behaviour problems.

- The simplest domains have only passive states (remember that a passive state may be event-reactive or state-reactive). The control machine can safely ignore the domain except during very short episodes of interaction in which the control machine causes a shared event and the domain reacts either immediately or not at all.

  Outside these episodes the domain will remain in whatever state it reached in the preceding episode (or in its initial state), and can be relied on not to initiate any event or state change whatsoever. The episodes are so short that during each episode the control machine can safely ignore all other domains: effectively each episode can be regarded as instantaneous. The light units in the one-way traffic lights problem is such a domain.

- Domains of the second class have active states, but all their active states are stoppable. The control machine can safely ignore the domain except during episodes of interaction that begin when the domain is in a passive state and the control machine causes a shared event.

  Some of these episodes are effectively instantaneous, when the domain responds either immediately or not at all, and does not enter an active state. Others have significant duration, when the domain enters a stoppable active state and remains in a stoppable active state for some time. The episode ends either when the domain spontaneously enters a passive state, or when the control machine causes a shared event that takes the domain into a passive state. Because all the active states are stoppable, the control machine can effectively override the domain behaviour at any time by forcing it immediately into a passive state.

  The sluice gate is a domain of this kind. Turning the motor on starts an episode in which the sluice controller machine must not ignore the sluice gate, but must wait for it to reach the end of its travel. Turning the motor off always terminates the episode, bringing the gate to an immediate halt.

- Domains of the third class are more complex. A domain of this class has active states that are not stoppable. That is, in some states its activity cannot be immediately halted by any externally caused event.

  The airport shuttle is an example of this third class of domain. The shuttle domain has passive states, in which it is stationary with the motor off. In its active states it is moving; all of these active states, except when movement is at the very lowest non-zero speed, are non-stoppable.

In an active state of the shuttle domain, the machine, by changing the motor and brake states, can cause the shuttle to reduce its speed. But deceleration is limited, and it takes some time for the shuttle to come to rest. During that time the shuttle is still active, and its position and speed are still changing.

Unsurprisingly, the hardest behaviour problems are those with the most complex class of controlled domain. The airport shuttle problem is a serious problem in control engineering. It is not at all clear how much motor power should be applied at each moment while the shuttle is accelerating, or how much braking power should be applied while it is decelerating. The skill that every car driver must learn – to bring the car smoothly to a halt at a desired stopping place – does not translate in any obvious way to a specification for the shuttle's control machine. If you are responsible for the shuttle control software you should certainly learn some control theory, and make sure you have a control engineer in your team.

Any questions?

It seems that a domain that reaches a pure passive state, or an event-reactive state, can't ever leave that state. Is this right?

Yes, it is.

Why do you say that the sluice gate 'transitions immediately' to a passive state? Surely the motor and gate mechanism must take some time to come to a full stop.

Yes, indeed they do. But the gate moves very slowly, and they don't take long. So 'immediately', as shown in the domain description, is a reasonable abstraction of the domain behaviour for our purposes in developing the sluice controller machine.

Is the famous cruise control problem as hard as the airport shuttle problem?

Well, it's certainly not trivial. If control is switched on when the set speed is 50mph above the current speed, how much acceleration should the machine try to apply? You must also address concerns that arise because the environment is changing. For example, road gradient and wind cause acceleration and deceleration even at a constant throttle setting. There's a nice discussion of the cruise control problem in these two papers:

Mary Shaw, *Beyond Objects: A Software Design Paradigm Based on Process Control*, ACM Software Engineering Notes, Volume 20, Number 1, pages 27–38, January 1995.
Mary Shaw, *Making Choices: A Comparison of Styles for Software Architecture*, IEEE Software, special issue on software architecture, Volume 12, Number 6, pages 27–41, November 1995.

6.5 Informal flavours

When you make formal domain descriptions, and use them in your problem analysis, you are doing something very ambitious. Think of it as a three-step procedure.

- First, you *formalise* the domain properties by identifying phenomena and writing down unambiguous formal statements about them. For example, you describe the way the traffic light units work by a state machine, and you specify the lights controller behaviour in another state machine.

- Second, you *reason* formally about your descriptions, and draw conclusions from your reasoning. For example, you show that combining the specification and the domain description gives another description, of a sequence of *Stop* and *Go* states.

- Third, you *interpret* the results of your reasoning in the domain. The third description, you claim, means that the *Stop* and *Go* sequence will show in the real light units.

This three-step procedure is based on a deep assumption about the domains.

6.5.1 The formality assumption

The deep assumption is that the domain is formal enough for the procedure to make sense. It may not be. Do you know the popular song: 'Everybody loves my baby, but my baby loves only me'? You can formalise it easily, using the logic symbols '$\forall$' and '$\to$'. The symbol '$\forall$' means 'for all', and '$\to$' means 'implies'. The formalisation is:

(a) $\forall x \bullet \text{Loves}(x, \text{MyBaby})$ // 'everybody loves my baby'

(b) $\forall y \bullet \text{Loves}(\text{MyBaby}, y) \to y = \text{Me}$ // 'my baby loves only me'

David Gries points out that you can now reason formally like this:

(c) What's true for all x must be true for MyBaby. Therefore from (a),
     $\text{Loves}(\text{MyBaby}, \text{MyBaby})$ // 'my baby loves my baby'

(d) $\text{Loves}(\text{MyBaby}, \text{MyBaby})$ is just a particular case of $\text{Loves}(\text{MyBaby}, y)$ in (b).
     Therefore from (b):
     $\text{Loves}(\text{MyBaby}, \text{MyBaby}) \to \text{MyBaby} = \text{Me}$
     Therefore I am MyBaby.

Something has gone badly wrong here. The formalisation seems appropriate; the reasoning is sound; but it has all led to nonsense. The cause of the breakdown is that the domain is too informal to be reasoned about in this kind of way.

To say that a domain is informal is to say two things:

■ first, that any formalisation and abstraction of domain phenomena and of their relationships is at best only *approximate*. Most interesting sets are fuzzy – you can almost always find a hard case whose membership is in doubt;

■ second, that you can't confidently limit the considerations that might affect the domain properties and behaviour you're interested in. So it's hard to make universal statements that apply in all cases. There is always much that has not been considered, and some of it may prove decisive – sometimes catastrophically.

A computer is carefully engineered so that for the practical purposes of software development you can reasonably regard it as formal. Its phenomena have reliably recognisable types: you can't be in doubt about whether something is an addressable byte of RAM or not. And all their instances have reliably recognisable values: you can't be in doubt about whether the value of a particular bit is one or zero. Events inside the computer have effects that can be correctly described by universal statements, for example, about the result of an arithmetic operation on any two 16-bit integers. On this basis you can build software that embodies a formal description of the machine's behaviour, and you can reliably predict what the machine will do at its interfaces with the world outside.

But most of the world outside is not formal. A lexical domain is formal – at least, in respect of its symbolic phenomena. But causal and biddable domains are always informal, at least to some extent. Sometimes the informality of a problem domain can be treated quite lightly – the flavour of informality is barely detectable, and you can get away with ignoring it. But sometimes the flavour is quite strong, and you have to be very careful in making your descriptions.

6.5.2 Designations

If you want to make a reliable description of an informal domain, your fundamental task is to establish the meanings of a set of ground terms that you can use in descriptions. The simple and appropriate way to do this is to write a *designation*, like this:

>Stop(i) ≈ state: the Stop light is on in light unit i

The designation gives the formal term *Stop(i)*. Then, after the designation symbol (≈), it says what kind of phenomenon it is: a state phenomenon. And it gives a *recognition rule* by which you can recognise whether what you are observing in the domain is, or is not, an instance of the designated phenomenon: *Stop(i)* is true exactly when 'the Stop light is on in light unit *i*' is true. When you write a designation you are introducing a new class of observation that you can make of the domain, and naming the newly observable phenomena so that you can refer to them in your descriptions.

Which phenomenon?

Designations can help you to avoid two forms of confusion. The first is confusing one phenomenon with another that is closely related. A contributory cause to the 1979 accident at the Three Mile Island nuclear power plant was a control panel indication that a certain valve was shut when in fact it was open. The true requirement for the information display problem of indicating the valve state on the control panel was something like this:

IndicateValveShut ↔ ValveShut

That is: the control panel must show that the valve is shut if and only if (↔) the valve is shut. But the machine specification did not directly satisfy the requirement. The indicator in fact showed whether the current was on or off in a solenoid that actuated the valve, not whether the valve itself was open or shut. The machine specification was therefore something like this:

IndicateValveShut ↔ SolenoidOff

To justify the claim that this specification ensured satisfaction of the requirement, there was an implicit assertion that the domain had this property:

SolenoidOff ↔ ValveShut

That is: the solenoid is off if and only if the valve is shut. The correctness of the specification relied on this assertion, but unfortunately the assertion was not true. The valve could stick in the open position with the solenoid off, and this is what happened. The absence of a clear and explicit designation for the term *ValveShut* allowed the mistake to be easily made and overlooked.

Is this an instance?

The second form of confusion that a carefully written designation will help you to avoid is uncertainty about whether a particular term applies in a particular case. But it will help only if the recognition rule is very carefully written. Suppose that you write this designation:

Mother(m,p) ≈ state: the person m is the mother of the person p

Then in many problem contexts your recognition rule will prove totally inadequate. Do you mean to include adoptive mothers? Surrogate mothers? Foster mothers? Stepmothers? Mothers-in-law? If you mean to avoid confusion you must test your recognition rule at least as carefully as you would test a program. If you can't find a recognition rule that captures your meaning well enough and survives your most rigorous testing, you have demonstrated that the term you had thought was useful must in fact be abandoned. You must find another ground term to use in describing the domain properties.

Designations are local to problems

It's not so hard as it looks to write a rigorous recognition rule. That's because you are writing it only for the problem context in hand. You do not have to take account of the whole universe, only of the part of the world where your problem is located; and you are free, within reason, to use words in locally acceptable senses. For example, in an inventory problem for the OfficeWorld Corporation – a company that supplies office furniture – you may need to designate the entity class *chair*. Perhaps you write this designation:

Chair(x) ≈ entity: x is a single unit of furniture whose primary use is to provide seating for one person

Philosophers have often cited 'chair' as an example of the irreducibly uncertain meaning of words in natural language. Is a bar stool a chair? A bean bag? A sofa? A park bench? A motor car seat? A chaise longue? These questions are impossibly difficult to answer – there are no right answers. But you do not have to answer them. The OfficeWorld Corporation has quite a small catalogue. It doesn't supply bar stools or park benches. Your recognition rule will do fine.

6.5.3 Defining further convenient terms

Being exact sometimes seems to make everything rather cumbersome and inconvenient. When we described the behaviour of each light unit in the one-way traffic lights problem by a finite-state machine, we marked the three unbroken states as 'Stop∧¬Go', 'Go∧¬Stop' and '¬Stop∧Go'. It would have been more convenient to write something like 'JustStop', 'JustGo' and 'Dark'. You can do this by defining these more convenient terms on the basis of the terms you have designated:

JustStop(i) ≜ state: Stop(i) ∧ ¬Go(i)
JustGo(i) ≜ state: Go(i) ∧ ¬Stop(i)
Dark(i) ≜ state: ¬Stop(i) ∧ ¬Go(i)

The definition symbol (≜) marks these as *definitions*, not designations. They introduce new terms that you can use in your descriptions, but they don't introduce any new observations or new phenomena. You can still only observe the *Stop* state and the *Go* state: you just have a more convenient way of referring to their combinations.

Here's another example. Suppose that you have designated the phenomena *Father(f,p)* and *Mother(m,p)*. Now you can define the terms *Child(c,p)* and *Sibling(c,d)* like this:

Child(c,p) $\triangleq$ state: Mother(p,c) $\wedge$ Father(p,c)

Child(c,p) is a term denoting a state; by this definition it means that *Mother(p,c)* is true or ($\vee$) *Father(p,c)* is true.

Sibling(c,d) $\triangleq$ state: $\exists$ p,q $\cdot$
                    Mother(p,c) $\wedge$ Mother(p,d) $\wedge$ Father(q,c) $\wedge$ Father(q,d) $\wedge$ c $\neq$ d

Sibling(c,d) is a term denoting a state; by this definition it means that there exist ($\exists$) some individuals *p* and *q* such that ($\cdot$) *Mother(p,c)* and *Mother(p,d)* and *Father(q,c)* and *Father(q,d)* are all true and *c* is not the same individual as ($\neq$) *d*. In other words, '*c* and *d* are siblings' means that they are different people who have the same mother and the same father.

Definitions are formal

Notice that the recognition rule in a designation is written in natural language: it's about observations in the informal world. But the definition rule is written in a formal language because it's not about the informal world at all: it's about a decision to use a formal term with a certain formal meaning.

Distinguishing definition from designation is vitally important. Suppose that in a university administration problem you have this designation:

Registered(p,d) $\approx$ state: the person p is registered for degree d

Now look at these lines:

(a) Enrolled(p) $\approx$ state: the person p is enrolled in the university
(b) $\forall$ p $\cdot$ Enrolled(p) $\leftrightarrow$ $\exists$ d $\cdot$ Registered(p,d)

The line (a) is a designation of another observable state, *Enrolled*. The second line (b) is a description that refers to those states. It says that *p* is enrolled if and only if ($\leftrightarrow$) there is ($\exists$) some degree *d* for which *p* is registered. This description (b) may be optative – part of a requirement – or indicative – part of a domain properties description. In either case you could look at the domain to see whether it's true or not. You might find a counter-example. John Brown is registered for a bachelor's degree but has been permitted, for conscientious reasons, not to enrol in the university; or Jane Green is enrolled in the university but is a part-time student and is not yet registered for any degree. Any counter-example shows that description (b) is false.

Now, keeping the same designation (a) of *Registered(p,d)*, look at this line:

(c) Enrolled(p) $\triangleq$ state: $\exists$ d $\cdot$ Registered(p,d)

The line (c) is a definition. It looks very like the description (b) in the first three lines, but it's not a description at all. It says that *Enrolled(p)* is a term denoting a state; by this definition it means that there exists some *d* such that the person *p* is registered for degree *d*. There can't be a counter-example to a definition because it can't be true or false. It can only be well-formed or ill-formed, convenient or inconvenient.

To sum up: when you write (a) and (b) you are adding a new class of observable phenomena *Enrolled(p)* to your view of the domain, and giving a domain description that refers to the new phenomena; when you write (c), you are just resolving to use the term *Enrolled(p)* because it's more convenient than *Registered(p,d)*. It matters a lot whether your description includes (a) and (b), or (c).

Definitions in state machine descriptions

You can write a definition in the text form with the definition symbol. You can also write it in other forms. It's often useful to write a set of definitions in a finite-state machine.

Look at these three finite-state machine diagrams:

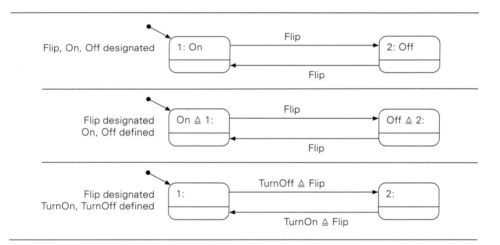

Definition in a finite-state machine

In the top diagram, all the terms used – the states *On* and *Off*, and the event class *Flip* – are designated. The description says something about the relationship between *Flip* events and *On* and *Off* states in the domain: initially, *On* holds, then *Flip* toggles between *On* and *Off*. The description might possibly be false. Someone might say: *On* was true, and I did a *Flip*, and *On* was still true. That would be a counter-example to the description.

In the middle diagram, the event class *Flip* is designated, but the states *On* and *Off* are defined. Effectively, *On* just means that an even number of *Flip* events (possibly zero) have occurred, and *Off* means that an odd number have occurred. The diagram says nothing about the domain. It's pure definition. There can't be any counter-example. It wouldn't make sense to say: *On* was true, and I did a *Flip*, and *On* was still true.

The bottom diagram also says nothing about the domain. The event class *Flip* is designated, but nothing is said about the states. The term *TurnOff* is defined to be the event class of odd-numbered *Flip* events, and *TurnOn* the class of even-numbered *Flips*.

You can write a definition in a separate box along with the diagram. Often that makes it easier to read. When we defined *SStop*, *SRaise* and *SLower* commands for the occasional sluice gate problem we did that.

Any questions?

Who is David Gries?
One of the two authors of David Gries and Fred B Schneider, *A Logical Approach to Discrete Math*, Springer-Verlag, 1993.

Is a lexical domain really formal? What about the underlying physical representation?
You're right. It's only formal if you restrict your attention to the symbolic phenomena and disregard their underlying physical representation.

Where can I read more about Three Mile Island?
Eugene S Ferguson, *Engineering and the Mind's Eye*, MIT Press, 1992.
Ferguson cites some full discussions of the accident, including: Anon, *An Analysis of Three Mile Island*, IEEE Spectrum, Volume 16, Number 11, pages 32–34, November 1979.

If you have to distinguish Valve Open from Solenoid On in the Three Mile Island example, don't you have to distinguish Stop Light Showing from Stop Light Switched On in the one-way traffic lights problem?
Yes. You're right. But in the traffic lights problem we are being less careful because it's not a safety-critical application to the same degree as Three Mile Island. Also, given the light unit equipment, there's nothing a software developer can do about it.

Surely the definition 'SStop ≜ Stop[2: or 3:]' wouldn't work if there were two outgoing transitions on Stop from state 2 or 3?
That's right – unless you want both of them to count as *SStop*. But then the state machine would be non-deterministic. You probably wouldn't want to use a non-deterministic machine as the basis for a definition. If you do want to, you must assign identifiers to transitions as well as to states.

6.6 Conceptual flavours

Some domains are hard to talk about because they seem to consist largely of concepts and intellectual constructs that are intangible and inconveniently slippery and subjective. Very often these constructs are denoted by nouns.

In English there's a very strong inclination, sanctioned by its great convenience and long history, to form nouns from verbs. If you lend money or a book you have made a *loan*; if you reserve a seat you have a *reservation*; if you steal something you have committed a *theft*; if you encounter a friend that's a *meeting*; if a company raises money it has an *equity structure*.

These nouns seem to denote intangible entities that can't be directly observed. They can cause a lot of trouble when you are trying to understand and describe what's going on in a biddable – human – domain, perhaps because it furnishes the real world in an information problem, or another domain in another frame. The difficulty is that the noun takes on a life of its own, and it can become hard to disentangle domain properties that involve it.

6.6.1 Concepts as entities

Let's start with a simple example that shouldn't cause us much trouble: a loan in the library administration problem. Suppose that we have designated:

> Borrow(e) $\approx$ event: e is an event in which a member borrows a copy of a library book of a certain title

Now we want to designate the concept of a *loan*:

> Loan(n) $\approx$ entity: n is a loan in which a member borrows a copy of a library book of a certain title

Entities from events

So far, so good. Now we must say how *loans* are related to *borrow* events. We need to designate the relationship – let's say it's a state:

> Origin(n,e) $\approx$ state: borrow event e is the origin of the loan n

We want to say that each *borrow* event is the origin of a unique corresponding *loan*, and that for each *loan* there is a unique *borrow* event that is its origin. The symbol '$\exists!$' means 'there is exactly one'. We can use it in this formalisation:

$$\forall\, e \bullet \text{Borrow(e)} \rightarrow (\, \exists!\, n \bullet \text{Loan(n)} \wedge \text{Origin(n,e)}\,)$$

$$\forall\, n \bullet \text{Loan(n)} \rightarrow (\, \exists!\, e \bullet \text{Borrow(e)} \wedge \text{Origin(n,e)}\,)$$

The roles of the *borrow* event seem to correspond naturally enough, by definition, to states associating the *loan* entity with the borrowing member, the borrowed copy, and the title borrowed. Given these designations:

BMember(e,m) ≈ role: member m is borrower in the borrow event e

BCopy(e,c)   ≈ role: book copy c is borrowed in the borrow event e

CTitle(c,t)   ≈ state: book copy c is a copy of title t

we can define:

LMember(n,m)   ≜ state: Loan(n) ∧
                          ∃ e · Borrow(e) ∧ Origin(n,e) ∧ BMember(e,m)

LCopy(n,c)   ≜ state: Loan(n) ∧
                          ∃ e · Borrow(e) ∧ Origin(n,e) ∧ BCopy(e,c)

LTitle(n,t)   ≜ state: Loan(n) ∧ LCopy(n,c) ∧ CTitle(c,t)

LMember(n,m) means that *m* is the member in *Loan n*, and so on. In the same spirit, we can define renewal of the loan as a renewal event of the book copy that was borrowed in the borrow event, and return of the loan as return of the copy.

How many loans?

We have chosen to assert that *loans* and *borrow* events are in one-to-one correspondence. That seems right. The uniqueness of each *borrow* event is essential to the uniqueness of the *loan* of which it is the origin.

But the uniqueness of each *borrow* event may not be enough on its own. If a *borrow* event can involve several book copies, we might not want to treat the event as originating only one *loan*. Instead we would have chosen that a *borrow* event could correspond to several *Loans*, one for each book copy. The origin of a *loan* is now a *borrow* event and a book copy:

Origin(n,e,c) ≈ state: borrow event e and copy c are the origin of loan n

∀ e,c • Borrow(e) ∧ BCopy(e,c) – (∃! n • Loan(n) ∧ Origin(n,e,c))

∀ n • Loan(n) – (∃! e,c • Borrow(e) ∧ BCopy(e,c) ∧ Origin(n,e,c))

Now we have asserted there is a unique *loan* entity *n* for each possible choice of *e* and *c* such that *Borrow(e)* is true and *BCopy(e,c)* is true. A *borrow* event originates as many *loans* as there are copies borrowed in the event.

Entities and requirement processes

I hope you feel at least slightly uncomfortable saying that a *loan* is an *entity*. It seemed attractive to think of a *loan* as an entity for two reasons. First, just because the word 'loan' is a noun. Nouns ought to denote entities. And second, because it seems certain that the library administration problem will involve a database, and equally certain that *Loan* will be an object class or entity class in that database. But these are bad reasons. The grammar of a natural language is not a reliable guide to understanding the world. And the database is not itself the domain of members and books and borrow events. It's a part of the solution, not a given domain in the problem. A *loan* entity in the database is a part of a *model* of the world, not a part of the world it models.

I also hope you feel uncomfortable treating our statements – about the relationship of *loans to borrow* events and to *BCopy* roles – as descriptions of domain properties. Domain property descriptions should be falsifiable assertions about the world. If you assert that each ICU patient has exactly one analog device, I can take you into the ICU and point to Mr Brown, who has two analog devices, and to Ms Jones, who has none. I have refuted your assertion by showing a counter-example. What counter-example might refute the statements about loans? None. They are not really statements, but definitions. Irrefutable statements usually are definitions.

Loans as processes

Instead of defining *loan* as an entity, it's better to think of it as a *process*: that is, as a collection of events ordered in time. In a human domain many, perhaps most, events are associated with agreements, undertakings, obligations, permissions and every kind of temporary social and legal relationship. If you borrow a book from the library you ought to return it eventually, and you ought not to keep it past its due date for return unless you have renewed it. If you reserve a book that is not available because it is out on loan, the library ought to keep it for you when it is returned, unless you have previously cancelled your reservation. Monitoring these obligations, enforcing them where possible, and reporting failure to satisfy them, is a *requirement* of the library system. It's a requirement that is best expressed as a process. The process describes how your customer wants the world to behave.

Suppose that more than one book copy may be borrowed in each *borrow* event. Then *loan* processes correspond one-to-one to (*borrow* event, book copy) pairs. For a *borrow* event in which member *m* borrows copy *c* of a title *t*, an incomplete sketch of the process may look something like this:

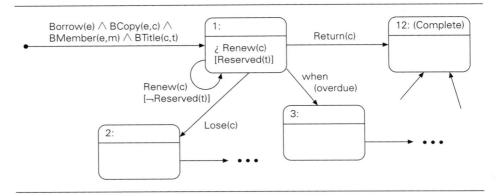

Library loan: incomplete sketch of a requirement process

The process begins, entering state 1, when the *borrow* event occurs. We don't show the *borrow* event as a transition out of an explicit initial state, because before the *borrow* event the process does not exist and has no state. If you are still thinking of the *loan* as an entity, the *borrow* event is not an event in its entity life history: it's the event that creates the entity. The inhibition of any event *Renew(c)[Reserved(t)]* in state 1, and the transition back to state 1 on an event *Renew(c)[¬Reserved(t)]* indicate that renewal of the loan is permitted in state 1, but only when there is no outstanding reservation for the title *t* of which the borrowed book is a copy. A *Return(c)* event in state 1 ends the process. If the due date for return passes, the process enters its state 3; if the book is lost, it enters state 2. To complete the process description we must consider whether: renewal is unconditionally forbidden in state 3; how and when fines for overdue and lost books must be levied and paid; whether borrowing other books is forbidden in states 2 and 3; and other similar questions, culminating in the eventual ending of the process some time after it has entered state 2 or 3.

This *loan* process is a kind of *use case*. But it's on a larger scale than is normal because it is not confined to a single uninterrupted episode of interaction between the member and the library administration system. Also, it doesn't say anything about the behaviour of the machine: it just describes the required behaviour in the problem domain.

6.6.3 Tagging a process

The library *loan* example is simple in two important ways:

■ the one-to-one correspondence between (*borrow* event, book copy) pairs and *loans* – whether they are entities or processes – gives each *loan* a clearly defined identity;

- the member *m* and book copy c participants in the *borrow* event are the leading direct participants in other events and states of the *loan* process. The title *t* of the book copy *c* is, in a sense, an indirect participant, associated with the *loan* through the *CTitle(c,t)* relationship. So it's easy to see which events are relevant to the *loan* process we started to describe in the previous section.

Sometimes these simplicities are absent or obscured, and things become a little harder. Here's an example.

Meeting scheduler problem

A system is to be developed to support the organisation of meetings. Each meeting is planned by a meeting initiator. The date and place of the meeting are to be settled by negotiation with intended participants, the negotiation being conducted chiefly by email. Some considerations in scheduling are:

- participants can specify sets of preferred and excluded date ranges;
- some participants are more important than others;
- dates and locations may be interdependent because desired locations are not always available;
- the system must inform intended participants of planned and replanned dates and locations in time for them to attend the meeting;
- the system must also manage equipment needs at meeting locations (not all equipment is available at all dates and locations).

It seems clear that the concept of a *meeting* is central in this problem. We would like to treat it as we did *loan*, basing its identity on a correspondence with an event. But which event? And which other events will be relevant to the *meeting* process?

From the rough sketch of the problem it seems that the identity of a *meeting* must be based on the event in which the initiator conceives or plans the meeting. But 'conceives or plans a meeting' is not an event class that will be easy to designate. We'll need something more concrete. It's also not clear how to say which events are relevant to the *meeting*. Any event involving the book copy *c* is relevant to the library *loan*, and any event involving the member *m* or the title *t* is potentially relevant. But the *meeting* is not so simple. Events involving the same date and place? But the meeting date and place are not known initially, and can change during the process. Events involving a participant? The set of meeting participants also changes. The meeting initiator? The meeting initiator might drop out and hand responsibility for the meeting to someone else. Everything seems to be fluid. Nothing can be pinned down.

In this kind of situation what people do in the problem domain is to introduce a tag. A *tag* is just a name attached to the meeting: it's a kind of identifier, but it doesn't identify anything except the *meeting* process to which it's attached. The tag can be used by everyone involved in the domain to say which meeting process they are talking about. A sensible tag will be meaningful: 'Week 26 Project Review', or 'Joe's Leaving Present', or 'Ideas On the Disk Capacity Problem'. The identity of the *meeting* process is based on the event in which the original initiator chooses and assigns the tag. If the tags are unique, the *meetings* will be uniquely identified.

Relevant events and states can be associated with the process by the tag. For example, an intended participant can specify sets of preferred and excluded date ranges. But one very likely possibility is that a person who is a conscientious intended participant of two different meetings $m1$ and $m2$ will exclude the currently planned date of $m1$ in dealing with $m2$, and vice versa. So the designation for the excluded state of a date is something like:

Excluded(p,d,m)   ≈   state: date d is excluded by person p for the meeting
                      tagged m

Such a state, of course, arises from an event in which person p made the exclusion. That event is relevant to the *meeting* process m because the tag m participates in the exclude event.

Any questions?

In the loan process description, does 'renew(c)' mean a renew event in which copy c participates'?
Yes. I conflated the event and role for brevity. If you like to be more rigorous, you need only make a suitable definition.

Why do you need origin(n,e)?
Because without it there would be no connection between the *loan n* and the corresponding *borrow* event e. All we would have is a set of loans and a set of borrow events, and no way of matching them up.

Why not just adopt the existing conventions of the people working in the application area?
Sometimes you can do that. But sometimes their conventions are confused and inadequate. Inadequate conventions can work fine in a manual system because people use their common sense to overcome the inadequacies. Airline flight numbers are a well-known example. Airlines often combine two flights, or split one flight into two legs. Airline employees overcome the resulting confusion by using their common sense in the awkward cases. If necessary, they will let you on a flight whose identifier doesn't match your ticket. But you can't base a software development on using common sense in the awkward cases. The machine hasn't got any common sense.

CHAPTER 7

Model domains and real worlds

A model – in the sense used in this book – is a distinct domain that corresponds by analogy to the real world domain in an information problem. A model domain separates and makes explicit some private phenomena of the information machine: the set of variables it uses to compute its display outputs. When you use a model domain, you split the problem into two subproblems: one builds the model, and the other uses it. A model domain can fulfil many purposes: remembering past events and states of the real world; summarising the past; supporting inferences about private phenomena of the real world; anticipating lengthy calculations. A model domain can also diverge from the real world in many ways, for example, by incompleteness, by delay, and by simple error.

7.1 Information problems

We have already seen the information display problem frame, and looked briefly at one or two simple examples. Here is the problem frame diagram, from Chapter 4:

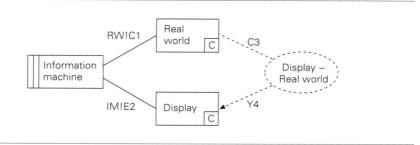

Information display: problem frame diagram

The part of the world about which information is required is called the real world. It's an autonomous causal domain. The display is the domain where the information is to be shown. The requirement, to be satisfied by the information machine, is to ensure that the state of the display, in terms of its symbolic phenomena Y4, corresponds (~) in a stipulated way to the state of the real world in terms of its causal phenomena C3.

The machine obtains the information to be displayed by inferring the phenomena C3 from the shared states and events C1. To address the frame concern you need a careful domain description of the real world, describing how the machine can do this.

We have already mentioned three problems of this class:

- the odometer display problem. The real world is the car on the road, and the display is the fascia display in the car. C3 phenomena are car speed and distance; C1 are the pulses caused by road wheel rotation;

- the local traffic monitoring problem. The real world is the vehicles and the road and the sensor tubes. C3 phenomena are the passage of various kinds of vehicle; C1 are the states of the four sensor tubes. The display is the report printed on the strip printer;

- the library membership reports problem. The real world is the library members, enrolling, resigning and paying fees. The display is the printed report.

In this chapter we're going to look a little more deeply at two new problems of this class. We'll use them to explain and discuss the origin of a model, the idea of introducing a model domain into the problem, and the decomposition of the problem into two subproblems connected by the model. These two new problems illustrate different aspects and principles of the use of a model domain.

7.2 A first example

Here's the first of the two problems. We'll look at this problem in quite a lot of detail. First, we'll use it to illustrate the way a model domain grows naturally out of the information machine. Then we'll explore the nature of an appropriate model and how it works.

7.2.1 The problem

This is the problem.

Lift position display

A somewhat primitive lift in a small hotel has been installed and successfully operated for many years. Now it is to be fitted with an information panel in the lobby, to show waiting guests where the lift is at any time, so that they will know how long they can expect to wait until it arrives.

The panel has two lamps for each floor. There is a square lamp to show that the lift is at the floor, and a round lamp to show that there is a request outstanding for the lift to visit the floor. In addition there are two arrow-shaped lamps to indicate the direction of travel. There is a lobby, and there are eight other floors, so the panel looks like this:

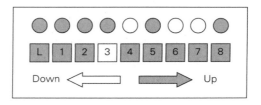

Lift position display panel

Our job is to drive the panel display from a very minimal interface with the existing request buttons and floor sensors of the lift. A floor sensor is on when the lift is within 6 inches of the rest position at the floor. Pressing a button is detected as a pulse. There is one button at each floor to summon the lift, and a set of buttons inside the lift car – one button to direct the lift to each floor.

This is the problem diagram, fitted to the information display frame:

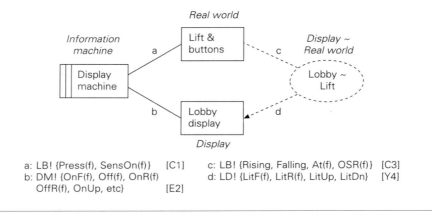

a: LB! {Press(f), SensOn(f)}   [C1]
b: DM! {OnF(f), Off(f), OnR(f)
     OffR(f), OnUp, etc}   [E2]

c: LB! {Rising, Falling, At(f), OSR(f)}   [C3]
d: LD! {LitF(f), LitR(f), LitUp, LitDn}   [Y4]

Lift position display: fitted to information display frame

The indexes (f) in the interface annotations refer to floor f; the lobby is floor 0. *Press(f)* is an event in which one of the two buttons for floor f is pressed (one in the lift car, one at floor f). *SensOn(f)* is the state in which the sensor at floor f is on. *OnF(f)* and *OffF*(f) events turn on and off the lamp for floor f, and *OnR(f)* and *OffR(f)* events turn on and off the lamp for an outstanding request at floor f; *OnUp* etc events turn on and off the lamps for the up and down directions.

LitF(f) is a state phenomenon that holds when the lamp for floor f is lit, and so on. *Rising* and *Falling* are states of the lift; we have not yet said exactly how they are designated. *At(f)* holds when the lift is visiting or passing floor f; we have not yet said how close it must be to the rest position at floor f for *At(f)* to hold. *OSR(f)* is a state that holds when there is an outstanding request for floor f.

Investigating the lobby display, you find that it is very simple. The lamps are mutually independent, and each one is robust. In any state, *OnF(f)* sets the floor lamp f on so that *LitF(f)* is true, and *OffF(f)* sets it off so that *LitF(f)* is false. The other lamps are similar.

7.2.2 From variables to models

One way to think about models in information problems is as a natural development from private phenomena of the information machine. In programming terms, these private phenomena are variables. In the very simplest cases the machine needs no such variables. In a slightly more complex case one or two variables are needed that can be understood purely in terms of the machine specification. But when the complexity reaches a certain level you must start thinking of the variables as *model variables*, their values corresponding to states of the real world. The next stage is to treat them as a distinct *model domain*, embodying an explicit model of the real world. A fully developed model domain is likely to be a database held on disk, or an elaborate structure of persistent objects.

No variable needed

Let's start by looking at only one part of the lift position requirement:

> R1a: the lamp corresponding to floor f must be lit if, and only if, the lift is at
> floor f.

We'll begin by taking the simple view that *At(f)* holds if and only if *Sens(f)* holds. Knowing that the display is robust, you might make the machine specification as simple as this:

```
forever {
  for f := 0 to 8 {
    if ( SensOn(f) ) OnF(f) else OffF(f);     // Light off unless Lift is At(f)
} }
```

Viewed as a program this is inefficient. The machine repeatedly polls all the sensors; if the lift is at a floor, the light corresponding to that floor is turned on, and all other lights are turned off.

The variable *f* here is just a control variable of the for-loop; its value tells you which floor sensor the machine is inspecting at any moment. If you could look inside the machine and observe the successive values of the variable *f*, you would learn nothing about the lift & buttons. The machine doesn't need any model variables: all it does is to translate between the *SensOn(f)* phenomena it shares with the lift & buttons and the *OnF(f)* and *OffF(f)* phenomena it shares with the lobby display. The translation is more or less direct, subject only to the frequency with which each sensor is polled.

A model variable: most-recent-floor

But this very simple machine turns out to be not good enough. The hotel customers complain. They say the floor lamp flashes so briefly when the lift passes a floor that they have to stare intently at the display not to miss it. So you must instead satisfy this more demanding partial requirement:

> R1b: the lamp corresponding to floor f must be lit if, and only if:
> - the lift is at floor f, or
> - the lift is not at any floor, but was most recently at floor f.

Now you need to use a global variable *r*, so that the machine can remember which floor the lift was at most recently. The lift is initially at floor 0, so your machine specification might be:

```
{ for f:=0 to 8 {OffF(f);}          // Turn off all floor lights
  r:=0; OnF(0);                      // At floor 0, turn light 0 on;
  forever {
    if ( ¬ SensOn(r) )               // if lift has left floor r ...
      if ( r>0 ∧ SensOn(r-1) ) {     // ... and reached floor r-1
        OffF(r); OnF(r-1); r:=r-1;   // light r off, light r-1 on
      }
      else if (r<8 ∧ SensOn(r+1)) {  // ... or reached floor r+1
        OffF(r); OnF(r+1); r:=r+1;   // light r off, light r+1 on
} }               }
```

This specification (or program) is more efficient. It exploits two domain properties:

- the lift is initially at the lobby floor 0;

- if the lift was most recently at floor *r*, the next floor (that is, other than *r*) must be $r-1$ or $r+1$.

The specification satisfies the partial requirement R1b: the light for floor *r* will stay on until the lift is at an adjacent floor. Again, the variable *f* (in the first line) is just the control variable for a loop. But the variable *r* is a *model variable*. Its value tells you which floor the lift is currently at, or was at most recently. It's a vestigial *model* of the lift.

7.2.3 On being a model

What does it mean to say that the variable *r* is a model of the lift? It means two things: the variable and the lift jointly satisfy a *correspondence requirement*, and each one satisfies a *common description*.

Correspondence requirement

The correspondence requirement is that *r* in the display machine must always correspond to *f* in 'At(f) or was most recently At(f)' in the lift & buttons domain. The display machine uses this model to maintain the required display. You can think of the correspondence and the usage as satisfying two requirements. They are shown very informally in this partial pseudo-problem diagram:

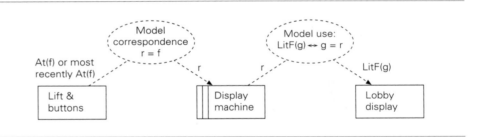

Model correspondence and model use

In the diagram distinct identifiers *f* and *g* have been used to emphasise that there is no necessary or causal relationship between the lights and the lift position: the relationship must be mediated by the variable *r*.

The common description

Because *r* is a model of *f*, there is a common description that applies to both of them:

> 'Its initial value is 0. Its minimum value is 0. Its maximum value is 8. In the complete history of its successive values, the absolute difference between any two adjacent values is 1.'

You can see that this is a description of the behaviour of *f* in '*At(f)* or was most recently *At(f)*'. It captures a domain property of the lift running in the lift shaft. It is also, of course, a description of the behaviour of the machine's model variable *r*.

The common description is different from the model correspondence requirement. Here is a pair of histories that satisfies the requirement but not the common description:

```
f:  7   2   5   9 ..
r:  7   2   5   9 ..
```

and here is a pair that satisfies the common description but not the requirement:

```
f:  0   1   2   3 ..
r:  0   1   0   1 ..
```

This model consisting of the one integer variable *r* is vestigial. But it illustrates the two notions – the correspondence requirement and the common description – that underlie more elaborate and realistic models.

7.2.4 Many more variables

Now we can turn to the next part of the requirement:

> R2: the request lamp for floor f must be lit if, and only if, there is an outstanding request for the lift to visit that floor.

You can see this is going to be a lot harder. It's easy enough to detect when a request is made: each button press event is a request. But it's harder to detect when it is satisfied. The lift display machine has no access to direct information about the behaviour of the people who use the lift. So it can't detect that a request is no longer outstanding because the person who pressed the button has now entered or left the lift at the requested floor. It can't detect whether the lift control computer is still treating a request as outstanding. It can't even detect whether the lift doors are open or closed. All it can detect is button press events and sensor states.

For the very simple requirements R1a and R1b we just jumped straight into the machine specification without making an explicit domain description. For R2 we'll certainly have to make a careful description of the lift & buttons domain, describing how the relevant requirement phenomena – *At(f)* and *OSR(f)* – are related to the *Press(f)* and *SensOn(f)* specification phenomena. And when we have made it we'll still have to write the machine specification.

What global variables are you likely to need this time? Surely something like the variable *r*. And surely another variable associated with each floor, to remember whether there's an outstanding request for that floor. There's enough here to need an explicit model domain. That means a decomposition into two subproblems, with the model domain to connect them.

Any questions?

In the problem statement you used values of the index f to identify the nine floors and the nine lamps. But what exactly connects each lamp and floor with its index value?

That's a very good question. It's pointing to a particular concern (the *identities* concern) that we'll come to in a later chapter.

What does 'robust' mean?

We discussed that in the previous chapter. It means that you can't break the domain by any externally caused event. Each lamp can tolerate any sequence of *On* and *Off* events; at any moment the lamp is *Lit* if and only if the most recent event in the sequence was an *On*.

Why is 'lobby' different from 'floor 1'?

It's the British convention. In Britain the first floor in a house is the floor immediately above the ground floor.

Why are you writing programs instead of giving declarative specifications?

Implicit, declarative specifications are seldom good for specifying behaviours: the procedural kind are better. Also, because our problem analysis is explicit, we don't need to embed the problem analysis in the machine specification.

7.3 Introducing a model domain

Let's be clear about one thing at the outset. When you introduce a model domain, you are introducing something that was not given in the original problem. From the point of view of the original problem, the model domain is definitely a part of the solution, not a part of the problem. That's obvious, really, because the model domain is just an elaborate version of the model variables needed in the information machine. The model domain lets you decompose the original problem into two subproblems by providing a link between them that would otherwise be missing.

Here's the information display problem frame decomposed into its two subproblems:

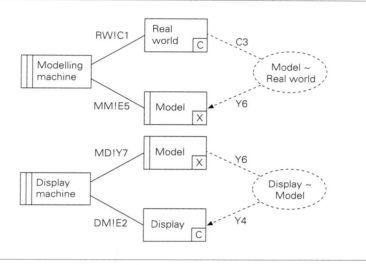

Information display with model: composite problem frame

Decomposing a problem means decomposing the requirement and decomposing the machine that is to satisfy it. The original requirement – that the display phenomena Y4 should correspond to the real world phenomena C3 – has been decomposed into two parts:

- the part to be satisfied by the modelling machine, that is, that the model phenomena Y6 should correspond to the real world phenomena C3;

- the part to be satisfied by the display machine, that is, that the display phenomena Y4 should correspond to the model phenomena Y6.

The model domain, and in particular its symbolic phenomena Y6, form the necessary link in the full description of the original requirement. Instead of a direct correspondence between C3 and Y4, we now have a correspondence between C3 and Y6 and another between Y6 and Y4. The display machine has no direct interface with the real world; instead, it relies entirely on the model for the information it displays.

Any questions?

Why show the two subproblems separately? Why not combine them by superimposing the two rectangles for the common model domain?

We never show two subproblems in one problem diagram. It's convenient to separate them because often you'll want to show a common domain differently in the two subproblems, or to combine two domains in one subproblem into one domain in another.

Isn't the distinction between the model and the real world just the old distinction between the physical and the conceptual schemas?

No. physical and conceptual schemas are two descriptions of the same domain – the database. The model and the real world are different domains.

The terms physical and conceptual were established by the CODASYL committee in the 1960s. They lost a unique opportunity. They saw that the implementation details of a database did not reflect anything in the real world – two descriptions, at least, were necessary. They could have called them the database schema and the real world schema. That would have written their names in the golden book of benefactors of the human race. Instead, alas, they called them the physical schema and the conceptual schema. A near miss, perhaps, but definitely a miss. What a shame.

7.3.1 The model and the real world

The model domain is completely distinct from the real world domain. The model is a lexical domain, while the real world is a causal domain. As you can see from the composite problem frame, they have no phenomena in common at all: the phenomena of the real world are C1 and C3; the phenomena of the model are E5, Y6 and Y7.

Let's look at the first subproblem. As a general rule, building the model is more interesting than using it, and this is no exception. Here's the problem diagram for the first subproblem in the lift position display problem:

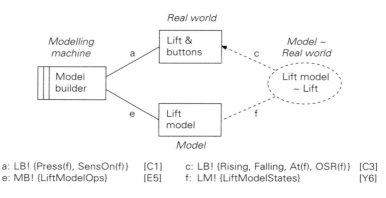

a: LB! {Press(f), SensOn(f)}   [C1]   c: LB! {Rising, Falling, At(f), OSR(f)} [C3]
e: MB! {LiftModelOps}   [E5]   f: LM! {LiftModelStates}   [Y6]

Lift position display: model building subproblem

The details of the lift model operations – the E5 phenomena in interface *e* – and the lift model states – the Y6 phenomena in interface *f* – have not yet been decided. After all, you still have to design the lift model domain.

Obviously, the first thing to do is to set about making your domain description of the lift & buttons domain. You can then base the design of your model on devising appropriate phenomena and relationships analogous to those of the lift & buttons. To keep the discussion reasonably short, we will concern ourselves only with what is needed for the lift model equivalent of *OSR(f)*, that is, the state in which there is an outstanding request to visit floor *f*. We will, incidentally, be doing much of the work for other parts of the model, but our focus will be on *OSR*. Our purpose is to make a description of the domain properties that relate *OSR(f)* to *Press(f)* and *SensOn(f)*.

7.3.2 Real world domain properties

The first relevant domain property is that an outstanding request is discharged when the lift becomes *accessible* at the requested floor, that is, when the person who made the request has had an opportunity to enter or leave the lift. If they don't take the opportunity – perhaps because they are daydreaming, or too slow, or the lift is full or going the wrong way – we can assume that they will repeat the request when they realise their mistake. This may be after the lift has gone, or it may be when they see the doors closing. We won't try to state this more formally.

The second relevant domain property is that the lift is not accessible if it just passes the floor without stopping, or if it is temporarily stuck at the floor because of a malfunction but does not open the doors. You can describe these episode classes like this:

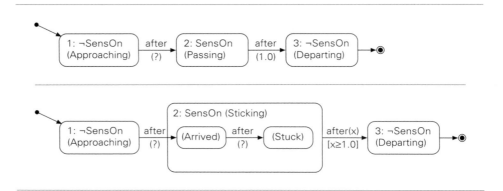

Real world domain description: processes for passing and sticking at a floor

When the lift passes a floor, it is first approaching from an adjacent floor in state 1, and *SensOn* is false. After some time *SensOn* becomes true, and then remains true while it is passing. The lift travels at 1ft/sec, so it is within 6 inches of the rest position at the floor for one second (half a second on either side of the rest position); after that, *SensOn* becomes false and the lift is departing in state 3. The parenthesised words, such as '(Approaching)', are just informal comments; they don't denote designated or defined phenomena.

When the lift gets stuck at a floor, it spends an indeterminate period of time there. Eventually, in not less than one second after *SensOn* first becomes true, *SensOn* becomes false and the lift is departing. (Conscientiously, we have checked that even if the lift reverses direction on getting stuck, it can't arrive and depart in less than one second.)

The lift is accessible in response to requests only while it is serving the floor, and only in certain states during the service visit. People often run to catch a lift whose doors are closing, and they may press the call button before rushing between the closing doors. So you must consider the possibility that a *Press* event occurs while the lift is visiting the floor, and that such a request may, or may not, be too late for the requester to enter or leave the lift. You must examine and describe the serving process in some detail. It looks like this:

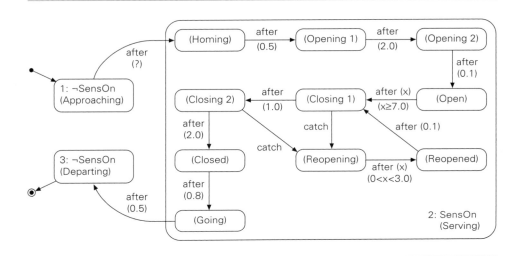

Real world domain description: process for serving a floor

SensOn first becomes true when the lift starts (Homing) on the rest position at the floor. After 0.5 seconds the lift has travelled 6 inches: the rest position is reached and the doors start (Opening1). It takes three seconds to open or shut the doors. It's possible for a person to enter or leave the lift whenever the doors are at least two-thirds open. So the lift is first accessible in the state (Opening2), one second into the opening cycle. It remains accessible while the doors stay (Open) for at least seven seconds, and during the first one third (Closing1) of their closing cycle. If the safety device catches an obstruction in the doors during the closing cycle, the doors reopen fully and the closing cycle is repeated. 0.8 seconds after the doors are fully closed, the lift is (Going); 0.5 seconds later *SensOn* becomes false and the lift is (Departing).

If you look carefully at this description, you'll see that when the lift serves a floor, the lift first becomes accessible 2.5 seconds after entering the *SensOn* state, and it becomes finally inaccessible for the visit when it starts (Closing2) and catches no obstruction before *SensOn* becomes false 3.3 seconds later.

Any questions?

Why do you not designate or define the phenomena of the domain description more formally, instead of writing comments such as '(Approaching)' in the state symbols?

Partly to keep the discussion short, and partly because the way it has been done is formal enough for the present purposes.

7.3.3 Designing the model

The model will eventually be driven by the model building machine from *Press(f)* events and *SensOn(f)* states. The model building machine drives the model by causing the lift model operations (the E5 events). We have to decide what these operations should be. We also have to decide what Y6 phenomena are needed if the model is to serve its purpose.

Model operations

Let's assume that the lift model operations are these:

- *MAsk(f)*, in response to which the lift model will be updated to reflect a request;

- *MArr(f)*, in response to which the lift model will be updated to reflect the arrival of the lift at a floor;

- *MLv(f)*, in response to which the lift model will be updated to reflect the departure of the lift from a floor.

Let's also assume that the model builder machine will behave like this:

- when a *Press(f)* event occurs, the model building machine will cause a *MAsk(f)* model operation;

- when *SensOn(f)* changes from false to true, the model building machine will cause a *MArr(f)* model operation;

- when SensOn(f) changes from true to false, the model building machine will cause a *MLv(f)* model operation.

Model symbolic states

For our focus on the outstanding requests we want the model to have distinct states (Y6 symbolic phenomena) that correspond to the *OSR(f)* states of the real world. Let's call the corresponding model states *MRq(f)*.

To determine *MRq(f)*, we'll need a model phenomenon *MAxsbl(f)* corresponding, as closely as possible, to the accessible and inaccessible states of the real world that we discussed informally earlier. To determine *MAxsbl(f)*, it turns out to be convenient to have three states, *MAway(f)*, *MHere(f)* and *MStaying(f)*, and two defined event classes: *MStay(f)* is an event in the model that corresponds to the lift becoming accessible; *MGo(f)* corresponds, very roughly, to the lift ceasing to be accessible.

Here's a sketch of the resulting lift model behaviour in response to *MAsk(f)*, *MArr(f)* and *MLv(f)* operations. The index (*f*) is omitted from the names in the diagram:

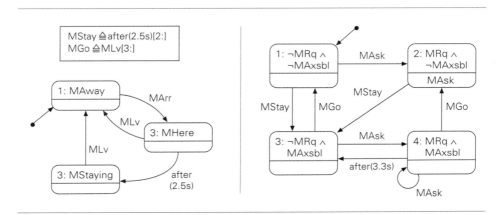

Lift model domain description: two behaviours for a floor

The diagram on the left shows the model's direct response to *MArr* and *MLv* operations for one floor. Initially the model is in the *MAway* state; an *MArr* operation puts it into the *MHere* state; if an *MLv* does not occur within 2.5 seconds it then enters the *MStaying* state. Intuitively, *MAway* corresponds to the lift being away from the floor; *MHere* corresponds to the (Passing) state or the earlier part of the (Serving) state when the doors are not yet open; and *MStaying* corresponds to the latter part of (Serving). Unfortunately, *MStaying* may also correspond to the (Sticking) state, when the lift is stuck at the floor for more than 2.5 seconds. *MStay* and *MGo* events are defined to be entry to, and exit from, the *MStaying* state.

The diagram on the right shows how the *MRq* state is determined. *MAsk* operations switch from ¬*MRq* (states 1 and 3) to *MRq* (states 2 and 4). *MStay* and *MGo* events, as defined in the diagram on the left, switch between ¬*MAxsbl* (states 1 and 2) and *MAxsbl* (states 3 and 4). If a *MAsk* operation occurs in the *MRq* ∧ *MAxsbl* state, it is not considered to be served unless the *MAxsbl* state persists for at least a further 3.3 seconds, this being the time taken for the final states (Closing2), (Closed) and (Going) of the real world serving process.

Model object structure

If the model is to be an assembly of objects, it may have this class structure:

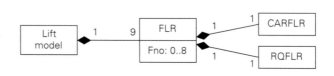

Lift model domain description: class diagram

A lift model object – of which there is just one – has nine FLR objects, which will be models of the floors. Each FLR object has a different value of its integer attribute *Fno*, and has one CARFLR and one RQFLR object:

- ■ CARFLR will model what the lift car does at the floor. The CARFLR object will embody the behaviour of the model with respect to *MArr* and *MLv* operations – that's the behaviour diagram on the left;

- ■ RQFLR will model what the requests for the floor do. The RQFLR object will embody the model's behaviour with respect to the *MRq* and *MAxsbl* states – that's the behaviour diagram on the right.

The detailed design of the objects will include a mechanism for sharing the *MStay* and *MGo* events.

Did you notice that the domain descriptions and the model behaviours we have shown are valid only for intermediate floors? The top and bottom floors are different because the lift cannot pass those floors. Also, the initial state of the real world lift is (Open): that is, at rest at the lobby floor, with the doors open. These differences must be treated with care, both in the domain descriptions and in the corresponding model objects. Probably subclasses of CARFLR and RQFLR will be needed. We won't treat these concerns here.

7.3.4 Maintaining and using the model

The shared events of the lift model, so far as we have discussed it, are *MArr(f)*, *MLv(f)* and *MAsk(f)*; the shared states are *MRq(f)*. We have already said how the model building machine causes the operations according to *Press(f)* events and changes in *SensOn(f)* states in the real world of the lift & buttons.

Using the model is equally straightforward. The display machine in the second sub-problem drives the request lamps, using the model state *MRq(f)* as a surrogate for the unavailable real world state *OSR(f)*.

The treatment of the floor lamps and the direction arrows is rather simpler than the outstanding requests, and we will not discuss it further.

Any questions?

Wouldn't it be more realistic to connect the machine to the existing lift control system?

In some cases, perhaps. But the control system may be an old electromechanical system. Or it may be a fragile software system that is best left untouched – any attachment might upset its execution timings and hence its operation.

Why don't you show how the model objects interact?

Because we are interested here only in their interface phenomena to the two machines and the two requirements. It's quite enough for our purposes to show how their symbolic states change in response to the operations performed by the model builder machine.

Isn't MStaying just the same as MAxsbl?

Yes, but they are states of different model objects. In this model design, objects are allowed to share events but not to share states.

Why is an MAsk ignored in state 2, while in state 4 is causes a self-transition?

Because in state 4 the self-transition implicitly restarts the calculation of the 3.3 seconds of accessibility that must remain if the request corresponding to the *MAsk* event is to be served in the current visit to the floor.

Why is it necessary to make such a meal of introducing MRq, MAsk, MArr and MLv, when you already have OSR(f), Press(f) and SensorOn(f), and of introducing MAway, MHere and MStaying?

Because the introduced phenomena are phenomena of the model domain, not of the real world. That has two consequences.

First, using the real world names for the model phenomena can be confusing when two phenomena with the same name don't correspond perfectly. In spite of our best efforts, *MRq* is not in perfect correspondence with *OSR(f)*.

Second, you can't avoid using different names for the lift model operations *MAsk*, *MArr* and *MLv*, and the specification phenomena *Press(f)* and *SensorOn(f)* of the lift & buttons domain. They all appear in the specification of the model builder machine, and must be clearly distinguished there.

7.4 Another model example

In the lift position display problem the model was strongly constrained by the original requirement and the very limited interface of *Press* events and *SensOn* states shared between the machine and real world. Often you have a freer choice in deciding the content of the model domain. You can see some of these possibilities in the second new problem. We won't treat this one in so much detail; we'll use it chiefly to illustrate some general points and some choices that face you when you introduce a model domain into a problem.

7.4.1 The problem

Here's the sketch of the problem:

Experimental voltages

In a simple laboratory experiment electrical voltages are measured at 32 points in a circuit and communicated to a computer by analog-digital devices. The devices convert the voltages into register values that are directly accessible to the computer. The points are identified by integer values 1-32.

The computer must maintain a display showing the 32 voltages as columns side by side on the screen. It must also display the average voltage over all the points, and, eventually, certain other information yet to be determined.

Here is the problem diagram, fitted to the information display frame:

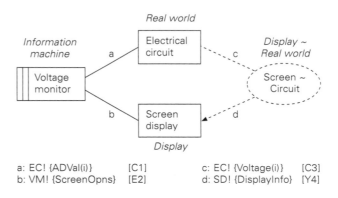

a: EC! {ADVal(i)}   [C1]   c: EC! {Voltage(i)}   [C3]
b: VM! {ScreenOpns}   [E2]   d: SD! {DisplayInfo}   [Y4]

Experimental voltages: fitted to information display frame

The interfaces marked *a* and *c* are simple and self-explanatory. The analog-digital devices are considered to be entirely reliable, and are regarded as a part of the electrical circuit domain.

We're treating the *b* and *d* sets of phenomena very casually here. The set *d* is roughly identified as *DisplayInfo* states because we don't know yet exactly what information is to be displayed. The set *b* is roughly identified as *ScreenOpn* events, that is, the operations by which the voltages monitor machine drives the screen display. For our present purpose of focusing on the use of a model, we aren't particularly interested in the properties of the screen display and how it is driven.

7.4.2 A version without a model

If the information to be displayed is strictly limited to 'a display showing the 32 voltages as columns side by side on the screen ... also ... the average voltage over all the points', there is no need for a model domain at all, and no need for problem decomposition.

The reason is that the real world phenomena and relationships to be displayed are all available at exactly the time when they are needed. The machine behaviour specification can be:

```
forever {
  sum := 0;
  for i:=1 to 32 {
    sum:= sum+ v[i];
    setScreenColumnHeight (i, v[i]);
  }
  display 'Average = ', sum/32;
}
```

Essentially, the voltages monitor machine makes repeated passes over all 32 points displaying their values as the heights of columns on the screen. In each pass it computes the averages of the 32 values found, and displays it at the end of the pass.

The machine uses variables *sum* and *i*. *i* is local to the for-loop. *sum* is also local to the loop: its value corresponds to the sum of the voltages over the 32 points just for the brief moment during execution of the display statement and before execution of *sum:=0* at the start of the next iteration. Neither *sum* nor *i* is a model variable.

7.4.3 A harder version

Only the very simplest information problems can be solved without a model domain. You need to introduce a model domain when your problem becomes more demanding. In the experimental voltages problem, any of these information requirements will demand a model.

- *All Averages*: the average voltage at each point since the experiment began.

- *Maximum Recent Average*: the identity of the point that has had the highest average voltage over the past five minutes, and that average.

- *Maximum Difference of Two Points*: the greatest difference during the whole experiment so far between the voltage at point 3 and the voltage at point 17.

- *Maximum Point Range*: the identity of the point that has exhibited the largest range between its highest and its lowest voltage over the whole experiment so far.

To provide information like this, the machine must not only continually detect the voltages in the real world, it must also remember at least some part or extract or summary of this information for use later when it is needed. In short, it must maintain and use a model of the electrical circuit. Just to remind you, here is the decomposed problem diagram, omitting the interface annotations:

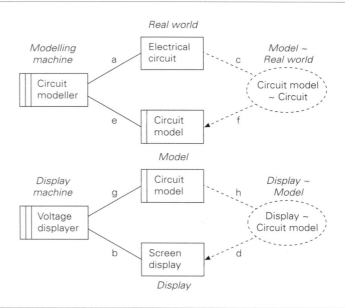

Experimental voltages: fitted to decomposed information display frame

As we saw in the lift position display problem, you must make a domain description of the circuit domain and then design and describe the circuit model domain.

Domain description

There's not much to describe in the electrical circuit domain. It has 32 continuously varying voltage states, which belong to the set *a* of phenomena shared with the circuit modeller machine. The requirement phenomena of set *c* are all *defined* in terms of the 32 voltage states. To deal properly with these definitions you need to recall a little of your elementary calculus. The 32 voltages vary as functions of time. The average of a continuously varying voltage V(t), from time *t0* to time *t1*, is the integral of its value over the period divided by the length of the period. That is:

$$\int_{t0}^{t1} V(t)dt/(t1 - t0)$$

However, the circuit modeller machine will have to treat these continuous voltages by a discrete approximation, polling their values at regular intervals. As a result, the circuit model phenomena corresponding to the 32 continuous voltages will be 32 sequences of polled voltage values. The model phenomena corresponding to the averages over a time period will be averages over suitably chosen subsequences.

7.4.4 A naïve circuit model

The simplest model in any problem is one that just stores an analogue of every instance of every phenomenon at the machine interface. In this problem, that means a model that remembers the complete history of the polled voltages. If the circuit modeller machine does a complete pass, polling each voltage point, once every five milliseconds, the circuit model will have state phenomena *CMVoltage(i,t)*, corresponding to the value of the electrical circuit voltage at point *i* at time *t*.

If you implement this circuit model as a simple data structure, it can be a two-dimensional array of voltage values. Each row contains the 32 point voltages found in one pass. The rows are ordered by time, each row being understood to contain values five milliseconds later than the preceding row. If you implement the model as a relational database, it can be a single relation with three columns. Because the tuples in a relation are unordered, each tuple must contain not only a voltage value and the identifier of a point but also the time at which the voltage was detected by the circuit modeller machine.

These models, of course, have an unavoidable imperfection. Being discrete models, they can be only approximations to the continuous phenomena of the electrical circuit. Worse, because the circuit modeller machine must take some time to make each pass over the 32 points, the time at which the voltage at point 1 is detected will be different from the time at which voltage 32 is detected. The polling must be fast enough and frequent enough for this imperfection to be tolerable by the experimenters who will use the displayed information. In short, the electrical circuit real world has a continuous flavour, with everything that this implies.

Subject to the inevitable approximation it involves, you can use this naïve model to provide any information about the real world electrical circuit domain that can be expressed in terms of present or past voltage values. The voltage displayer machine inspects the circuit model states *CMVoltage(i,t)* for all relevant values of *i* and *t*, and calculates the required information directly. The harder questions – *All Averages*, *Maximum Recent Average*, *Maximum Difference of Two Points*, and *Maximum Range Point* – are now no longer hard.

7.4.5   A more practical model

The naïve model that remembers the complete history is very simple. But it is also very inconvenient for two reasons. First, there is a space problem. The space needed for the model grows without limit: another row is added to the array, or another 32 tuples to the relation, every five milliseconds, on each pass over the electrical circuit register values.

Second, there is a response-time problem: the amount of calculation needed to answer some of the questions may be large and, for some questions, unlimited. To display the *Maximum Recent Average* (which point has had the highest average voltage over the past five minutes?) the machine must calculate the average of 60,000 values for each of the 32 voltages. To display the *All Averages* (what has been the average voltage at each point since the experiment began?) the number of values to be used in the calculation grows without limit as the experiment proceeds. The machine will, eventually, be unable to keep up.

Space reduction

To deal with the space problem you must obviously redesign the model so that parts of the history that can be regarded as out of date and no longer useful are deleted. You can then use the space they occupied for new information. But it's not clear that any part of the history can be regarded as no longer useful. To answer the *Maximum Recent Average* question we need only the history of the most recent five minutes, but for the *All Averages* question we seem to need the whole history, right back to the beginning of the experiment. The solution is, of course, to maintain a rolling summarisation of the past history that we delete. The summary will be much more compact than the full history, so we will save most of the space that the deleted history had occupied.

Response-time reduction

An appropriately designed summary will also help with the response-time problem. You can try to arrange matters so that in maintaining the rolling summarisation you are simultaneously contributing partial results to the calculations whose response time is in question. For example, you might decide that the model will have these state phenomena:

■ *CMVoltage(i,t)*: the voltage values for each point *i* and all values of *t* in the most recent five minutes; earlier values *CMVoltage(i,t)* are deleted and forgotten;

■ *OldTotal(i)*: the total of the deleted voltage values *CMVoltage(i,t)* for each point *i* and all values of *t* preceding the most recent five minutes;

■ *NewTotal(i)*: the total of the voltage values *CMVoltage(i,t)* for each point *i* and all values of *t* in the most recent five minutes;

■ *MaxVoltage(i)*: the maximum voltage value detected at point *i* during the experiment so far;

■ *MinVoltage(i)*: the minimum voltage value detected at point *i* during the experiment so far;

■ *OldPassCount*: the number of inspection passes made before the most recent five minutes;

■ *NewPassCount*: the number of inspection passes made during the most recent five minutes.

These state phenomena of the circuit model domain are easily maintained by the circuit modeller machine as it makes each pass over the electrical circuit states. They also allow most of the required information to be calculated reasonably quickly. For example, to calculate the *Maximum Recent Average (*which point has had the highest average voltage over the past five minutes?) the average voltage of each point can be quickly calculated as *NewTotal(i)* divided by *NewPassCount*.

However, the *Maximum Difference of Two Points* (what has been the greatest difference during the whole experiment between the voltage at point 3 and the voltage at point 17?) can't be answered from the model we have just described. As a general rule, any reduction of the simple complete history model will lose some information, and must therefore make some potentially required displays impossible to produce. Whenever you are designing a model domain, it is helpful to ask yourself the question: What information will be impossible to produce from this model?

Any questions?

If the experiment were important enough – such as a space probe – you would keep all the data for ever, wouldn't you?

Yes. But you would need a big budget.

Surely that last question (what has been the greatest difference during the whole experiment between the voltage at point 3 and the voltage at point 17?) can be answered by just maintaining the maximum difference between point i and point j for all pairs (i < j)?

Yes, it can. But if that wasn't planned when the model was designed it's too late to do anything about it when the requirement is recognised.

Isn't this problem rather silly? Surely the questions to be answered should be decided at run time, not when the model is being designed?

Of course. You're completely right. We're coming to information problems with run-time questions in the next chapter.

But it's also worth remembering and stressing that when you design a model domain you are implicitly deciding which questions the system will be able to answer and which questions it won't. This was a central idea of the JSD method more than 20 years ago. It was first described in this paper:

M A Jackson, *Information Systems: Modelling, Sequencing and Transformations*, in Proceedings of the Third International Conference on Software Engineering, pages 72–81, May 1978.

and then in: M A Jackson, *System Development*, Prentice Hall International, 1983.

John Cameron, *JSP & JSD: The Jackson Approach to Software Development*, IEEE CS Press, 2nd Edition, 1989.

7.5 Control and definitions in models

The problem frame for the subproblem of building a model is:

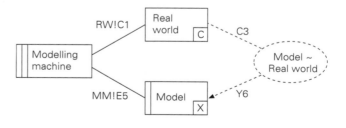

Model building subproblem: problem frame

Essentially, you introduce the model domain to provide new model phenomena Y6 that can act as surrogates for the real world requirement phenomena C3. The Y6 phenomena will then be readily available to the display machine of the second subproblem in a way that the C3 phenomena cannot be. The modelling machine maintains – more or less – a one-to-one relationship between C1 events or state changes and E5 operations; So the vital correspondence between C3 and Y6 relies on these relationships:

- the relationship between E5 and Y6. This is the responsibility of the designer of the model domain;

- the relationship between C1 and E5. This is the responsibility of the specifier of the model building machine;

- the relationship between C3 and C1. This is governed by the nature of those phenomena and the domain properties of the real world.

Three different possible relationships between C1 and C3 give somewhat different characters to the resulting model domains. The three are:

- C3 cause C1;

- C3 are defined in terms of C1;

- C1 cause C3.

We'll look at all three in the three sections that follow.

7.5.1　C3 cause C1

First, C3 may be the cause of C1. For example, the upwards and downwards travel of the lift (*Rising* and *Falling*) and its dwelling for various periods of time at the different floors (*At(f)*) are C3 phenomena; they are the cause of the lift states *SensOn(f)* that the machine can detect directly. Another example, which we have not discussed in this chapter, is in the local traffic monitoring problem. There, the passage of vehicles of various types causes changes in the states of the sensor tubes.

When the C3 phenomena are the causes of C1, the purpose of the model domain can be regarded as *diagnosis:* the C1 are the symptoms, and the C3 are the causes. In real world terms, the diagnosis runs, 'If these C1 phenomena have occurred, they must have happened because of an occurrence of such-and-such a pattern of C3 phenomena.' Translated into model domain terms, 'If these E5 operations have occurred, they should be reflected in such-and-such states Y6.' In the terms of the local traffic monitoring problem: 'If this pattern of changes to the sensor tube states has just occurred, it must have been because a car has just passed, so the count of cars should be one higher than it was.' In terms of the lift: 'If this pattern of *SensOn(f)* states has occurred, it must have been because the lift is now serving floor *f;* and that real world state should be modelled by the lift model state *MStaying(f)* and *MAxsbl(f).*'

The crucial difficulty of diagnosis, as every medical practitioner knows, is that different causes can give rise to the same symptoms. The lift sensor states may be a symptom of the lift being stuck, not of serving the floor. The traffic monitoring sensor tubes may have been affected by children playing, or by a falling tree. A secondary difficulty, that can sometimes be serious, is that there may be a significant time lag between the occurrence of the cause and the occurrence of the symptoms. We'll look briefly at that concern later in this chapter.

7.5.2 C3 defined in terms of C1

Second, the C3 phenomena may be *defined* in terms of C1. In the experimental voltages problem, the average voltage at a point, or the maximum difference between two points, is not a distinct phenomenon in its own right. It is related to the 32 voltage values by a definition.

Examples of such definitional relationships occur frequently, especially in biddable domains. Phenomena that at first sight seem to be distinct turn out, on further thought, to be related by definition. An important and common case is the relationship between entity states and entity participation in events. For example, a person may participate in an *enrol* event, thus becoming a member of the library. But the state of 'being a member' is not a distinct phenomenon in its own right: it is, by definition, the state of any person who has participated in an *enrol* event and has not yet participated in a *resign* event.

This definitional relationship is much easier to deal with in modelling than the causal relationship of the previous section. When you design the model domain you have a choice between two simple possibilities.

■ One possibility is to let the C1/C3 real world definitional relationship be modelled by a similar E5/Y6 definitional relationship. When the display machine in the second subproblem needs access to Y6, it must then calculate Y6 according to the definition.

■ The other possibility is to model the C1/C3 definitional relationship by a causal relationship in the model domain. The Y6 phenomenon is designated as a phenomenon in its own right in the model domain; the domain is designed so that when the modelling machine causes an E5 operation the appropriate change is made to Y6. Provided that the modelling machine and the model domain are perfectly reliable, no harm comes of replacing the definitional relationship by a causal relationship in this way. Another way of thinking about this replacement is that the model is being used to precalculate Y6 in anticipation of its need.

7.5.3 C1 cause C3

Finally, C1 may be the cause of C3. This is the case we have not yet seen. Consider the following – admittedly rather contrived – problem.

Traffic light display

The one-way traffic light system now needs a little display to show the Stop and Go states of the light units on a small panel that the road repairers can easily see. To avoid disturbing the existing design, it is decided to add the display to it as a separate module. The new module will share the RPulse and GPulse events of the existing system.

The problem diagram, without decomposition, is:

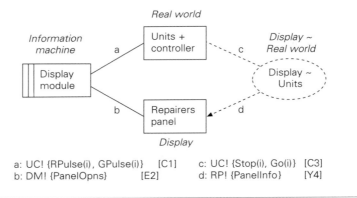

a: UC! {RPulse(i), GPulse(i)} [C1] c: UC! {Stop(i), Go(i)} [C3]
b: DM! {PanelOpns} [E2] d: RP! {PanelInfo} [Y4]

Traffic light display: fitted to information display frame

The real world is the combination of the light units domain and the lights controller from the original problem. The new module is the display module. It is the machine in this present problem. It shares the pulse events of the set *a* with the real world of the light units domain and the original lights controller. The *PanelInfo* to be shown is some convenient representation of the *Stop* and *Go* states of the units + controller domain. The *GPulse* and *RPulse* events are the C1 phenomena, and they cause the *Stop* and *Go* states which are the C3 phenomena.

On decomposing as usual, the modelling subproblem is:

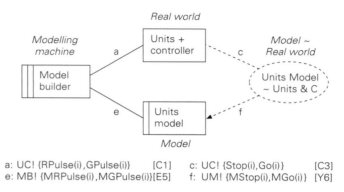

a: UC! {RPulse(i),GPulse(i)}   [C1]   c: UC! {Stop(i),Go(i)}   [C3]
e: MB! {MRPulse(i),MGPulse(i)}[E5]   f: UM! {MStop(i),MGo(i)} [Y6]

Traffic light display: model building subproblem

The model operations E5 – *MRPulses* and *MGPulses* – match exactly the *RPulses* and *GPulses* that are the C1 phenomena. The model Y6 states – *MStop* and *MGo* – must correspond exactly to the *Stop* and *Go* states that are the C3 phenomena. Most significantly, the domain description of the units model will be exactly the same as the domain description of the units + controller: it will show how changes to the *Stop* and Go (or *MStop* and *MGo*) states are caused by *RPulse* and *GPulse* (or *MRPulse* and *MGPulse*) events.

This is, in a sense, the purest form of model domain. Except for the small inevitable delay between the model builder machine detecting an *RPulse* or *GPulse* and the ensuing *MRPulse* or *MGPulse,* the units model and the units + controller domains are perfect images of each other.

7.6 Some model concerns

The relationship between the model domain and the domain it models can be complex and difficult to understand. The purposes and advantages of a model in solving an information problem are fairly obvious. We have already mentioned and illustrated most (but not all) of them:

- it lets the machine remember phenomena from the past that may be necessary for providing information in the future;

- it lets the machine carry out some calculations incrementally that would be too burdensome if they were delayed until their results are needed;

- it can model defined terms as if they corresponded to separate designated phenomena, and maintain their values in accordance with their definitions;

- it can model processes of a conceptual domain – of the kind that are best understood in terms of tagging – as if they were physical entities;

- it can capture and embody inference rules derived from the properties of the modelled domain;

- using embodied inference rules, it can provide surrogates for private phenomena of the modelled domain that are inaccessible to the machine.

When you use a model in analysing and solving a problem it's also important to remember some concerns and potential difficulties that can arise. In this final section we'll just mention some of them briefly.

Model imperfection

The traffic light display is exceptional in having a model that is effectively perfect. That is, the correspondence between the model and the real world is perfect. In the two problems we have looked at more deeply, the correspondence is imperfect in more than one way.

The lift model is imperfect in at least these ways:

- if the lift is stuck at a floor for more than 2.5 seconds, the RQFLR object enters the *MAxsbl* state although the lift is not accessible at all. We are assuming that the lift doesn't get stuck very often;

- when the lift is in its (Closing2), (Reopening), (Reopened), (Closed) and (Going) states, the RQFLR object is in its *MAxsbl* state although the lift is not accessible at all in those states. In principle this is a serious imperfection. We dealt with it by a cunning expedient;

- state 4 in the RQFLR object is the cunning expedient. It means something like 'the model is guessing that the lift is accessible, but if it leaves within 3.3 seconds that will mean that it wasn't accessible after all'. This is a suspect – but perhaps unavoidable – blend of modelling the real lift and modelling the limitations of the available information;

- the CARFLR *MHere* state corresponds to a similar blend. It means something like 'the real lift car has arrived at the floor, and is either (Passing), (Arrived), (Stuck) or (Serving); if it hasn't left within 2.5 seconds that will mean that it was in the first 2.5 seconds of (Serving)';

The circuit model is imperfect in at least these ways:

■ the continuously varying voltages are modelled by discrete samples;

■ the samples collected at different circuit points in each pass are, inevitably, collected at different times;

■ because some of the historical data has been discarded, the information available is reduced.

If your model is imperfect, you must be aware of the resulting imperfections in the information produced from it. The crisp tidiness of a lexical model domain can distract your attention from the messy faults in its correspondence with the real world.

Time lag

In information systems that use databases there is commonly a time lag between the occurrence of a real world event or state change and the detection of that event by the modelling machine. Even when communication is online – for example, by access to the web – there may be other sources of delay. For example, insurance policy holders often wait a long time before notifying the insurance company of a significant event.

This time lag can have different consequences in different applications. For example:

■ in a national census office the consequences are probably negligible. The delays – even in a country with poor communications – are small in relation to the period between one census and the next so it makes sense to accept the delay and wait for the model to reach a more up-to-date state before using it;

■ in a billing problem it's normal to carry over an unspecified balance from one period to the next. Neither the customer nor the billing organisation expects the model to be fully up-to-date in respect of either part of the real world. The customer is not distressed if a postal payment is somewhat delayed in reaching the company; the company is not distressed at the thought that the customer has consumed more water or electricity or gas than the model shows;

■ in a banking problem it is common to strike a daily balance. Items not processed today will be handled tomorrow.

But in some cases – for example, in some insurance applications – the consequences of time lags must be dealt with meticulously. If a claim arises around the time of policy renewal, it is essential to determine the true order of events: lapse of the old policy; renewal of the policy; payment of the premium; occurrence of the incident giving rise to the claim; claim notification. In a problem like this it may be necessary to distinguish three significant times for most real world events: when the event occurred; when notification reached the insurance company; and when the model was updated. In effect, the primary model is combined with a meta-model. The meta-model models the updating of the primary model.

Incompleteness

A model may be incomplete. Because of time lag, unavailability of information, or other causes, some of the model phenomena have never been brought into correspondence with the real world. For example, if an analog-digital device fails temporarily in the experimental voltages problem, there will be a gap in the sequence of voltage samples at a particular point. A library member may have no address recorded in the database. This is different from having information that is out of date: it is having no information where information is, by default, assumed to be present.

Incompleteness causes much difficulty when the model and the modelled domains are not properly distinguished and described, and the required correspondence between them carefully stated. A notable example of difficulty is the use of NULL values in relational databases. A NULL value might occur because:

- it corresponds to a real world individual – an entity or a value – that does not exist. For example, a compassionate library might allow street dwellers to become members. Street dwellers don't have addresses, so the tuples that model them have NULL values in the address column;

- it corresponds to a real world individual who does exist but is not known. For example, a patient being monitored in the ICU might have been brought in unconscious and has not yet been identified. The patient's model has a NULL name;

- it corresponds to a defined term in the real world for which the definition does not apply in the model. For example, *Recent Average* for a voltage point in the electrical circuit domain is defined to be the average at that point over the past five minutes. If failure of the analog-digital device has prevented any sampling at the point during the past five minutes, the real world average is well-defined but the corresponding model value must be NULL.

Errors

In administrative and business applications an unreliable *connection domain* is often interposed between the real world and the model building machine. Failures in this connection – such as keyboarding errors in data entry – are likely to corrupt the correspondence between the model and the real world.

Detecting and correcting these failures often becomes a major concern in the problem analysis. In later chapters we'll say more about connection domains and about detecting and correcting failures.

Any questions?

How can I deal with all these concerns that can arise in using a model?

Some of them are special to particular applications, for example, life assurance. Some are special to particular model implementations, for example, a relational database. So you may need to acquire particular expertise or to draw on expert help there. But you always need a solid understanding of how a model domain is related to its real world.

Is it really necessary to make separate domain descriptions of the real world and the model?

What can I say? Is it really necessary to keep your eyes open while you're driving? Not if you're driving a dodgem car in a fairground. Is that how you see your development work?

If the effort seems too much, you could cut it down like this. Start by making a description of one of the two domains. Choose either one of the two, but be sure to choose it explicitly. Document your choice, and stick to it rigidly. Let's suppose you choose to describe the real world domain. Then take the resulting description and write another document that states precisely:

(a) which parts of the real world description apply to the model domain, and how;

(b) which parts of the real world description don't apply to the model domain, and why;

(c) the additional properties of the model domain that don't apply to the real world, and so are not mentioned in its description.

If the model domain is part of the solution, why are we discussing it in this book?

Because in analysing and structuring a problem you can't avoid straying some way into the structuring of a solution. Try thinking about the problem context as a black box, with only the requirement phenomena visible from the outside. From that point of view, it's often very hard to state the requirement intelligibly, and even harder to show that there can be a machine to satisfy it. Black boxes are like top-down. They're useful for describing problems that have already been solved and systems that have already been designed. But not much help in solving and designing.

CHAPTER 8

Variant frames

The set of basic problem frames and their flavours can be extended by frame variants. Typically – but not necessarily – a variant adds a domain to the problem context. Most variants can be applied to several basic frames. Example variants are description, operator, connection and control. The first three add a domain, the fourth modifies the control properties of interfaces. More than one variant can be applied simultaneously to the same basic frame.

8.1 Frames and variants

Problem frames are patterns to which you fit particular problems and subproblems. The closer the fit, the more useful the frame. There's an infinity of possible problems and subproblems, but only a small set of problem frames. The set is extended by *variants,* in which a basic frame is varied or elaborated in some way, often by the addition of another domain to the problem diagram. The variant shares the central concern that characterises the basic frame, but extends it to deal with some problems that don't fit the unmodified basic frame. As you would expect, the modification introduces additional concerns on its own account.

In this chapter we'll discuss four kinds of variant.

- A *description variant* modifies the basic frame by introducing a description domain. A description domain is a lexical domain that describes a part or aspect of the requirement, or describes some other domain that may or may not be present in the problem context. You can introduce a description domain into any basic frame, but they are most commonly found in behaviour and information problems.

- An *operator variant* introduces an operator into the basic frame. We have already seen one such variant in an earlier chapter: the commanded behaviour frame is an operator variant of the basic required behaviour frame. The basic information display frame has a similar variant.

■ A *connection variant* introduces a connection domain between the machine and the central domain in the basic frame. There are connection variants of behaviour and information problems. They are very common in administrative and business applications. One well known development method assumes a connection variant of the required behaviour frame.

■ A *control variant* introduces no new domain. Instead it varies the basic frame by altering the control characteristics of interface phenomena. There are control variants of the basic transformation and workpiece problem frames.

8.2 Description variants

The simplest description modifies the required behaviour frame: the required behaviour of the controlled domain is explicitly represented in a lexical *description domain*. The control machine uses the description domain to determine the behaviour to be imposed on the controlled domain. Here's an example.

Regulated one-way lights

The equipment company that manufactures the traffic light units has realised that its existing product is very inflexible. The regime of Stop and Go lights is preset in the factory. Sometimes this preset regime doesn't fit the road conditions very well. In a new design the manufacturers have incorporated a magnetic card reader. The regime is encoded on the card as a simple ASCII text. For example:

(S1,S2:50; S1,G2:120; S1,S2:45; G1,S2:100;)*

When the road repairers set up the lights they first select a card carrying the encoding of the desired regime, and then insert it into the card reader. The computer reads the card and controls the lights accordingly. To change the regime only the card need be changed. The manufacturers supply a range of cards to suit any condition tolerably well and most conditions perfectly.

This is an archetypal use of a description domain. You can think of it as a kind of *late binding*. The decision 'what lights regime is required?' is no longer bound at the time the software is designed and written, that is, when the machine is built. Instead, it is encoded in an exchangeable or modifiable description domain, and needn't be bound until the machine runs. Here are two examples of such description domains:

■ the *program text* for a computer. The computer's behaviour is bound at run time by choosing the program to be executed. The different between a Turing machine and a Universal Turing machine is that the universal machine has a description domain encoding the program, while the simple machine has the program permanently built in;

■ *type objects* (sometimes called meta-objects) in object-oriented programming. Instead of fixing the behaviour of each instance of an object class permanently in the class definition, you encode it in one or more type objects. If each object instance is associated with a type object at run time, its behaviour can be different from other objects of the same class and can even be changed during its lifetime.

8.2.1 Problem diagram

Here's the problem diagram for the regulated one-way lights:

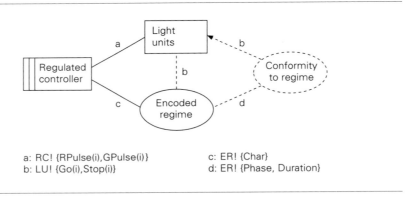

a: RC! {RPulse(i),GPulse(i)}
b: LU! {Go(i),Stop(i)}

c: ER! {Char}
d: ER! {Phase, Duration}

Regulated one-way lights: problem diagram

The description domain is the encoded regime. It is represented by a solid oval. That means that it's a *tangible description*, embodied in a physical domain. A tangible description is always a lexical domain. The encoded regime has an interface of shared symbolic phenomena with the machine. These symbolic phenomena are *Char* – the characters of the encoded description, which the machine can read.

The dashed line connecting the encoded regime to the light units domain indicates that the description *refers to* light units phenomena. This reference is like the reference by a requirement (which is an *intangible description*) to a domain. This reference – to the *Stop* and *Go* states – has exactly the same phenomena as the requirement reference *b*, so it is identified with the same letter.

The requirement in the original version of the problem was called lights regime, because it stipulated the particular regime of *Stop* and *Go* lights to be shown. Now, in this description variant, the requirement is called conformity to regime. It doesn't stipulate the regime of lights to be shown but instead that the lights shown must conform to the encoded regime.

8.2.2 The description domain

To analyse this problem and address its central concern you must, of course, investigate and describe the encoded regime domain. Because the encoding takes the form of an ASCII string, your description will be in a language suitable for describing the grammar of which any regime encoding is an instance. For example, you could use the notation we used to describe the email files in the mailfile analysis problem. Your description will then be like this:

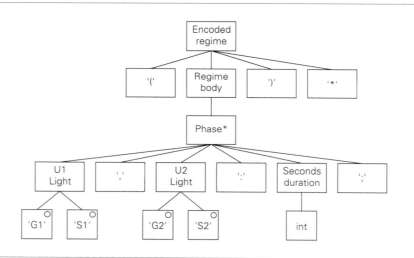

Domain description: syntax of encoded regime

The characters *Char* in the set *c* of phenomena shared with the machine are the leaves of this tree. The regime consists of a regime body in parentheses; the regime body is any number of phases; each phase has a U1 light, a comma, a U2 light, a colon, an integer seconds duration, and a semicolon. For example, the description

    (S1,S2:50; S1,G2:120; S1,S2:45; G1,S2:100;)*

has a regime body containing four phases, with seconds durations of 50, 120, 45 and 100. In the second phase, light unit 1 shows Stop and unit 2 shows Go, and so on.

8.2.3 Transformation problem description variant

Here's an example of a description variant of a transformation problem:

Lexical analysis

As part of a small and simple compiler you need a program to perform lexical analysis on the input text. The lexical analyser must recognise tokens appearing in the input – integers, floating-point numbers, identifiers, comments and so on – and produce an output stream in which each token appears as a separate record with a field for the token type and a field for the token value. For example, from the input

(123 + 56 – abc)

the analyser must produce

Lpar,"(" Int,"123" Op,"+" Int,"56" Op,"–" Ident,"abc" Rpar,")"

where the token types are Lpar, Int, Op, Ident and Rpar.

This is a straightforward basic transformation problem. Treating it that way, you would write the definitions of the token types into the lexical analysis program itself. A more flexible way of treating the problem is as a description variant. The token type definitions are encoded in a description domain that the lexical analyser interprets during its analysis of the input.

Here is the problem diagram:

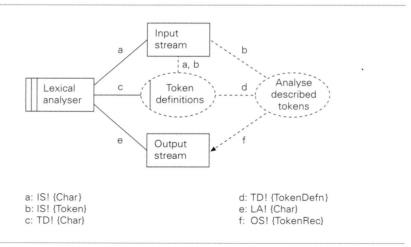

a: IS! {Char}
b: IS! {Token}
c: TD! {Char}

d: TD! {TokenDefn}
e: LA! {Char}
f: OS! {TokenRec}

Regulated one-way lights: problem diagram

The token definitions domain is a description domain to be designed. It describes the relationship between characters and tokens in the input stream domain. The requirement is that the output stream should contain token records corresponding to the input stream tokens, in accordance with the definitions in the description domain.

The form of a token definition might be like this example:

Letter = [_,a-z,A-Z]
Digit = [0-9]
Token(Ident) = (Letter (Letter | Digit)*)

An identifier token is a letter followed by zero or more occurrences of letter or digit, where letter is an alphabetic character or an underscore and digit is a numeric character.

8.2.4 Information problem description variant

In a problem that fits the basic information frame, the information machine selects the information to be displayed. The selection criteria are given in the requirement and built into the machine. Instead, you can encode these criteria in a description domain, with the same benefits of flexibility as in a behaviour or transformation problem.

A subproblem of patient monitoring provides an example. Here's the subproblem sketch, extracted from patient monitoring:

Device failure detection

A patient-monitoring program is required for the intensive care unit in a hospital. Each patient is monitored by an analog device which measures factors such as pulse, temperature, blood pressure, and skin resistance. If an analog device fails the nurses' station is notified.

This subproblem fits the basic information display frame. The problem diagram, omitting the interface annotations, is:

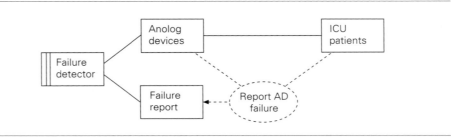

Device failure detection: problem diagram

The failure that matters, and must be detected and reported, is failure of an analog device to transmit the patient's vital factor correctly to the monitoring machine. So the requirement refers not only to the failure report and the analog devices domains but also to the ICU patients domain. Unfortunately, there is a serious difficulty. The failure detector machine has access to the patients only through the very analog devices whose failure it is trying to monitor. You can't give the failure detector an interface to the ICU patients domain that bypasses the analog devices. If you could, the analog devices wouldn't be needed at all.

But you can discover and exploit the strongest reliable constraints that can be placed on the possible time series of values of each kind of vital factor. For example, the temperature of a living human being is always greater than 88° and less than 110° Fahrenheit. The maximum rate of change of temperature is very small: it is significantly less than 1° Fahrenheit per minute. So if the readings from the analog device fall outside these limits, then certainly some kind of failure has occurred. For each type of device and each vital factor it will be possible to establish constraints of the kind you are looking for.

The failure may be a breakdown in the device itself, or the device may have become detached from the patient, or, if it is a surface device, it may have been affected by some external interference such as a spilled liquid. All these possibilities, of course, are just particular kinds of failure.

Having established the constraints you could write them into the requirements and embody them in the program text of the failure detector machine. But it would be better to record them in a description domain, like this:

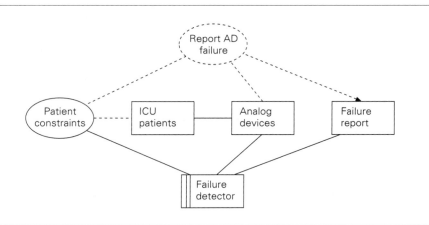

Device failure detection: adding a description domain

The patient constraints domain describes the constraints for each vital factor and hence for each type of analog device. The ICU patients domain is included in the problem diagram because it is the domain described by the patient constraints.

Any questions?

Is the lexical analyser something like Lex?

Yes and no. Yes, because Lex uses a description domain just like ours. No, because Lex works by generating a special-purpose lexical analyser program: the description domain is interpreted when lex generates the analyser, not when the input stream is analysed.

Now here's a question for you. How would you show Lex in terms of problem and subproblem diagrams?

Surely the periods & ranges would specify an alarm if the patient's temperature was less than 88 or more than 100 Fahrenheit?

Yes, but there are probably different alarm notifications. Also, the periods & ranges domain doesn't specify a maximum rate of change. These differences reflect the fact that monitoring the patients is a different subproblem from detecting device failure. You shouldn't be afraid of redundancy between subproblems.

Is the description in a description variant always static, or can it change while the machine is running?

That's a good question. In the patient monitoring example the description captures constant truths about patient factors – physiologically determined maxima and minima – so it's static. But in the home heating system the machine must construct and maintain a dynamic description of the room occupancy behaviour. It changes this description continually, and uses it in deciding when to turn the heating on and off in the different rooms.

8.3   Operator variants

We have already seen one operator variant in Chapter 4. In the basic required behaviour frame the control machine must ensure that the controlled domain behaves as described in the requirement; but in the commanded behaviour frame, an operator is introduced and the machine must ensure that the controlled domain behaves in accordance with the operator's commands. There is a similar very common variant of the basic information display frame. The variant and basic frames are often combined to give a more complex requirement.

8.3.1 Information problem operator variant

In the basic information display frame you fix the choice of information to be displayed in the requirement. In the lift position display and odometer display problems this was realistic. In the experimental voltages problem it was less realistic – a useful system would surely allow the experimenter to choose the information to be displayed according to the progressive results of the experiment, and to enter enquiries that the machine would answer.

You can think of the kind of information problem in which the purpose of the machine is to answer questions as an operator variant of the basic frame. We'll call it the commanded information frame. Here's the frame diagram:

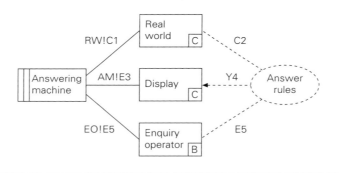

Commanded information: frame diagram

The operator is called the enquiry operator. The enquiries are regarded as commands, and are shared with the machine as events E5. The machine is called the answering machine, and produces its information outputs in the display domain. The requirement is the answer rules, and stipulates the answers to be produced for each combination of a real world state C2 with an E5 enquiry. The answers are the symbolic phenomena Y4.

As in the commanded behaviour frame, it's an important concern to reject commands that makes no sense in the context of the preceding commands. In the commanded information frame this form of the concern is usually missing. The commands embody enquiries about the real world. There is no reason to relate a command to the preceding commands: each command is to be treated as completely independent. But often there will be very many types of enquiry, and an elaborate command syntax provided to express them. A command that does not conform to the required syntax is not sensible and must be rejected.

8.3.2 The commanded information requirement

In capturing and describing the requirement for a commanded information problem, one of your most important concerns is to determine the set of possible enquiries that the machine must be capable of answering. You can't leave your customer to decide about this kind of requirement: few customers will be able to make a coherently informed decision.

The set of possible enquiries will be limited by three things:

- the interface between the real world and the answering machine limits the shared phenomena that are directly available to the answering machine;

- domain properties limit the inferences that can be drawn – with or without an explicit model – from the shared phenomena about real world phenomena that are not directly available to the machine;

- the command syntax of enquiries forms a language, and the expressive power of this language limits the enquiries that can be formulated.

Suppose, for example, that you are dealing with a commanded information version of the experimental voltages problem. You have to decide what enquiries the experimenter can enter and the machine must answer. At one extreme – far too feeble – the experimenter is allowed to enter a number in the range 1-32, and the machine answers with the present voltage at that point. At the other extreme – far too ambitious – the experimenter is allowed to enter any mathematical expression using variables $v[p,t]$ to represent the voltage at point p at time t, and the machine evaluates the expression and displays the resulting value.

An appropriate choice will almost always lie somewhere between the extremes. If your commanded information problem is a subproblem of the library administration problem, and the real world is the borrowing of books by members, you certainly won't want to limit the enquiries to 'which member is borrowing this book?' and 'which books is this member borrowing?'. But you also won't want to spend effort on analysing and describing a requirement to answer enquiries such as 'in the past month, which members have borrowed more than two books that have also been borrowed by members who borrowed either no book or more than four books last week?'.

In a commanded information problem that needs an explicit model, the design of the model domain will usually impose further limits on the set of possible enquiries. Real world phenomena that have no surrogate in the model domain are placed for ever out of reach. We mentioned this point when we talked about model domains in the last chapter.

8.3.3 Combining the basic and variant frames

Problems with operators – both information and behaviour problems – often combine the basic and variant frames. The basic frame gives a default information display or a default behaviour of the controlled domain, and the variant is superimposed on that to give an additional information display, or to give modified or overriding behaviour of the controlled domain.

The combination frame is just the frame of the commanded variant. But the requirement is a composite of the basic default requirement and the superimposed commanded requirement. You must then address a concern that focuses directly on the superimposition: How are the two requirements put together to form the combined requirement, and what are the effects elsewhere in the development?

Here's a very simple example of the combination. The operator's commands modify the required behaviour; they don't override it.

Operated one-way lights

An alternative new version of the one-way traffic lights provides for a traffic overseer who can override the default regime of Stop and Go lights. The machine is equipped with two buttons marked 'Hold' and 'Change'. The overseer can extend the current phase of the light sequence by pressing the Hold button, or curtail it by pressing the Change button. Pressing a button causes a pulse shared by the machine.

Here's the problem diagram:

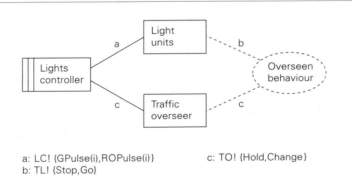

a: LC! {GPulse(i),ROPulse(i)}   c: TO! {Hold,Change}
b: TL! {Stop,Go}

Operated one-way lights: problem diagram

For simplicity we're assuming that the requirement embodies the default regime and also the rules for overriding it in response to *Hold* and *Change* commands from the traffic overseer. The default regime is as before:

```
forever {
        show only Stop(1) and Stop(2) for 50 seconds;
        show only Stop(1) and Go(2) for 120 seconds;
        show only Stop(1) and Stop(2) for 50 seconds;
        show only Go(1) and Stop(2) for 120 seconds;
}
```

8.3.4 Modifying default behaviour

The rules for modifying the default behaviour may be something like this:

- on a Hold command the current phase is extended from the point already reached by its default length. So, for example, if a Hold command is issued when the Stop(1) and Stop(2) phase has been current for 35 of its normal 50 seconds, the phase is extended to 85 seconds in total;

- on a Change command the current phase is terminated and the next phase is immediately begun;

- if two Hold commands are issued within one second, the current phase is extended until a Change command is issued. Other Hold commands issued after the first Hold in a phase, and before the end of the phase or a Change command, are ignored.

The domain properties are, of course, entirely unaffected by the introduction of the operator and the composition of the two requirements, and are exactly as given before. Your machine behaviour specification will be based on these unchanged domain properties, and on the required behaviour as modified by the operator's commands.

8.3.5 Overriding default behaviour

When the operator commands must override the default required behaviour, rather than modify it, you will often find it easier to treat the required behaviour and the commanded behaviour as distinct subproblems. The subproblem machines are combined to give a machine that switches between the required and the commanded *modes*. The modes are never combined. They alternate, depending on the operator's commands, subject to restrictions derived from the domain properties. These restrictions may be concerned with ensuring that the switch does not take place until the domain has reached a state in the current mode that is an acceptable initial state in the new mode. We'll come back to this topic in Chapter 11, when we discuss composite problem frames.

Any questions?

Why not just use a general query language, such as SQL, instead of trying to decide what enquiries the machine must be able to answer?

SQL is a programming language for relational databases. Most enquiry operators aren't programmers, and don't think of the real world as a relational database. The machine must present an intelligible interface to the enquiry operator. Almost always that will mean giving up full generality in favour of something more closely related to experience in the real world.

Wouldn't you want to relate enquiry commands to the context of the preceding commands if you were trying to optimise the enquiries, for example, as a Web browser optimises page retrieval by caching?

Yes, you might. But that would be a more elaborate variant, and would probably need decomposition into two subproblems.

8.4 Connection variants

In an information problem the belief problem domain is the real world. In a behaviour problem it's the controlled domain. In an ideal world, the machine you are building would always have a perfect interface of shared phenomena with the chief problem domain. The interface would be rich enough to give the machine direct access to all the phenomena it must detect or control to satisfy the requirement. But the world is not always perfectly arranged. Often the connection between the machine and the chief problem domain is indirect, through another domain that interposes its own properties and behaviour. We'll call such a domain a *connection domain*.

Reliable connection domains

When the connection domain is specifically designed to act as a connection – for example, a purpose-built sensor or an actuator – it may be very reliable. The floor sensors in the lift position display problem never fail. You can be very confident that if *SensOn(f)* holds, the lift car is indeed within 6 inches of the rest position at floor *f*. If an *RPulse* is sent to the light unit in the appropriate state, the unit will indeed enter a *Stop* state. When a connection is reliable in this kind of way you usually absorb it into the domain it connects. So the electromechanical relay or semiconductor device that switches the power in the light unit is treated as an integral part of the light unit; and the floor sensor is treated as an integral part of the lift & buttons domain.

Unreliable connection domains

But sometimes the connection is a complex domain in its own right, and can introduce many kinds of uncertainty into the connection. Its interposed behaviour and properties then demand your attention quite separately from the central problem domain that it connects to the machine and that is the chief subject of the requirement. This is particularly likely to happen in business and administrative problems, where the problem domain may be separated from the machine by substantial data entry and data output domains. For example:

- in the library administration problem the requirement is chiefly about the library books and the members and the affiliated libraries. The library manager machine must exercise some kind of control over the borrowing and return of books, and the payment of membership subscriptions and fines for overdue books. But the connection between the library manager machine on one side, and the library books, the members and the affiliated libraries on the other side, is through the library staff. The library staff are interposed between the machine and the other domains, and constitute a complex connection domain in their own right. That's why they had to appear as a separate domain in the library administration problem diagram;

- in the meeting scheduler problem the requirement is chiefly about the people who initiate and participate in meetings, and about their diaries and time commitments, and about the availability of meeting rooms and necessary equipment. But the connection between the meeting scheduler machine and these domains is through email messages, and through conversations with secretaries. The email system and the secretaries are interposed between the machine and the chief problem domains, and they are complex domains in their own right.

When a problem has this kind of complex connection we'll say that it is a *connection variant*, and that it has a *remote problem domain*. Talking in this way helps to focus your attention on the problem domain at the far end of the connection from the machine. That's an essential focus because it's what the requirement is chiefly about. You have to pay attention to the connection domain because it complicates the problem in a way you must not ignore. But you mustn't forget that the remote problem domain is what the problem is really about.

8.4.1 A required behaviour frame with connection domains

Complex connection domains are also found in other contexts. The 'four variable model' is a method for developing software for certain kinds of behaviour problem. It uses a connection variant of the basic required behaviour frame. Here's its implicit problem diagram:

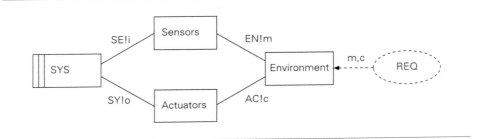

Four variable model: standard problem diagram

The control machine is called SYS. The controlled domain is called environment. There are two connection domains – sensors and actuators – interposed between the machine and the controlled domain.

The requirement is called REQ. It stipulates a condition on the phenomena m and c of the environment: m are controlled by the environment, and c are controlled by the actuators. In the terminology of the four variable model, m are the *monitored variables,* and c are the *controlled variables.* The specification phenomena shared by the machine are i and o; they are the *input variables* and *output variables.* Hence the 'four variables': m, c, i and o.

Descriptions

The method demands the construction of five descriptions:

■ REQ is an optative relation between the variables m and c. It is the requirement;

■ NAT is an indicative relation between the variables m and c. It describes the domain properties of environment;

■ IN is an indicative relation between the variables m and i. It describes the domain properties of the sensors connection domain, that is, how the sensors translate the environment phenomena m to phenomena i shared with the machine SYS;

- OUT is an indicative relation between the variables o and c. It describes the domain properties of the actuators connection domain, that is, how the actuators translate the phenomena o controlled by the machine SYS to environment phenomena c;

- SOF is an optative relation between the variables i and o. It is the specification of the machine SYS.

The four variable method emphasises mathematical rigour. Its range of applicability is somewhat smaller than appears at first sight. It is restricted by these underlying assumptions:

- the requirement phenomena are exactly the variables m and c that are shared by the environment with the sensors and actuators. So if you think of the sensors and actuators as parts of the machine, the method assumes that the requirement phenomena and specification phenomena are the same sets;

- the phenomenon sets m and c are disjoint. That is, no phenomenon may belong to both sets;

- the sensors and actuators are mutually independent in their operation.

To some extent, these restrictions can be circumvented. For example, if the phenomenon mi belongs to m and to c, it can be renamed cj in its incarnation in c, and the description NAT can then include a statement that the values of mi and cj are always equal. This statement would be a definition masquerading as a domain property.

8.4.2 A causal remote domain

Here's an example of a remote domain in a purely causal behaviour problem.

Lathe control

An automatic lathe is a computer-controlled metal-working tool that makes metal parts by cutting or drilling, the parts being held in a rotating clamp during the process. We are to develop the lathe controller for using the lathe to make brass bushes from brass rod. A bush is a cylindrical part, made from a blank piece of metal that must be drilled, shaped to fit into a housing, and cut to length, all on the automatic lathe.

Here is the problem diagram, with the interface phenomena very roughly annotated:

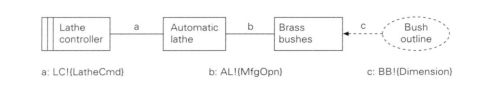

Lathe control: problem diagram

There are two given problem domains: the automatic lathe itself and the brass bushes. The brass bushes domain is both the brass rod stock from which the bushes are to be made and, eventually, the bushes themselves. The machine you must build is called the lathe controller. The brass bushes are a remote domain in this problem; the automatic lathe is the connection domain.

The phenomena *a* shared by the lathe and the machine are the *LatheCmd* commands by which the controller can order the lathe to perform such manufacturing operations as selecting a cutting tool, moving the tool, feeding the material to be cut, and setting the motor speed. The phenomena *b* shared by the lathe and the brass bushes are the manufacturing operations that the lathe can perform.

The requirement is called the bush outline. That reflects the fact that it describes the required outline shape of the finished bushes. It describes the outline by giving the required dimensions *c* with respect to a fixed basic shape. For example, if a bush has the fixed form of a simple circular cylinder with an axial hole, there would be three dimensions to be described: the internal radius, the external radius and the length.

8.4.3 Domain property descriptions

To solve this problem you must make separate domain descriptions of the automatic lathe and the brass bushes. The first of these describes the properties of the lathe that connect its phenomena *a* and *b,* that is, how the lathe performs operations in response to commands. The second describes how the brass stock reacts to the operations it is subjected to by the lathe by changing its form and dimensions, relating the phenomena *b* and *c.*

Along with the usual specification, describing the behaviour of the lathe controller, and the requirement, describing the required fixed form and dimensions, these two domain descriptions fit into the frame concern argument for the problem as shown in this diagram:

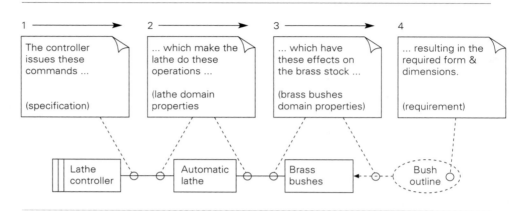

Lathe control: frame concern

Because there are two domains there are four descriptions instead of the usual three needed for a simple behaviour problem.

Is it really necessary to make and use both of these descriptions? Yes, it is. Here's why.

- If you leave out the brass bushes domain and its description, the requirement would have to be expressed purely in terms of the lathe manufacturing operations *b*. There would be no explicit description of what is being made.

- If you leave out the automatic lathe domain and its description, there would be no connection at all between the machine and the brass bushes. The problem as described would be entirely insoluble.

- If you combine the automatic lathe and the brass bushes into one domain – let's call it lathe & bushes – you would suffer two penalties. First, the lathe & bushes domain would be very complicated: it would be hard to understand and hard to describe. Second, you wouldn't be able to use your lathe & bushes domain description again when you have another problem using the same lathe to make a different product, or a different lathe to make the same bushes.

8.4.4 Combining variants

Not surprisingly, different variants can be combined, and the same variant can be applied twice in one problem. Here is an example in which the connection variant is combined with two instances of the description variant.

Versatile lathe control

The automatic lathe system needs to be much more flexible. The dimensions and shape of the bushes to be turned are described in a file held on floppy disk. This allows not only bushes of different sizes and proportions, but also such variations as flanged and stepped bushes.

In addition, the system is to be applied to several different lathes in the factory, each with a slightly different set of commands. For example, the control screws by which the cutting tool holder is moved are of different pitches, so they need different amounts of rotation to produce the same tool movement. The properties of the particular lathe to be controlled are described in a second floppy disk file. The computer is equipped with two floppy disk readers.

Here, without interface annotations, is the problem diagram:

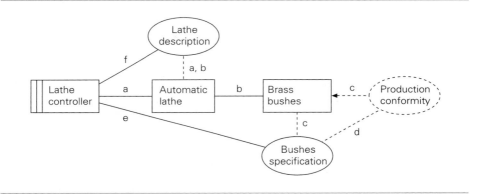

Versatile lathe control: problem diagram

There are two description domains: the lathe description and the bushes specification. The lathe description describes the properties of the automatic lathe, that is, how the commands *a* issued by the machine determine the manufacturing operations *b* performed by the lathe. The bushes specification describes the required dimensions of the brass bushes. The requirement is called production conformity: it stipulates that the brass bushes should conform to the description encoded in the bushes specification.

Why is the lathe description not referred to by the requirement? Because the requirement concerns only the bushes, not the lathe. Here's how the development concerns fit together:

- the requirement stipulates that the dimensions of the bushes produced must conform to the bushes specification;

- at run time the machine will calculate what manufacturing operations *b* must be performed. The rules for this calculation are fixed at development time – in the machine specification – from the properties of the brass bushes and bushes specification domains;

- at run time the machine will calculate what commands *a* must be issued to cause the calculated manufacturing operations *b*. The rules for this second calculation are also fixed in the machine specification at development time, from the properties of lathe description and the automatic lathe.

Use of the lathe description, then, is implicit in the program context and the requirement as shown in the diagram. The lathe description would be referred to by the requirement only if there were a further requirement to operate the automatic lathe in a certain way that is not a prerequisite for producing the bushes – for example, to observe some cutting speed restriction intended solely to reduce wear and tear on the lathe.

8.4.5 Biddable remote and connection domains

Here's another, rather different, example of a connection and a remote domain, from a subproblem of the library administration problem. It's about administering library membership.

Library membership control

It is required to restrict the way library membership is acquired and exercised. The membership rules must be enforced, as they relate to the privileges and obligations of membership in terms of enrolling, resigning, paying fees, and similar matters.

Here's the problem diagram, roughly annotated:

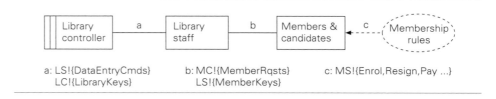

Library membership control: problem diagram

The machine, directly accessible at interface *a* only to the library staff, is called the library controller. At this interface the staff enter data into the machine, and the machine controls the issue of 'library keys'. The keys might be just authorisation numbers; or perhaps they might be encoded membership cards produced by the machine (but not shown in this diagram).

The staff interact at *b* with members and candidate members. Some of this interaction is face to face in the library, and some is by telephone (we're ignoring postal interaction here). At this interface the members & candidates can make requests of the staff. The staff can give out 'member keys' – perhaps in the form of member Ids and PINs – without which the rights and privileges of membership cannot be exercised.

The membership rules requirement stipulates the privileges and obligations of membership and restrictions on the behaviour of members that concern enrolling, paying fees, and so on.

The library staff are a connection domain to the remote domain, which is the members & candidates. You can't ignore either of these domains in this problem. The staff can't be ignored because they introduce a large element of unreliability into the connection between the machine and the members & candidates domain. For example:

- a member may pay a fine or a fee to a staff member who then omits to enter a record of the transaction in the machine;

- a membership card or PIN is mistakenly given to the wrong person;

- a new member's age is wrongly recorded, resulting in the wrong fee rate for their membership.

You certainly can't ignore the members & candidates. They are the chief domain here: the problem is about administering membership, not about staff interaction with the machine. Members' properties and behaviour affecting membership are certainly not restricted to their interactions with the staff. For example:

- members may forget their member Ids or PINs;

- members may change their names;

- members may change their addresses;

- someone who is not a member may find or steal a member Id or PIN, and use it to impersonate a member.

If you insist on identifying these events with interactions between members and the staff, you won't be able to deal properly with the problem as it really is.

8.4.6 Documents as connection domains

If the membership control problem uses membership cards, they can be understood as a connection domain in their own right. Machine-readable documents of this kind can be used to connect the machine to a domain from which it would otherwise be disconnected.

Sometimes the connection is used only to identify people – such as the library members – who are authorised to perform certain actions – such as borrowing books. Then it can be used to separate authorised from unauthorised people, and to distinguish one authorised person from another. But it can also be used in other ways. Here are some examples of documents as connection domains:

- bank account cards that can be used in ATMs;

- smart phone cards of the kind common in Europe, which encode a credit amount that depends on the original price of the card and is reduced by the charge for each call made;

- bar-coded labels on goods in supermarkets;

- bar-coded address labels on parcels in a parcel delivery system;

- anti-theft tags on high-value items in stores;

- bar-coded identifying tags on library book copies.

Models of document connection domains

Connection domains consisting of documents share phenomena with the machine only when the document is accessible to the reader that is attached to the machine. The phone company can't check the remaining credit on your pre-pay phone card when it's not inserted into one of their phones; the library machine can't check the bar-coded labels on a book unless the book is swiped at a barcode reader.

You can deal with this intermittent accessibility by an information system using an explicit model domain. The real world for this information system is the domain of documents. If the information system machine shares the events in which the documents are produced – either by itself or by another machine – it can build a model of the connection domain that includes all the documents in the domain. As each document participates in subsequent events shared with the machine, the machine updates its model accordingly.

The information system about the documents is, of course, just a subproblem of the larger problem in which they are a connection domain. And, as always, you must remember that in this larger problem your chief concern is with the remote domain.

Any questions?

Where is the four variable method described?

The four variable method is the work of David Parnas and his colleagues. It also provides most of the basis of the CORE method for describing real-time requirements. These methods are described in:

A John van Schouwen, David Lorge Parnas and Jan Madey, *Documentation of Requirements for Computer Systems*, in Proceedings of the IEEE International Symposium on Requirements Engineering, pages 198–207, January 1993.

David Lorge Parnas and Jan Madey, *Functional Documents for Computer Systems*, Science of Computer Programming, Volume 25, Number 1, pages 41–61, October 1995.

Stuart Faulk, John Brackett, Paul Ward and James Kirby Jr *The Core Method for Real-Time Requirements*, IEEE Software, Volume 9, Number 5, pages 22–33, September 1992.

If there are plastic membership cards, wouldn't they be a problem domain in their own right?

Yes, they would be. If you're going to deal seriously with the library problem you'll have to consider what can happen to the cards, including loss, theft, degradation of the magnetic encoding, etc. It will probably be helpful to treat the handling of the cards as a separate subproblem from dealing with the membership.

8.5 Control variants

Any event has three control aspects:

- control of the event class or type: what class of event is to happen?

- control of the event occurrence: when is the event to happen?

- control of the event roles: which individuals are to participate in the event?

When an event is shared between two domains, the question arises for each aspect of control: which domain has control? Very often, especially for causal events, control of all the aspects lies with the same domain. So, for example, in the one-way traffic lights problem the interface between the lights controller machine and the light units domain consists of the *GPulse* and *RPulse* events. In this case, the lights controller controls all aspects: it controls whether a *GPulse* or an *RPulse* is to happen, when it is to happen, and whether unit 1 or unit 2 is to participate.

If you want to think about the situation in programming terms, you can think of the lights controller as invoking an external procedure of the light units domain, and choosing the parameters: the light unit plays no part in the decision. In Ada the procedure declarations would be:

GPULSE (U: **in** LIGHT_UNIT) ..   and   RPULSE (U: **in** LIGHT_UNIT) ..

or perhaps:

PULSE (U: **in** LIGHT_UNIT; P: **in** PULSE_TYPE)

Control of the event class and the time of occurrence always go together: the same domain determines what should happen and when it should happen.

But control of the roles is sometimes separated from control of the event class and time. The commonest case is an event in which a machine reads a data record stored in a lexical domain. In the mailfiles analysis problem, if you look in finer detail at the interface between the mail analyser and each mailfile that it accesses, you'll see this:

■ the mail analyser determines whether the next event should be an open or a read event;

■ if it is a read event, the mailfiles domain determines:
   – which record value (which message line) should participate, or ...
   – ... if there are no more message lines, that no record value should participate.

In programming terms, the mail analyser invokes the read procedure of the mail-files domain, but the mailfiles domain determines the parameter. In Ada the procedure declarations would be:

OPEN ( ) ..   and   READ (R: **out** DATA_RECORD) ..

In the problem frames we have looked at already in earlier chapters, each interface has its own particular control characteristics. Some of those frames have variants in which control of event class, occurrence time, and roles are differently assigned.

8.5.1 A transformation problem

The simplest transformation problems are those in which the inputs and outputs domains are sequential files that map easily on to each other. Here is a very simple example.

Summarising online usage

Joe has discovered that the software supplied by his ISP (Internet service provider) writes a monthly log file to disk, with one record for each logged-on session. Each month's log file looks like this:

```
04/03/2000   08.15   10.23
04/03/2000   13.21   16.47
05/03/2000   08.10   12.49
06/03/2000   09.02   10.36
06/03/2000   11.18   12.34
06/03/2000   18.44   20.05
...
```

There are three fields in each record: the date, the log-on time, and the log-off time. Joe wants to produce monthly summary reports looking like this:

```
04/03/2000   2    5.34
05/03/2000   1    4.39
06/03/2000   3    4.11
...
All 03/2000  84   197.31
```

There is one record for each day and a total for the month. Each day record has three fields: the date, the number of logged-on sessions, and the total logged-on time for that date. The month record has the total number and duration of sessions in the month.

This is a classic, very simple transformation problem. We'll give the problem diagram in a slightly unusual form. Because we're interested here in control variants, we'll give the annotations for the specification interfaces in more detail than usual. Where we would normally show just the symbolic values at each interface, we'll now show the events and their roles. Here's the diagram:

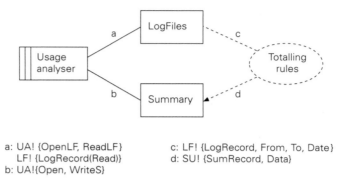

a: UA! {OpenLF, ReadLF}   c: LF! {LogRecord, From, To, Date}
   LF! {LogRecord(Read)}   d: SU! {SumRecord, Data}
b: UA!{Open, WriteS}

Summarising online usage: problem diagram

As the annotation for the phenomena *a* shows, the usage analyser machine controls the *OpenLogFile* and *ReadLogFile* events, and the logFiles domain controls the logRecord participating in each *ReadLogFile* event. When a *ReadLogFile* event occurs at the end of a logFile – that is, when the records of the file are exhausted – the logFiles domain ensures that no logRecord participates in that event; the usage analyser recognises the absence of a participating record as indicating the end of the file. Equivalently, the absence of a record may be represented by a special EOF (end-of-file) or NULL record.

The usage analyser controls phenomena *b*, the *OpenS* and *WriteS* events of the summary domain. It also controls the participation of the *SumRecord* and its constituent data in each *WriteS* event.

A transformation control variant

Now let's look at a control variant of the same problem. Suppose that Joe investigates the interface between his ISP software and the logFiles. He discovers that it's a simple procedure call interface: an initial *ISPOpen* invocation establishes each logfile, and successive *ISPWrite(LogRecord)* invocations write the logfile records. An *ISPClose* invocation writes the EOF record. He realises that he could connect his usage analyser directly to the ISP software, cutting out the storage of logfiles on disk. Instead of storing the logfiles, he can just store his monthly summary files.

He also realises that this doesn't change the problem in any deep way. In fact, the problem diagram will be almost the same. Here it is:

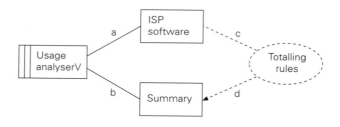

a: IS! {ISPOpen, ISPRWrite, ISPClose}   c: IS! {LogRecord, From, To, Date}
b: UA!{OpenS, WriteS}   d: SU! {SumRecord, Data}

Summarising online usage variant: problem diagram

What has changed? We have named the machine usage analyser V – for variant. The inputs domain of the transformation problem frame is now the ISP software instead of the logFiles themselves. And as the annotation for the interface *a* shows, the interface between inputs domain and the transformation machine now consists of the *ISPOpen*, *ISPWrite* and *ISPClose* events, which are controlled by the ISP software domain, not by the machine. The *ISPClose* events correspond to the *LFRead* events in the original version in which no record participates because the logfile is exhausted. Because the associated role (the participation of a *LogRecord* in a read or write event) is now controlled by the same domain as the event, it is not shown separately in the annotation.

Machine as program procedures

Essentially, the new machine is very much like the old one, except that it has relinquished control of the events it shares with the inputs domain; control of the associated roles was, and remains, with the inputs domain. The sequence of records received by the machine at interface *a* is the same in both versions.

If you want to think of the machine in programming terms, the old machine was a *main program*. The new machine is a *procedure* with local static variables that persist from one invocation to the next. Or, you could say, the new machine is a *server*. The old machine invoked a procedure of the logFiles domain to obtain each successive logRecord, and a procedure of the summary domain to output each successive sumRecord. The new machine is invoked by the ISP software whenever another logRecord is available. As before it writes each successive sumRecord to the summary when it has computed its data.

These two different invocation hierarchies, represented as module charts in the style of structured design, are:

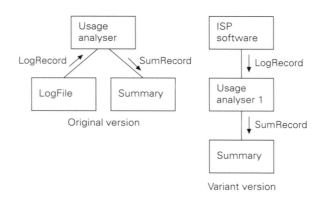

Original and variant represented as procedure hierarchies

Obviously, it would be nice to be able to take advantage of the similarity of the two versions in programming terms; and that is possible. What interests us more here is this: the original problem and its variant are essentially the same so far as the sharing of symbolic phenomena is concerned; the differences are only in the control aspects, which are often of relatively minor importance in a transformation problem.

8.5.2 Other control variants

Control variants of this kind can appear wherever these conditions hold:

- the interface to be varied is essentially a sequence of event occurrences of a single type;

- in each event a symbolic value is transmitted, except that no value is transmitted in the final event of the sequence;

- the timing of the interface events and of any events that depend on them is unimportant.

Here's an example.

Simple stream editor

A stream editor is to be built to support simple editing operations on ASCII text files. The sequence of operations to be performed is given in a command file, each operation being a simple global find-and-replace; Find-and-delete operations can be specified as find-and-replace with an empty replacement string. The operations are to be performed in the order in which they appear in the command file.

This is essentially just a control variant of a workpieces problem. The ASCII text files are the workpieces domain, and the file of operation requests is the user domain. In the conventional form of a workpieces problem, the user sits at the computer waiting for each operation to be completed before requesting the next. The editing tool rejects requests that are not sensible, and may perhaps ignore premature requests that it is not yet ready to act on.

You can think of the command file as a control variant of the user. In the summarising online usage problem, the machine in the basic transformation frame controls the logFiles *OpenLF* and *ReadLF* events; in the variant this event control is given to the logFiles domain in the form of the ISP software. In the stream editor, the control moves in the other direction. Instead of the user domain controlling the edit command events, as it does in the basic workpieces problem frame, control of those events is given to the editing machine. The command file is a passive lexical domain, to be viewed as a description, substituted for the autonomously active biddable user domain.

Here is the problem diagram:

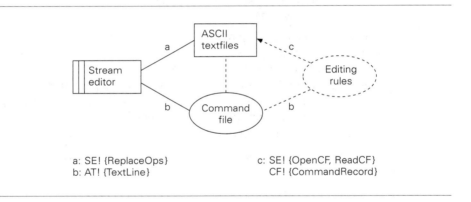

a: SE! {ReplaceOps}
b: AT! {TextLine}

c: SE! {OpenCF, ReadCF}
   CF! {CommandRecord}

Stream editor: problem diagram

The variant is appropriate to the problem because the timing of the commands in the command records is not significant. The desired result of the editing is unaffected by eliminating the user's control over the speed with which commands are presented to the machine.

Any questions?

Isn't the separation of control of the event and the role in the control variant undoing the abstraction of the phenomena?

Yes, in a way. Or perhaps it is explicitly recognising a different realisation of the abstraction.

Does the separation of control of the event and the role occur only in programming?

Not at all: I'm sorry to have given that impression. It can occur anywhere. For instance, when a member borrows a book, the member controls the event, but the librarian, or the machine, controls the due-date role.

Why don't behaviour and information frames have control variants?

Because timing and control are more fundamental to them than to workpiece and transformation problems. If the interface control properties were significantly different for a behaviour or information problem, the problem would have changed enough to merit a different frame and different frame concern.

Is there a way of taking advantage in programming terms of the similarity between the two machines?

Yes. There is a technique, called *program inversion,* by which this can be done for simple sequential programs. For more elaborately structured object-oriented programs you need something like callback and event-driven patterns. You can read about program inversion in M A Jackson, *Principles of Program Design,* Academic Press, 1975; and about callback in Frank Buschmann, Regine Meunier, Hans Rohnert, Peter Sommerlad and Michael Stahl, *Pattern-Oriented Software Architecture: A System of Patterns,* John Wiley, 1996.

Can you do the same trick with the outputs – the summary – as with the inputs domain?

Yes. It's the same seperation of event and role. The summary controls the event and the usage analyser controls the record role The same inversion or callback techniques work in much the same way.

Isn't unix sed a stream editor like the example here?

Yes, it is, but it is far more elaborate and powerful.

Can't you get over the restriction to a single event type by encoding the event type in the transmitted symbolic value in some way?

Yes. But only if the event type and the transmitted value role are controlled by the same domain.

In the summarising online usage problem, what does the log file show for a session that continues past midnight? Or for a session lasting more than 24 hours?

Hmm ... It's time for the next chapter.

CHAPTER 9

Particular concerns

In addition to the frame concern, other concerns must often be addressed in analysing a problem. Some are common to almost all problems, some arise out of the nature of particular requirements or interfaces or problem domains. Examples of such concerns, briefly discussed in this chapter, are overrun, initialisation, reliability, identities, and completeness.

9.1 Frame concerns and others

Addressing the frame concern of a problem is absolutely necessary. If you can't show that you have addressed the frame concern successfully, you can't show that you have understood the problem and how to solve it. But what is necessary is not always sufficient. Usually other particular concerns must be addressed; some are independent of the frame concern, some are aspects of it, some arise out of the nature of a problem domain, some from more general sources.

In this chapter we will look at some of these particular concerns and at how they can be recognised and addressed. The concerns we will look at are:

- *overrun*: the overrun concern is about a domain's ability or inability to respond to each externally controlled event before the next event occurs;

- *initialisation*: the initialisation concern is about the initial state of the problem context in which the machine will run;

- *reliability:* the reliability concern is about the failure of a domain to conform to a description on which your development relies;

- *identities:* the identities concern is about identifying distinct individuals in a domain where multiple instances of a class have independent existences;

- *completeness*; the completeness concern is about ensuring that the problem requirement, problem domain, and machine descriptions are complete.

These are only some of the particular concerns that can arise in a development. There are others that we are saying nothing about: for example, the inputs domain in a transformation problem may be difficult to parse correctly. Recognising particular concerns, and building up a repertoire of familiar concerns to look for in each problem, is an important part of using problem frames.

9.2 The overrun concern

The overrun concern can arise wherever there is a mismatch of speeds at a domain interface. This concern is not limited to problems of any particular class. Wherever events or state changes are shared between two domains it is possible, in principle, for the domain that controls the phenomena to initiate them too quickly for the other domain to react. For example:

- John and Lucy may enter commands faster than the party plan editor can handle them;

- the *WheelPulses* may occur at a faster rate than the odometer microchip can rework its speed and distance calculations;

- the lights controller may cause an *(RPulse,GPulse)* pair for the same light unit with too little intervening delay to allow the unit to detect and react to the second pulse of the pair;

- the monitor computer in the local traffic monitoring problem may produce information output events faster than the strip printer can print them.

In the first of these examples, the mismatch is caused by an over-energetic user in a workpieces problem. The problem domain is too fast for the machine. In the second it's caused by the real world in an information problem. Again the problem domain is too fast for the machine. In the third and fourth examples it's caused by the machine in a behaviour problem and by the machine in an information problem. In both of these cases the machine is too fast for the problem domain.

9.2.1 When the machine is too fast

When the machine is too fast, the concern is usually easy to address. The machine is slowed down by introducing delays into its execution. The delays may be unconditional. If the light units require at least 10msec to intervene between successive pulses to the same unit, each pair 'RPulse(2); GPulse(2);' can be replaced by 'RPulse(2); wait(10msec); GPulse(2)' and so on.

In some cases the machine shares phenomena with the problem domain by which it can determine whether the problem domain is ready for further interaction. For example, the strip printer in the local traffic monitoring problem may use a form of flow control: the machine may send data only when the printer has signalled that it is ready to accept it.

9.2.2 Strategies for overrun

An overrun concern is harder to address when the problem domain is too fast for the machine. Then you have three possible strategies for addressing the overrun concern:

- *simple inhibition*: the machine inhibits the shared events whenever it is not ready to participate;

- *ignoring*: the machine ignores any event in which it is not ready to participate;

- *buffering*: any event in which the machine is not ready to participate is buffered. The machine participates later.

We'll look at each of these in a little more detail.

Simple inhibition
Simple inhibition means that the machine prevents the shared event from occurring. You shouldn't use it when the problem domain is a causal domain. The result of inhibiting an event controlled by a causal domain is almost certain to be deadlock in the causal domain: the irresistible force has met the immovable object.

But simple inhibition may be appropriate when the controlling domain is a biddable human domain. Humans are adaptable enough to avoid deadlock: they wait, or try something else. When a command requesting an operation on a workpiece in a PC brings up a dialogue box with a progress bar, other commands requesting operations on the same workpiece are inhibited until progress is complete and the dialogue box goes away.

Ignoring
The machine may simply ignore any event that occurs when it is not ready to participate. For the machine, the effect is as if the event had not occurred. This strategy can work well when two conditions are satisfied:

- the shared events are commands, and the domain controlling them is a human, biddable, domain;

- a clear indication is given that the command has been ignored, for example, by an audible beep, or by the state of the workpiece or controlled domain as it appears to the user or operator.

The second condition is important. Suppose, in the occasional sluice gate problem, that the sluice operator first issues a *Raise* command. This is then followed by *Stop* and *Lower* commands, issued in such quick succession that the machine is unable to react to the *Lower* and ignores it. Can the sluice operator tell from the appearance of the sluice gate & motor domain that the *Lower* command has been ignored? Not really. There are many reasons why the command may appear to have had no effect – or no effect yet. The result will be that the operator is left in a state of uncertainty and confusion. In this case, an audible beep, or a similar signal, is essential.

If you adopt this strategy in a problem in which the controlling domain is causal, you must be careful to consider the effect of ignoring the event on the causal domain's behaviour. For example, if the causal domain is the machine in another subproblem, and has been specified on the assumption that the events it causes have certain effects in another domain, the effect may be catastrophic.

Buffering

Buffering is an attractive strategy. But you must use it with great care when the problem domain is biddable: it can lead to situations in which a domain previously thought to be passive – event-reactive or state-reactive – confuses the user or operator by appearing to behave actively. This caution applies particularly strongly when a command is buffered because current conditions don't allow it to be obeyed. The point is well illustrated by an anecdote about a military avionics system:

> '... a computer issued a "close weapons bay door" command on a B1-A aircraft at a time when a mechanical inhibit had been put in place in order to perform maintenance on the door. The "close" command was generated when someone in the cockpit punched a close switch on the control panel during a test. Two hours later, when the maintenance was completed and the inhibit removed, the door unexpectedly closed.'

What is called 'the inhibit' here was, in fact, a form of buffering, not of inhibition. The error in this use of buffering was allowing excessive delay between the occurrence of a command and the machine's action in response. When the door closed, the user or operator who punched the switch had long ago forgotten that the command was pending.

Buffering can be used to handle the overrun concern in the odometer microchip problem. The machine buffers all WheelPulses. It recalculates speed and distance at fixed intervals, emptying the buffer and taking account of the buffered pulses each time. When the car is travelling slowly the buffering has no effect. When it is travelling at a constant fast speed, the effect may be that recalculation occurs only on every second pulse.

Any questions?

Surely overrun can't occur in a transformation problem?

That's true for the basic transformation frame. But a control variant, in which the machine is driven by the inputs domain, can have an overrun concern.

Isn't the light units example really a breakage concern?

Yes, if the unit would be put into an unknown state by too little delay between pulses, then this would be a breakage concern. If, instead, it would ignore the premature pulse, it's reasonable to regard it as an overrun concern.

It's broadly true that pure overrun concerns, that can't be regarded as anything else, are about machines that are too slow, rather than machines that are too fast. An overrun concern when the machine is too fast can often be regarded as a part of the proper treatment of the domain properties.

Can the different strategies be combined?

Yes, certainly. For example, you can combine buffering with the ignoring strategy. Events occurring when the buffer is full are ignored or inhibited.

Where does the avionics anecdote come from?

From an account of safety concerns in software development. You can read it in Nancy G Leveson, *Software Safety: What, Why and How*, ACM Computing Surveys, Volume 18, Number 2, pages 125–163, June 1986.

9.3 The initialisation concern

If you have ever programmed, you know how important initialisation is. Program variables must be initialised before they are used. Using the value of an uninitialised variable is a common programming error. In some programming languages initialisation may be automatic. In Java, each object's instance variables are given default initial values – such as zero, or space, or the empty string – when the object is created. But local variables of the object's methods are not. So if you forget to initialise a local variable in a method, the result will be surprising or worse.

Initialisation matters in problem analysis too: for the specification of machine behaviour, for domain property descriptions and for requirements. But the initialisation concern is often harder to address properly in problems than in programs.

9.3.1 Initialisation in the machine and the world

There's no special difficulty about initialising the machine. Each machine you build, considered separately from its context, can be started or restarted at any time. Whenever it is started, it goes through the behaviour you have described in your specification, from the beginning: in the terminology of PCs, the operators or users can *boot* or *reboot* the machine whenever they like.

In the simplest version of the one-way traffic lights problem, this was the specification for the lights controller machine:

```
{   RPulse(1); RPulse(2);                        // set Stop(1) Stop(2) only
    forever {
        wait 50 seconds; RPulse(2); GPulse(2);   // change Stop(2) to Go(2)
        wait 120 seconds; GPulse(2); RPulse(2);  // change Go(2) to Stop(2)
        wait 50 seconds; RPulse(1); GPulse(1);   // change Stop(1) to Go(1)
        wait 120 seconds; GPulse(1); RPulse(1);  // change Go(1) to Stop(1)
}   }
```

Whenever the road repairers start up the lights controller machine, it begins execution at the first line of its behaviour specification. If the machine has local variables needing initialisation, their initial values can be set at the beginning of the specification, just before the initial *<RPulse(1);RPulse(2)>* event sequence.

But problem domains in the world outside the machine may not be so easily started or restarted. In the one-way traffic lights problem, the two light units are identical, and each one behaves like this:

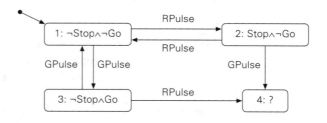

Behaviour of one traffic light unit

Each light unit has its own internal state, and its response to *GPulse* and *RPulse* events depends on that internal state. For the initialisation concern, the essential question is this: Can you assume that the initial state 1 of the light unit coincides with the initial state of the lights controller machine?

Certainly not. There is no reason to assume that at all. The light unit is not a Java or Smalltalk or C++ or Eiffel object that will be *created* when the machine begins its specified behaviour. It's a light unit, not a model of a light unit. It's part of an independent domain in the world outside the computer. It's marching to its own drum beat. In problem analysis, this is where the initialisation concern begins to bite.

9.3.2 Initialisation and description span

So what are we entitled to assume about the light unit? Let's put that question differently. How fully and accurately did we describe the light unit properties in our domain description? More exactly, what *time span* in the whole life of one light unit did our domain description really describe?

Perhaps you have been asking that question impatiently ever since Chapter 4. If so, I'm sorry you have been kept waiting so long. Many people never ask that question. But we're asking it now.

Here are some possible answers. The description describes:

- *one machine execution*: the time span is exactly one execution of the one-way traffic lights system, from the moment the machine is installed, switched on and started in a particular road repair site to the moment the machine is switched off when the repair works are completed;

- *one uninterrupted power episode*: the time span is from connecting electrical power to the light unit to the next occasion on which the power supply is interrupted for any reason. This span surely won't include more than one machine execution span, and may include less than one if the power fails or someone mistakenly pulls out the plug or cuts the cable;

- *one reset episode*: the time span is from one pressing of the light unit's *reset* button to the next occasion on which the *reset* button is pressed. (We forgot to mention the reset button in our description.) This span is more or less independent of the machine execution span;

- *full unit lifetime:* the time span is from the original release of the light unit from the factory where it was made to its final decommissioning and scrapping; you would expect this span to be much longer than one machine execution span.

The most convenient answer is the first: one machine execution span. That's what we would like to assume. Then we could claim that there is nothing wrong with our original development – there is no unaddressed initialisation concern. Unfortunately, this isn't very plausible. It can be true only if some phenomenon corresponding to the *start machine* event is shared with the light unit. That shared phenomenon can't be an *RPulse* or a *GPulse* – we have already accounted for all of those.

The uninterrupted power span and the reset episode span are more plausible, but less convenient. The unit lifetime span is not particularly plausible, it's also very inconvenient indeed.

9.3.3 Operating instructions and domain descriptions

For every machine you build in a software development you must provide operating instructions for starting execution. Think about it. The machine doesn't start itself. It relies on a human being to turn it on. You need the operating instructions to say when it's all right to turn the machine on: that is, in what circumstances you can turn it on and expect it to ensure that the requirement is satisfied.

Sometimes, of course, there are no restrictions: you can turn the machine on whenever you like. But if the problem context includes any given domains, the operating instructions may tell you that some preparation is necessary. Perhaps you mustn't start the lift position display machine unless the lift car is at the lobby floor with the doors open; or you mustn't start the home heating controller unless the furnace has been off for at least five minutes; or you mustn't start the lights controller until both light units are connected to the computer and to their power supply.

If the operating instructions include events that affect the behaviour or state of a domain, those events must appear in the domain description so that you can relate the initialisation to the subsequent behaviour. Suppose, for example, that in the one-way traffic lights problem the span of the original – inadequate – domain description was one uninterrupted power episode. Then the *powerOn* and *powerOff* events will be included in the operating instructions:

'Starting procedure:
(1) Ensure that both units are powered down (by performing *powerOff* if necessary) and the computer is not running.
(2) Connect the pulse lines between the computer and the units.
(3) Perform *powerOn* for each unit.
(4) Start the computer.'

The *powerOn* and *powerOff* events must also appear in the domain description of the light unit behaviour. That means that it must have a larger span. Here it is:

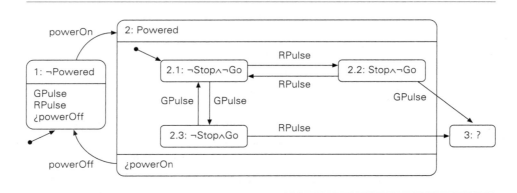

Behaviour of one traffic light unit: larger span

The light unit has three outer states, and state 2 has three substates. Initially, in state 1, before a *powerOn* event, *GPulses* and *RPulses* are ignored, and *powerOff* events are inhibited; a *powerOn* event causes a transition to substate 2.1 of state 2. In state 2, *powerOn* events are inhibited, and a *powerOff* event causes a transition back to state 1. Most of the behaviour originally described is in state 2, except that this state does not include the unknown state. Nothing is said about behaviour after the unknown state has been reached: even switching the power off and on may fail to restore the unit to health.

The operating instructions for the starting procedure, combined with the larger span of the new domain description, allow the system to be restarted whenever necessary, provided that neither light unit has reached the unknown state. So if power fails, or a power connection or pulse line is broken, the road repairers can simply perform the start procedure and the system will return to normal operation, from the beginning.

9.3.4 Initialisation by the machine

The procedures necessary for starting and restarting depend on the properties of the domains involved and on the way the machine exploits those properties.

When initialisation is impossible

Let's go back for a moment to the case we mentioned earlier, in which our original domain description described the full lifetime of a light unit, from manufacture to final scrapping. This was the case that we said was very inconvenient. Here's why. The state of each light unit persists across *powerOn* and *powerOff* events, and there is no *reset* button. The pulse needed to cause a change to a new state depends on the old state; worse, the state is not shared, so the machine can not detect the old state; and worse still, the unit is fragile, so the wrong pulse can break it. The initialisation concern is virtually impossible to address. It's more than inconvenient. Buy your light units from a different manufacturer.

Domain initialisation from any state

Now let's go to the other extreme. Let's suppose that the light units are much simpler. The *Stop* and *Go* states in each unit are independent and robust: they're like the lights in the lift position display problem. The events that change them are *OnStop(i), OffStop(i), OnGo(i) and OffGo(i):* immediately after an *OnStop(i)* event in any state the *Stop(i)* state holds, and so on. The machine specification can be like this:

```
{ OffGo(1); OnStop(1); OffGo(2); OnStop(2);      // set Stop(1) Stop(2)
    forever   {
        wait 50 seconds;
        OffGo(1); OnStop(1);                      // set Stop(1) ...
        OffStop(2); OnGo(2);                      // ... and Go(2)
        wait 120 seconds;
        ...
} }
```

Now the machine initialises the light units. Whatever the initial states of the units, the machine will set them as required when it starts.

It's often possible to initialise a controlled domain from an arbitrary current state like this. In the sluice gate control problem our domain description said that the initial state was '¬MOn ∧ DCl': the motor is off, and the direction is set to clockwise. A machine behaviour that will achieve this initial state from an arbitrary current state is simply:

```
{ Off; Clockw;                    // set "¬MOn ∧ DCl"
    ...
```

This initialisation must be explicitly included in the specified machine behaviour. If we had also asserted that the gate is *Shut* in the initial state, it would have been necessary for the machine to achieve this too in initialising the domain. A little more elaborate, but still straightforward.

9.3.5 Initialisation in an information problem

In a behaviour problem the machine may be able to bring the controlled domain into a desired initial state. This is never possible in an information problem, where the real world is autonomous and not subject to any control by the machine. In this case it's necessary to apply some control to the machine, to bring it into alignment with the real world.

One way is to restrict – in the operating instructions – the circumstances in which the machine may be turned on. In the lift position display problem, our domain description said that initially the lift is at rest at the lobby floor, with the doors open. The lift manufacturers leave the lift in this state when it is originally installed. It is also the state in which the lift maintenance and repair engineers, and the safety inspector, are expected to leave the lift on completion of their work. So you could very reasonably insist in the operating instructions that the display machine must not be started unless the lift is at rest at the lobby floor, with the doors open. A repair engineer who leaves the lift in the wrong state must be recalled to put it in the right state before the display machine can be started.

You might instead specify a machine behaviour that imposes something like this operating restriction on itself. The behaviour could include a preliminary phase in which the machine waits until *SensOn(0)* has held for at least 2.5 seconds. The main behaviour is not activated until this preliminary phase is complete, and the real world is known to have reached the described initial state.

Initialising the model

In an information problem with a model domain, you may need to force the model into correspondence with the state of the real world at the time the machine is started. You often need to do this in an administrative or commercial system in which the model is a database. You must provide for 'populating the database'. A safe approach is to initialise the model by rerunning the prior history of the real world. But sometimes it costs too much time or money. Then you must elaborate the model building subproblem by introducing events specifically designed to establish the initial state of the model. Often this must be done piecemeal, the initial state being established at different times for different parts of the model.

This model initialisation may be hard to get right. In the model building subproblem without initialisation, the states and the evolution of the model domain must correspond to those of the real world in the way stipulated by the requirement. The model initialisation can be in conflict with that requirement, because intermediate states in the initialisation process may not correspond to any actual state of the real world. If you resolve the conflict by a liberal policy – giving the initialisation all the freedom it seems to need – you may find that you have undermined the correspondence between the model and the real world. If you adopt a more restrictive policy you may find that it's very awkward and inconvenient – perhaps even impossible – to initialise the database in some cases.

Any questions?

Surely some machines will be started by other machines, and won't need operating instructions?

Yes. Then only the 'outermost' machines need operating instructions.

Aren't some machines started only once?

Yes. But they still need operating instructions just for that one occasion.

How can the light unit have a reset button if it wasn't mentioned in the original domain description?

It's surprising. How can the original domain description have omitted something so important as the reset button? I don't know.

Is it really necessary to address the initialisation concern directly in the lift position display problem? Won't the machine and the model settle down automatically after a short while , perhaps after the lift has been both to the lobby and to the top floor?

Well, perhaps the machine and model will 'settle down'. But the initialisation concern hasn't gone away. It now requires you to show that the machine and model really do 'settle down' from any initial state of the lift and buttons.

9.4 The reliability concern

The machine you build in a software development satisfies the requirement by exploiting the domain properties captured in your domain description. In a behaviour problem the machine exploits the properties of the controlled domain to ensure the required domain behaviour: the sluice gate controller relies on the properties of the motor and the gate mechanism to open and shut the gate. In an information problem the machine exploits the properties of the real world to infer requirement phenomena from the shared specification phenomena that it can access directly: the display machine relies on the properties of the lift mechanism to detect the lift position and movement from the floor sensor states. In a transformation problem the machine exploits the lexical properties of the inputs domain to parse the inputs and transform them into the outputs: the mail analyser relies on the directory structure and the mailfile syntax to allow it to analyse the messages correctly. The same thing applies to a workpieces problem.

But problem domains are parts of the physical world, even when they are lexical domains such as the mailfiles domain, or the encoded regime in the regulated one-way lights problem. So their reliability is always in question. The mailfiles directory structure may have been damaged by an operating system fault; the floppy disk containing the encoded regime may be unreadable or may have an undetected error; the sluice gate & motor mechanism may break down; a floor sensor may stick in the *SensOn(f)* state; a library member's card may be duplicated by forgery. The reliability concern is about dealing appropriately with these worrisome possibilities.

9.4.1 Assessing the reliability concern

When you put effort into addressing the reliability concern in respect of any particular property of a particular domain, you are paying an insurance premium to cover the system against some risk of failure. Whether this *reliability premium* is worth paying depends on the size of the premium, the likelihood of the failure, and the seriousness of the damage that the failure would cause. In a safety-critical system the seriousness of the damage may be so great that you must be willing to pay even a very high premium to insure even against a very unlikely failure. However reliable the analog devices are in the patient monitoring problem, you must still diagnose and report their failures because lives are at risk. In a non-critical system you may be willing to insure even against a remote risk of minor damage if you can do it very cheaply, but not if it's expensive.

The rule of the greater disaster

There is another factor to take into account: the rule of the greater disaster. There's no point in worrying about the arrangement of the deckchairs on the Titanic. So in the sluice gate control problem it makes sense to consider the possibility that the motor is stuck, but it makes no sense at all to consider the possibility that the whole sluice gate and its mechanism have been swallowed up in an earthquake or swept away in a mudslide. If that has happened, your customer will be too preoccupied with other things to question the adequacy of your control software. In the lift position display it makes sense to consider the possibility that the lift is stuck at a floor. But it makes no sense to consider the possibility that the lift jumps out of the lift shaft. If that has happened no one will be worrying about the correctness of the lobby display.

9.4.2 Separating the reliability concern

One way to address the reliability concern is to make a more accurate domain description that takes account of the possible failures. We did that to a small extent in the lift position display problem. We described the possible behaviours of the lift car at a floor: one of the possible behaviours was getting stuck, and staying at the floor for some time without opening the lift doors.

Reliability of a lexical domain

Here's another example. We didn't take account of possible failures in our domain description of the mailfiles domain, but we can think about it now. Here (once again) is the domain description we made of one mailfile:

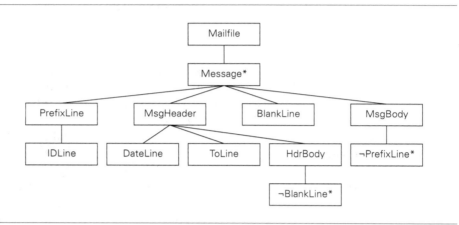

One mailfile: partial domain description

What can go wrong in one mailfile? If the file has been corrupted, or the email client software that writes it is faulty, there are several obvious possibilities:

- the PrefixLine may be omitted from a Message;

- a spurious line may be inserted before a MsgHeader;

- the DateLine may be omitted from a MsgHeader;

- a DateLine may be faulty, that is, it does not contain a valid date following 'Date:';

- a spurious line may be inserted in a MsgHeader between the DateLine and the ToLine;

- the ToLine may be omitted from a MsgHeader;

- a ToLine may be faulty, that is, it does not contain a valid email address following 'To:';

- the BlankLine may be omitted from a Message;

- a MsgBody may contain a PrefixLine.

One approach to the reliability concern in any problem is to make a more elaborate domain description. For example, instead of saying that a message begins with a PrefixLine, you could say that it begins with a PossiblePrefixLine, which is either a PrefixLine or nothing; and you could say that between the PossiblePrefixLine and the MsgHeader is a SpuriousGroup consisting of zero or more lines that are not DateLines, and that instead of a DateLine there is a PossibleDateLine, which is either a DateLine or nothing, and a DateLine is either a GoodDateLine or a BadDateLine, and so on, for all the faults you can think of. Part of your domain description might then look like this:

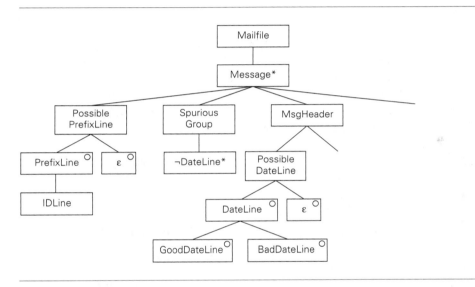

One possibly faulty mailfile: partial domain description

There are two things to say about this description. First, it's going to make it hard to interpret each mailfile. If the PrefixLine of a message is present, and the next line is not a DateLine, does that next line belong to the SpuriousGroup, or has the DateLine been omitted? That's a difficult part of the *parsing concern*. Perhaps we need a different description. Second, by accommodating all these faults we have hidden the description of a correct mailfile behind a description of all the things that can be wrong. It's now very hard to see what a correct mailfile consists of.

You need to separate the description of the correct mailfile from the description of the faulty mailfile. We can go further: you need to separate the problem of dealing with correct mailfiles from the problem of addressing the reliability concern for the mailfiles domain.

9.4.3 Addressing reliability by decomposition

The reliability concern arises in many kinds of problem. The characteristics of each particular problem will determine how you should address it. But as a general rule you should deal with it in a separate subproblem. The subproblem requirement will always include *detection,* that is, recognising that some failure has occurred. It may include *diagnosis:* determining the cause of the particular failure that has been detected. Sometimes it will include *repair:* for a lexical domain it may be appropriate to repair the domain to eliminate the fault. The subproblem that addresses the reliability concern will fit into the original problem in different ways. We'll look at two of them. First, the sluice gate.

Sluice gate reliability concern

In the simple required behaviour version of the sluice gate control problem there is an obvious reliability concern. The requirement can be satisfied only by relying on the gate & motor domain properties: when the motor state is *On* and *Clockwise* the rotating vertical screws raise the gate; *On* and *AntiClockwise* lowers it; when the motor state is *Off* the gate does not move; when the gate is *Open* the *Top* sensor is on; and so on. There are many ways in which the gate & motor domain can fail:

■ the *Top* or *Bottom* sensor may stick *on* or *off*;

■ the motor may burn out;

■ the power may fail;

■ the drive pinion may become loose on the motor shaft;

■ the gate may become detached from the vertical screws;

■ debris may be jammed in the gate, preventing it from closing.

Is it worth paying the reliability insurance premium in this problem? Yes, it is. If the gate is jammed, or in any other way failing to move in concert with the motor and the vertical drive screws, there's a danger of further damage to the mechanism. Not catastrophic, but probably expensive. The sluice controller machine should set the motor *Off,* and not allow it to be turned on again. There's not much need for diagnosis: the gate & motor will certainly need inspection by a repair engineer, and the cause of the failure will reveal itself. There's no possibility of repair by the machine: this is not a lexical domain.

How can failure be detected? The phenomena shared between the machine and the gate & motor are the *Top* and *Bottom* sensor states, controlled by the gate & motor, and the *On, Off, Clockw* and *Anti* pulses, controlled by the machine. If you think of the sluice controller combined with the gate & motor as a real world domain, detection can be based on the relationship between the sensor states and the motor pulses. Recall that the gate moves at 1 inch per second, and the vertical travel is 48 inches. So, for example, if the motor has been set *On* and *Clockwise* for more than 48 seconds, and *Top* is not yet true, some failure has occurred.

We're separating the reliability subproblem from the behaviour subproblem. The behaviour subproblem machine must have the responsibility to set the motor *Off*, so the failure must be communicated to it. You can regard this communication as playing the part of a very simple *safety operator*. The resulting decomposition is:

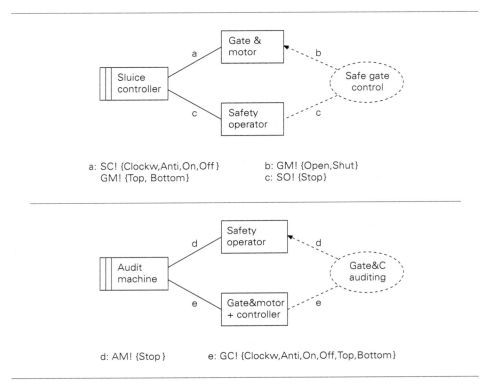

Sluice gate control: auditing reliability

The original required behaviour problem is the upper subproblem in the diagram, with the addition of a commanded behaviour: when the safety operator issues a *Stop* command, the machine must cause an *Off* command for the motor.

The lower subproblem deals with the reliability concern as an information subproblem. We're regarding its requirement as an auditing requirement, Gate&C auditing. The audit machine is the information machine; the gate & motor + controller is the real world; the safety operator is the display; the requirement is to produce output in the form of a *Stop* event whenever the behaviour and state of the gate & motor + controller indicate that failure has occurred. The sluice controller responds to the operator, who can override the default gate regime, commanding the gate & motor to stop immediately.

9.4.4 Mailfiles: reliability decomposition

In the mailfiles analysis problem it is reasonable to attempt some repair where a mailfile or a message is not too badly damaged to be used in the analysis. For example:

- if the PrefixLine of the first message is missing it could be supplied, with a dummy identification number;

- a bad DateLine, in which the date part is not in the correct format, could be repaired by replacing the erroneous field with the date of the previous or next message in the same file, if there is one;

- missing DateLines and ToLines could be sought in the later lines of the MsgHeader;

- SpuriousGroups could be dropped.

The choice whether to attempt this kind of repair, and which particular repairs to attempt, depends on many factors. If you judge, perhaps wisely, that the whole mailfiles analysis problem doesn't merit too much effort, you might decide just to eliminate everything that is not a correct message. That decision makes the repair problem easier, but not totally trivial: you still have to decide where each correct message begins and ends.

The repair is a transformation problem in its own right. The decomposition is like this:

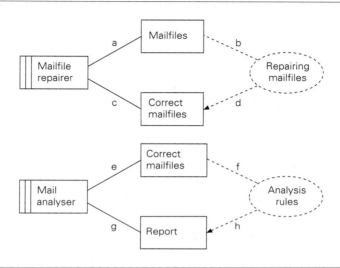

Mailfiles analysis: reliability by repair

The original transformation problem has been decomposed into two transformation subproblems. The second subproblem is the original mailfile analysis problem, but now with a cast-iron guarantee that its correct mailfiles input domain conforms to the domain description of correct mailfiles. The first subproblem achieves correctness by applying whatever repairs are judged appropriate as it transforms its unreliable mailfiles input domain to its correct mailfiles output domain. The repairs judged appropriate are described in the repairing mailfiles requirement. The unreliable input domain is described in a domain description that allows it to be parsed for purposes of the repairing mailfiles requirement.

9.4.5 Reliability in an information problem

You can apply the technique we used in the mailfiles problem to information problems too. In the local traffic monitoring problem, the monitor computer must detect and count the passage of road vehicles of different kinds: cars, motorbikes and commercial vehicles. It's connected to the real world of the road by the *On/Off* states of sensor tubes, and it must use those changes in the sensor states to recognise the passage of the different kinds of vehicle.

A major part of the difficulty is that there is really no limit to the possible patterns of sensor states. The road is a narrow local road. So sometimes there will be an orderly pattern, caused by a procession of easily recognisable vehicles, well separated and travelling at moderate speeds. But not always. Sometimes there will be unusual incidents, giving rise to unusual patterns: children jumping up and down on the sensor tubes; a local unicycle rider; a motorbike rider who accelerates enough to lift the front wheel off the road; a pile of building material falling off a truck – anything is possible.

You can regard this difficulty as a reliability concern. In one subproblem the sequence of sensor state changes is examined and purged of exceptional features that don't conform to easily recognisable vehicle patterns; in the second subproblem the original required analysis is made and the results printed on the strip printer.

9.4.6 The difficulty of diagnosis

As our last word on the reliability concern, it's worth pointing out that failure diagnosis is inherently much harder than failure detection. It's one thing to detect that a domain is not conforming to a given description of correct behaviour; it's another thing to say why.

The source of the difficulty is that many different causes can result in the same effects. In the sluice gate problem the motor state has been set to *On* and *Clockw* for 48 seconds but *Top* still doesn't hold. Why? There are many possible explanations:

■ the motor is burnt out;

■ the *Top* sensor is stuck off;

■ the pulse line for the motor *On* pulse is disconnected;

■ the power supply has failed.

And there are many others.

To do the best possible job of diagnosis you must use all the available evidence. In the sluice gate problem there isn't much evidence available. But in other problem contexts there may be more than you can see at first. For example, in a technical text such as a source program there are often imperfect but important clues to the cause of an error. A missing right delimiter (such as '}' or 'end' or '>') can be accurately located if the text has been consistently indented following a simple rule. Programmers who normally use identifiers structured according to an elaborate coding standard don't suddenly use a single-character identifier, especially 'i' or 'l' or 'o', that they have forgotten to declare: the mysterious identifier is probably a typo for '1' or '0'.

It's a major benefit of separating out the reliability concern that you can pay serious attention to diagnosis without being distracted by the transformation or behaviour or information problem you started with.

Any questions?

In the transformation problem we're not really repairing the failures. We're making a fresh copy of the whole domain, aren't we?

Yes. In analysing and structuring the problem you must treat correct mailfiles and mailfiles as distinct domains. But the implementation may blur the distinction. A control variant of the mail analyser problem can be a subroutine of the mailfile repairer, invoked for each record of correct mailfiles. Then correct mailfiles appears in the implementation only as a sequence of records passed between the two subproblems.

What would the domain description of the unreliable mailfiles domain look like, then?

It's still not trivial, remember! There's discussion of this kind of problem in M A Jackson, *Principles of Program Design*, Academic Press, 1975.

Would it be a good idea to introduce an explicit description domain to say what the rules for a correct mailfile are?

Perhaps. But an explicit description doesn't buy you much unless the described domain's properties are likely to change.

Won't the mailfiles correction have to happen at the level of individual files? We won't be correcting the directory, will we?

We might. For example, a directory entry may fail to point to a file. This is an error condition, different from pointing to an empty file.

9.5 The identities concern

In his book about computer-related risks, Peter Neumann records an air crash that took place in England some years ago:

> 'A British Midland Boeing 737-400 crashed at Kegworth in the United Kingdom, killing 47 and injuring 74 seriously. The right engine had been erroneously shut off in response to smoke and excessive vibration that was in reality due to a fan-blade failure in the left engine. The screen-based "glass cockpit" and the procedures for crew training were questioned. Cross-wiring, which was suspected – but not definitively confirmed – was subsequently detected in the warning systems of 30 similar aircraft.'

The cause of this particular crash may have been pilot error – the cockpit voice recorder showed that the pilot and co-pilot were arguing, unsure which engine had failed and which had been shut off. But the cross-wiring found in the 30 other aircraft was clearly a potential cause of other disasters. The warning light indicating malfunction in the left engine was connected to the right engine, and vice versa. The term 'cross-wiring' itself denotes precisely a failure to address an identities concern.

Multiplex domains
You have an identities concern when the machine has an interface of shared phenomena with individuals in a *multiplex* domain. A multiplex domain consists of multiple instances of a class of things, often a class of entities, that are not connected into any structure that identifies them, and that do not identify themselves.

The mailfiles domain in the mailfile analysis problem is not a multipledomain: the domain contains the directory that gives access to the individual mailfiles and identifies them. But the light units domain in the one-way traffic lights problem is a multiplex domain: there are two individual light units, and nothing in the domain to connect them. The rooms in the home heating problem are a multiplex domain. The members & candidates in the library administration problem are a multiplex domain: there is a coherent behaviour relating all the events in which each member or candidate participates, but there is nothing in the domain to connect one of them with another.

Of course, the identities concern only arises if it's necessary for the machine to distinguish one individual in the multiplex domain from another. You could certainly say that the vehicles in the local traffic monitoring problem form a multiplex domain. But the monitor machine doesn't distinguish them: if the same vehicle passes twice it's counted twice, and that's what's wanted. In the one-way traffic lights problem, there's no need to distinguish one light unit from another, provided that they are required to adhere to the same regime of *Stop* and *Go*. But if the regime must favour one direction over another – for example, because the road is on a hill and uphill traffic must be given longer to clear the controlled segment – then you have an identities concern.

9.5.1   Interfaces in an identities concern

The focal point in an identities concern is the interface of shared phenomena. The machine may be connected to just one individual at a time, or to several simultaneously. In either case, for each shared event or state, the concern is: which individual is the machine sharing with?

Sometimes, when the machine is connected to only one individual at a time, the identities concern may dissolve away. For example, in a smart-card system for pre-payment of public transport fares, customers top-up the credit on their cards by inserting money into a machine. The customer inserts the card into a reader attached to the machine, and makes a payment by inserting money into the machine; the machine increases the credit stored in the card by the amount paid. The smart cards form a multiplex domain. The identities question would be: which individual card is to be updated by the credit increment? The answer is simply: whichever card is participating in the read event by having been inserted into the card reader. The identities concern is dissolved.

The identities concern can also be simplified or altogether dissolved if the multiple individuals are in some way self-identifying. Creating and attaching formal identi-fiers such as account numbers, insurance policy numbers, telephone numbers, ISBNs, and hundreds of others, is a very old practice – so old that we don't even realise that it once had to be invented. In a very different context, placing multiple devices on a bus and communicating with each one by its unique ID exploits the same idea.

Identities interfaces in patient monitoring
But often the multiple individuals are not self-identifying, and the answer 'whichever individual is participating in the shared event' isn't good enough. Here's a partial problem diagram of the patient monitoring problem:

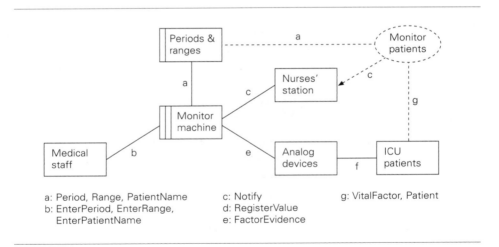

a: Period, Range, PatientName
b: EnterPeriod, EnterRange,
   EnterPatientName

c: Notify
d: RegisterValue
e: FactorEvidence

g: VitalFactor, Patient

Patient monitoring: partial problem diagram

The machine must monitor the patients according to the periods and ranges speci-fied by the medical staff. The medical staff identify the patients by name when they enter the periods and ranges at interface *b*, and the machine has access to those names as values shared at interface *a* with the lexical domain periods & ranges. Each patient is connected, at interface *f*, to one or more analog devices. Each device is physically attached to the patient, for example, a skin resistance device may be strapped to the patient's arm. Each analog device is also connected at interface *e* to the machine, where the device and the machine share the value of a register accessed at a machine port or storage address.

Somehow, each patient must be associated with the right set of devices and registers, and with the right name. This is the identities concern as it arises in this problem. Addressing it adequately is, literally, a matter of life and death.

9.5.2 An identities model

It is not hard to see that you must address the identities concern by introducing a model domain from which the monitor machine can obtain the information it needs: that is, the correspondence relating the patient names, the analog devices with their types, and the shared registers. The machine will use this model to answer questions such as: 'What register must be inspected to find John Smith's current temperature?' So it looks at first sight as if the model should be a simple mapping from (patient,factor) pairs to shared registers, like this:

(PatientName,VitalFactor) $\mapsto$ SharedRegisterID

The symbol '$\mapsto$' means 'maps to'. This model completely omits any mention of the analog devices themselves. That is economical, but it may turn out to be a false economy for two reasons. First, as a general rule in designing model domains, it's not a good idea to restrict the model to the bare minimum that is needed for the problem in hand. It's better to include more, to make it more likely that the model will still be adequate for an enlarged problem.

Second, to address an identities concern properly you must always trace the whole path from the multiple instances in the multiplex domain to the connection point or points in the machine domain. Here, the steps in that path are:

- the machine can refer to PortId values;

- a PortId identifies a shared register;

- a shared register is shared with an analog device;

- an analog device measures a certain type of vital factor: for example, it's a thermometer;

- an analog device is attached to a patient;

- a patient is identified by a name.

Because the analog devices are important components in a critical medical system, they are prominently labelled with individual IDs. The devices with their IDs should be included in the model. When failure is detected, the report at the nurses' station will include the device ID in the notification, along with the device type and the patient's name.

The identities model now begins to look a little more elaborate. As an object class model it may be something like this:

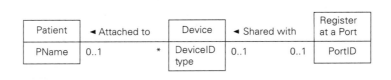

Patient	◄ Attached to	Device	◄ Shared with	Register at a Port
PName	0..1 *	DeviceID type	0..1 0..1	PortID

Patient monitoring: identities model

The model treats Type – that is, the type of vital factor that the device can measure – as an attribute of device. We might instead have shown a general device class with subclasses specific to the various factors, for example, a temperature device, a pulse device, and so on. The multiplicities 0..1 take account of:

- devices plugged into the machine but not attached to any patient;

- devices attached to a patient but having no shared register because they are not plugged into the machine;

- devices that are neither plugged into the machine nor attached to any patient;

- shared registers shared with no device because none is plugged in.

9.5.3 Model creation and maintenance

The creation and maintenance of the model is, as always, a separate subproblem from its use. The initial state of the model must be empty. Initially the monitoring machine is idle: there are no patients and no connected analog devices. Subsequently, whenever a patient to be monitored arrives in the ward or leaves the ward, and whenever there is any change in the set of devices connected to a monitored patient or plugged into the machine, the model must be updated.

The analog devices might possibly be self-identifying, returning their IDs and types in response to a query by the machine. But the machine can't obtain the patient's name except from a human informant. So creating and maintaining the model will certainly need human assistance. We will assume that paramedical staff are responsible for this.

The simplest way of handling the model creation and maintenance is to treat it as a workpieces problem. But this is not good enough. In a model building problem you must consider the modelled reality explicitly. So the subproblem diagram, omitting all interface details, will look like this:

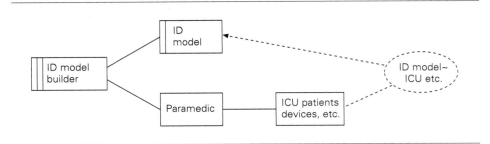

Identities model creation: problem diagram

The paramedic, who can observe the patients, devices, and machine ports they are plugged into, acts as an informant in creating and maintaining the model. The model is used by the machine that monitors the patients according to the periods & ranges description. In analysing this subproblem, you must pay careful attention to what the paramedic can see in the ICU domain.

This approach may prove to be too simple. The subproblem diagram excludes the periods & ranges domain. So the subproblem machine can't take account of that domain and any information that might be obtained from it. For example, the tool can't check whether a patient name entered into the identities model also appears in the periods & ranges description. A more careful approach is probably needed. You must also consider how the creation and use of the model are to be synchronised. But that belongs in another chapter.

Any questions?

I'm not quite sure how the ID model gets over the identities concern. What, exactly, is being shared?

The essential point is the use of names in the model. Each machine port has a PortID name – perhaps in the form of a hexadecimal address – by which it is already known to the machine. The model maps this name to a device, using the DeviceID, and the device to a patient, using the PName. All the names are symbolic values. Symbolic values, such as strings, characters and integers, belong to all domains. That's how they help to address the identities concern, by acting as IDs shared across domains.

What happens if a patient's name is changed?

That's a good question. The identities model must be synchronised with the periods & ranges. This synchronisation concern is just one aspect of dealing with the dynamic nature of this identities concern.

9.6 The completeness concern

The completeness concern is about ensuring that the software will do everything your customer needs. In an obvious sense this is an impossible task. People often can't think of, or don't recognise, their own needs. A major goal of requirements elicitation is to help your customers to identify what they need, sometimes using techniques drawn from sociology, ethnography, and other human disciplines.

But requirements elicitation, and the human disciplines it may draw on, are not the subject of this book. So we will say no more about completeness in this very informal sense. Instead we'll address a more sharply focused notion of completeness, starting from a formal notion and then broadening out to completeness in problem domains in general.

9.6.1 A formal kind of completeness

One of the earliest uses of finite-state machines was to describe regular languages. For example, if you want to describe the language each of whose sentences is any number of occurrences of either *b*, or *a* followed by *b*, followed by one final *c*, you might write the regular expression

(b I (a b))* c

or you might draw this diagram:

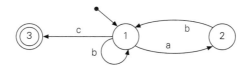

A state machine describing a language

The double circle for state 3 indicates that it is a final state, that is, a sentence can end at state 3, but not at any other state. State 1 has outgoing transitions on *a*, *b* and *c* because a sentence can start with any of those. State 2 has an outgoing transition only on *b* because after an *a* nothing else but *b* is possible. State 3 has no outgoing transitions at all because nothing can follow a *c*. The language is described both by the presence and by the absence of transitions.

Describing a causal domain

This is fine for describing the sentences of a formal language. But if you are using a state machine to describe the behaviour of a domain, and the transitions are associated with externally controlled events to which the domain responds, it's a lot less satisfactory to omit transitions in this way. There are three reasons.

- First, in software development you are likely to be dealing with more elaborate and less elegant state machines, and with a significant number of them. So it's easy to forget a transition that you should have included. It's helpful to have a positive indication that an omission was intentional.

- Second, if by omitting a transition on an externally controlled event you mean to indicate that the controlling domain will not cause this event in this state, you have severely damaged the modularity of your development. To validate the description of the domain whose behaviour you are describing, you must now examine the behaviour of the controlling domain also.

- Third, a causal domain has more behavioural possibilities than having or not having a transition on a particular event in a particular state. As we saw when we discussed dynamic domain flavours, there are at least these three:
  - the event is tolerated but causes no transition to another state;
  - the event causes a transition to another state;
  - the event is inhibited, that is, the domain prevents it from occurring.

If the description provides for actions to be performed on entry to a state, you must also distinguish two subcases of the first of these three possibilities:

- the event is tolerated and causes no transition at all;

- the event causes a self-transition to the current state, with a consequent performance of the state's entry actions.

This fragment of a state machine diagram illustrates all four possibilities:

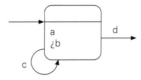

Treatment of an event in a state

In the state illustrated, *a* is tolerated and causes no transition, *b* is inhibited, *c* causes a self-transition to the same state, and *d* causes a transition to another state.

You can always make a description that's complete in this sense, even if you don't know all the facts. Because a domain may have an *unknown* state, in which subsequent state and behaviour is unknown and the domain should, conservatively, be assumed to be broken, it is always possible to choose one of the four possibilities for each event class in each state. If you don't know the effect of an event in a state, show it as a transition to the unknown state.

9.6.2 Description span

We have already referred to *description span* earlier in this chapter, when we discussed the initialisation concern. For a behavioural description, the span is a time span. The initialisation concern reminds you to extend the span as far as you need to, at least in the backwards direction. And not to forget that spells of interaction with the machine in use cases are only a part – sometimes a small part – of what happens in the problem domains.

There are other dimensions of description span. In the library administration problem it's easy to focus on the lending of books to members. But there may be other books that are never lent to members: most libraries have a reference section, and some a valuable books section, of books that are never lent. The span of the object class description that includes books must be large enough to include these too.

9.6.3 Two heuristics

One dimension of completeness is *description scope,* that is, the classes of phenomena you refer to in a description. One way of failing to address the completeness concern is to omit relevant classes. Two heuristics can be helpful here.

Widening participation

The first heuristic is to consider the relationships – in a very general and informal sense – that you are describing, and to ask yourself whether the same or similar relationships can exist elsewhere. Here are some examples.

- In the library administration problem, members borrow books from the library. Does anyone else borrow books from the library? Do the staff borrow books? Perhaps they have rarely used special privileges to do so. Is anything else borrowed, other than books?

- In a printer control problem, a behavioural description shows how the printer reacts to eject commands by feeding a sheet of paper. Can anything else make it feed a sheet of paper? Is there a page-throw button on the printer's manual control panel? Is there another command that can do it?

- In the home heating problem the machine can start and stop the fuel blower by causing *OnBlower* and *OffBlower* events. Can anything else cause these events? Can any other class of event start or stop the blower?

- Again in the library administration problem, members borrow and return books, and renew their loans, in events shared with the library staff. Can members and books share events in which the staff don't participate? Yes: they can lose them, steal them, leave them in the library by mistake, and damage them; and a member may lend a borrowed book to another member.

Often, you can think of questions of this kind by considering the roles in an event class and the individuals that can participate in each role. For the *borrow* events the roles are *borrower* and *borrowedItem*: perhaps a *borrower* need not be a member, and a *borrowedItem* need not be a book. You could even consider all possible pairs of individual, by class, and ask yourself whether there are any events in which they could both participate.

Complementary events

The second heuristic is to consider each of your event classes and ask yourself whether it has a complementary class. Here are some examples.

- Library members can *lose* books. Presumably they can also *find* them after they have been lost. Your customer surely doesn't want to be forced to treat a found book as a new acquisition. It would have to be an acquisition at zero price, with an unidentified supplier and no invoice – in short, a complete mess.

- You are developing a system for a utility company. The company pays money to its suppliers, and receives money from its customers. Does it ever pay money to a customer? Or receive money from a supplier? It's very unlikely that these things never happen at all.

■ Another library administration example. Members can order books that the library does not own, but will *obtain* from a larger library in a cooperative scheme. Because the library for which you are developing software is a small one, your customer may have forgotten that it's possible – in principle, at least – for your library to participate in the complementary event, in which a larger library in the cooperative scheme obtains a book from you.

■ In the patient monitoring problem an analog device can *fail*. Presumably it's then taken out of service. Perhaps it can then be *repaired* or *replaced*.

■ In the patient monitoring problem, a notification at the nurses' station is a form of alarm. If it can be turned on, it can surely also be turned off.

■ In the patient monitoring problem, medical staff may order additional factor monitoring for a patient, *adding* a new analog device. Presumably they can sometimes decide that an existing factor monitoring is no longer needed, and *remove* the device.

9.6.4 Avoiding deadlock

It's often useful to consider all the things you are expecting to happen in a problem domain and examine whether any of them could be prevented by *deadlock*: that is, they can't happen because they're caught in some circular dependency. Here are three examples.

■ In an insurance problem, a facility was provided for replacing customers' policy documents. The developers were thinking about replacing documents that had become unreadable by accidental damage or wear and tear, so the system would produce a replacement policy document only if the customer returned the old one. But, of course, the commonest reason for needing a replacement was loss or theft. The system didn't allow customers to replace a lost document – because they had lost it.

■ A sales order processing system sends out a bill for a zero amount when a customer's balance is reduced to zero by a credit for returned goods. There is no way of paying the bill because the receivables subsystem does not accept zero payments. The only way to prevent the system from sending repeated bills is to remove the customer completely from the system database, and re-enter all the information as if for a new customer.

■ An e-commerce Web site registers its customers, identifying them by email address. A would-be customer's first registration may be cut short – perhaps because of network connection failure – after recording their email address. On next visiting the site, the customer enters the same email address, which causes them to be treated as an existing customer. They are then required to confirm their identity by entering their password. But the aborted registration hadn't reached the password stage. The aborted registration blocks any attempt by the customer to register again on a later occasion with the same email address.

When deadlocks like this occur they are embarrassingly obvious. During analysis and development they can be hard to find.

9.6.5   A general observation

The completeness concern is hard to address in administrative and business systems. That's because in those systems the most important domains are often biddable human domains whose behaviour is largely unconstrained and unpredictable.

Making a complete description of the behaviour of a biddable domain may be easier if you adopt the approach we adopted to the reliability concern. Make one formal description of the 'correct' behaviour, and a separate description of the 'faulty' behaviour. The description of the faulty behaviour may be quite informal. Informal scenarios can be useful here, if their time span is long enough. Unobvious aspects of behaviour are often revealed only by a scenario with a very large time span – in some cases, a whole human lifetime.

Any questions?

What were the earliest uses of state machines?

A good book to read on this subject is Marvin Minsky, *Computation: Finite and Infinite Machines*, Prentice Hall International, 1972.

Why are informal scenarios helpful?

Because their informality reminds you that you are talking about the world outside the computer, and that plenty of interesting things can happen that don't involve the computer at all.

CHAPTER 10

Decomposition revisited

Problem decomposition is not an exact discipline. But it can exploit some useful heuristics, and it can be reasonably systematic. In this chapter we explore the decomposition of a realistic problem. The problem has an obvious initial decomposition into three subproblems. Considering the frame concern of each of these subproblems reveals further subproblems, and still more subproblems arise from particular concerns. Other, more sharply focused, heuristics can be applied in many cases.

10.1 Introduction

In Chapter 3 we began to discuss the relationship between problems and subproblems, and looked briefly at a few examples of subproblems – the panel display and safe furnace operation subproblems in home heating, the entering periods & ranges and reporting analog device failures subproblems in patient monitoring, and the membership reports subproblem in library administration. We recognised these subproblems in a very casual way, and justified them as examples of intuitively recognisable problem classes. Now, after looking more closely at some problem frames and some of their flavours and variants, it's time to revisit the business of decomposing realistic problems.

In this chapter we will decompose one realistic problem in some detail, using a number of heuristics: recognising subproblems that fit known frames, and addressing concerns that arise for particular domains or frames. Then we will look at some other heuristics and their application.

At the interface marked *b* the machine issues commands *ShowPkgId, ShowBin* and *ShowDestn* by which it reports misrouted packages on the display unit. Finally, at interface *d* the router operator causes *OnBut* and *OffBut* events, pressing the buttons that instruct the machine to start and stop the conveyor.

10.2.1   A simple decomposition

At first sight this problem is basically a required behaviour problem: to ensure that packages arrive at their destination bins. Adding two other parts of the overall requirement, we can easily decompose it into three independent subproblems of recognised classes. In fact, the decomposition is directly stated in the final paragraph of the problem sketch given above:

> *'The problem is to build the controlling computer to obey the operator's commands, to route packages to their destination bins by setting the switches appropriately, and to report misrouted packages.'*

The three subproblems are:

- *obey the operator's commands* – a commanded behaviour problem: the machine starts and stops the conveyor in response to the operator's commands;

- *route packages* – a required behaviour problem: the machine sets the switches ahead of each package as it travels through the tree of pipes and switches, ensuring that it reaches its destination bin;

- *report misrouted packages* – an information display problem: the machine detects misroutings and reports them on the display unit.

Obeying operator commands

The commanded behaviour problem seems quite straightforward. The problem diagram is:

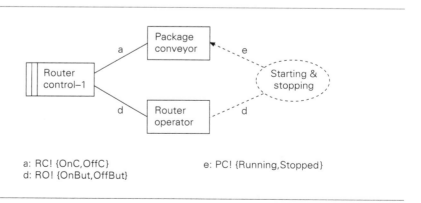

a: RC! {OnC,OffC}   e: PC! {Running,Stopped}
d: RO! {OnBut,OffBut}

Package router: commanded behaviour subproblem diagram

The requirement is simply that the conveyor should be in its *Running* or *Stopped* state in response to the operator's commands. In response to an *OnBut* it should be *Running*; in response to an *OffBut* it should be *Stopped*.

Package routing

The requirement to route the packages to their destination bins seems to be a straightforward required behaviour problem. The problem diagram is:

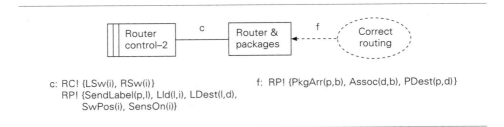

c: RC! {LSw(i), RSw(i)}
   RP! {SendLabel(p,l), Lld(l,i), LDest(l,d),
        SwPos(i), SensOn(i)}

f: RP! {PkgArr(p,b), Assoc(d,b), PDest(p,d)}

Package router: required behaviour subproblem diagram

The requirement is called correct routing. The requirement phenomena are *PkgArr(p,b)*, *Assoc(d,b)* and *PDest(p,d)*. The requirement stipulates that each package *p* must arrive at bin *b*, where the package destination is *d*, and the destination *d* is associated with bin *b*.

We are assuming here that we can designate *PkgArr* events and the other requirement phenomena, or can define them in terms of phenomena of the router & packages domain that are already known.

The phenomena of the specification interface *c* between the machine router control-2 and the router & packages domain are as in the context diagram. The machine controls the switch setting events, and the router & packages domain controls the switch position states, the sensor states, and the reading and transmission of the bar-coded label.

Reporting misrouted packages

The *PkgArr* events and the related phenomena will be equally convenient for the information display subproblem:

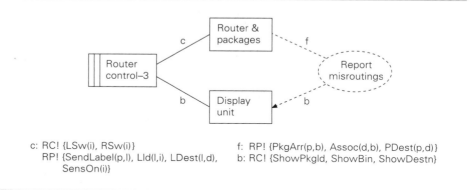

c: RC! {LSw(i), RSw(i)}
RP! {SendLabel(p,l), LId(l,i), LDest(l,d), SensOn(i)}

f: RP! {PkgArr(p,b), Assoc(d,b), PDest(p,d)}
b: RC! {ShowPkgId, ShowBin, ShowDestn}

Package router: information display subproblem diagram

The requirement phenomena at *f* are the same as for the package routing subproblem: package arrival at a bin, association of destinations with bins, and the destination of each package. The display unit phenomena at *b* are also the same as before.

We are assuming that the display unit is straightforward, allowing the machine to display package ID, bin and destination. The requirement is simply that when a *PkgArr* event occurs in which the bin and package destination are not correctly associated, the relevant information must be shown on the display unit.

We have also assumed that misrouting of a package is to be reported only when it reaches the wrong destination bin, not when it is first directed along the wrong path from a switch. This assumption is convenient because it simplifies the problem. If we choose to report misrouting at the earliest opportunity, the machine must handle every event in which a package leaves a switch. To avoid multiple reports of misrouting of the same package, it would need to distinguish the original misrouting – failing to take the correct exit from the switch – from subsequent occasions, when the switch has no correct exit.

It doesn't look as if there can be any objection to our assumption. There is nothing the operator can do with a misrouted package until it reaches a bin, so earlier information is of no practical value.

Any questions?

Why not have one machine to track each package?

An interesting idea. But you will still have to deal with the interaction among packages. The machine that tracks only one package can't set the switches for it in ignorance of the other packages' positions.

Remind me again: why is it acceptable to be so vague about the display unit phenomena?

First, because it keeps our discussion in the book within reasonable bounds. Second, because experience helps you to see what is going to be a source of concern and what is not. The display unit is not.

But haven't you been altogether too casual here? For example, where does the phenomenon Assoc(d,b) come from in the router & packages domain?

Absolutely right. We have been far too casual. We're going to be more precise when we look at the frame concerns in a moment.

You said that the requirement for the package routing subproblem stipulates that each package must reach the desired bin. But the problem sketch has already acknowledged that this may not be possible. Should the requirement have been stated differently?

That's a very good question. We have made no effort to state the requirements precisely. Later in this chapter we'll discuss a decomposition heuristic that might suggest splitting this subproblem just because of the shape of its requirement. But we will conclude there that we shouldn't split it.

10.2.2 Frame concerns

Having identified these three subproblems, we must now examine them to see what concerns they raise. We'll start, of course, with the frame concerns.

Subproblem: obeying operator commands

The conveyor domain proves, on investigation, very easy to deal with. In the *Running* and *Stopped* states packages are, and are not, being moved towards the reading station. In terms of the classifications discussed in Chapter 6, you discover that:

- when *Stopped*, it is in a *passive* state: it is not moving, and will do nothing on its own initiative; but it will respond to an *OnC* event by entering the *Running* state;

- when *Running*, the conveyor is in an *active* state: it is moving, and delivers any package placed upon it to the reading station. This is a *stoppable active* state, that is, it will respond to an *OffC* event by immediately entering the passive *Stopped* state.

You also discover that:

- in respect of the externally controlled *OnC* and *OffC* events it is a *robust* domain, that is, no event sequence puts it into an unknown state. *OffC* and *OnC* events that are not viable are tolerated and ignored, as you would hope.

So it's not necessary to reject any of the operator's commands. But you should bear in mind that there may be other sources of commands – perhaps issued by the machine in another subproblem – that must eventually be considered.

Subproblem: reporting misrouted packages

To address the frame concern for an information problem you must find and describe real world domain properties that bridge the gap between the requirement and the specification phenomena. Here, they are:

- *specification phenomena*: the machine receives the packageID and destination when the package label is read; it shares the switch position states and the sensor states; and it can set the switches;

- *requirement phenomena*: packages arrive at particular bins, destinations are associated with bins, packages have destinations.

One thing is very clear. There is no source in the specification phenomena for the association of destinations with bins.

Destination mapping

So there must be another domain, and a subproblem to create and edit it. Here's the subproblem:

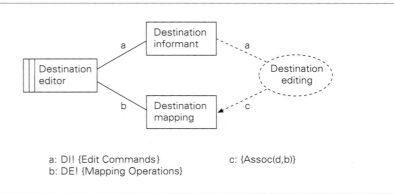

a: DI! {Edit Commands}   c: {Assoc(d,b)}
b: DE! {Mapping Operations}

Package router: editing the destinations mapping

The additional domain is the destination mapping. It associates destination string values with bins. It's not a model domain, it's just a designed lexical domain. You might say that it models some intention on the part of the people using the router – packages for the North West Islands should go into bin *B7*. But these intentions are certainly not observable, and the requirement can't be usefully formulated as a correspondence between a model and a modelled reality. So it's right to regard the subproblem of constructing this description as a simple workpieces problem.

The destination informant is the user in the workpieces problem. Since you have decided not to treat the destination mapping as a model, you need not concern yourself with the question: how does the destination informant get the information about the associations? That's their problem.

The destination mapping domain must be included in the problem context for the reporting misrouted packages subproblem. It provides the machine with the necessary requirement phenomenon Assoc(d,b) that it needs. On investigation this proves to be a many-to-one mapping: there are more destinations than router bins, but only one bin for each destination.

More difficulties
We seem to have provided a source for the association of destinations with bins. But more difficulties await us with the other requirement phenomena.

Neither the package destination nor the arrival of a particular package at a bin is straightforwardly available at the machine interface. The package ID and destination are transmitted to the machine when the package label is read at the reading station. But that event is a long way in the past when the package eventually arrives at a bin. The arrival of a package at a bin is partially available in the state of the sensor that leads immediately to the bin. But from the sensor state the machine cannot detect which package has arrived: only that some anonymous package has arrived.

These difficulties are also present in the package routing subproblem. There, it will be necessary to detect package destination and package arrival at each switch entry point. So we'll deal with them in considering that subproblem.

Subproblem: package routing
Let's start by considering the routing problem in the narrow sense: choosing the correct route to send each package to its destination bin. Of course, the destination mapping is needed, and must be added to the problem diagram.

The router & packages domain is fragile. Setting a switch while a package is in it causes a transition to the unknown state. The domain description also states dynamic properties such as the impossibility of one package overtaking another, and also static properties such as the tree structure: there is exactly one path from the reading station to any bin.

To achieve correct routing, the router control-2 machine must set the switches ahead of each package as it falls through the router. Because many packages are falling through the pipes and switches simultaneously, the machine must detect the arrival of each package at the sensor just above each switch. It then sets the switch to direct the package towards its destination bin:

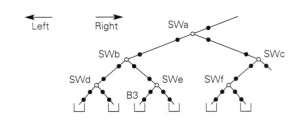

Routing a package to a bin

A package whose destination is at bin *B3* must be switched to the left exit when it arrives at switch *SWa*, right at *SWb*, and left again at *SWe*. There is no correct route to bin *B3* for a package arriving at switch *SWc*: it has already been misrouted. Of course, the machine does not set the switch if it is already set in the correct direction, or if it is not empty.

A static model

To set the switches appropriately, the machine must have access to information about the layout of the router: that is, how are the pipes, the switches, the reading station, the sensors and the bins connected? This information cannot come directly from the router itself. It must come from a model of the router. What's needed is a *static model*, from which the machine in the package routing subproblem can obtain answers to questions like these:

■   To which pipe is sensor *s* attached?

■   Is bin *b* reachable from the left or right exit of switch *w*, or from neither?

It looks as if this model, like the destination mapping description, must be produced by a human informant. But this time it's definitely a model, not just a description. Here's the problem diagram, with the interfaces very roughly annotated:

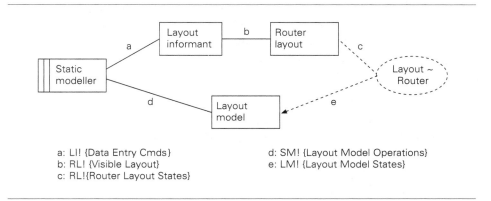

a: LI! {Data Entry Cmds}
b: RL! {Visible Layout}
c: RL!{Router Layout States}

d: SM! {Layout Model Operations}
e: LM! {Layout Model States}

Package router: building a static model

The router equipment layout is visible to the layout informant, who issues data entry commands to the static modeller machine. The machine responds to those commands by invoking operations of the layout model.

The requirement is that the layout model should correspond in a stipulated way to the router layout. We haven't given any detail of the model phenomena or operations at the connections *d* and *e*. The correspondence must provide the answers needed by the package routing machine.

Packages destinations and sensors

Let's return now to the difficulty of detecting package destinations and package identities when a package arrives at a sensor. In the subproblem of reporting misrouted packages, the relevant sensors are those that lead immediately to a bin. In package routing, the present subproblem, the relevant sensors are all the others. In both cases, when a package arrives at a sensor, the machine shares only the sensor state. It detects that some package has arrived. But it needs to know more: Which particular package has arrived? and what is its destination?

A dynamic queues model

You can see what kind of model could answer these questions. The essential domain property is that packages can't overtake each other in the pipes or switches. So the packages inside each pipe and inside each switch form a *queue*, behaving in a mannerly first-in first-out fashion. In each queue, the first package to arrive is the first to leave. You can base your model on this property.

The model will have one queue for each pipe, one for each switch, and one for the reading station. Packages correspond to model records with ID and destination fields. Records in the reading station queue correspond to packages that have been read but have not yet entered the topmost pipe. The model looks like this:

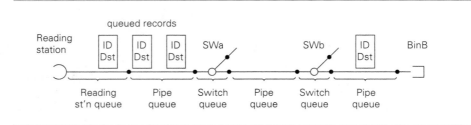

Queues model of packages in the router

Each queue is associated with its entry point: the reading station or the sensor at the queue entrance. The package records inside a switch form a queue, although it is a queue with two exit points. That's unusual, but it's all right in this case. A switch can't be flipped while there is any package inside it: the exit point can change only when the queue is empty. So if ever there are two packages simultaneously in the switch, they are both making for the same exit.

Here's the problem diagram for building the model:

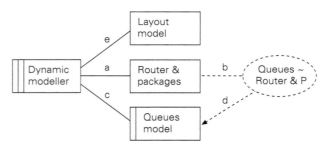

a: RP! {SendLable(p,l), Lld(l,i), Dest(p,d)   c: DM! {EnQ(r,q,s), DeQ(r,q,s), RecPkg(r,p,d)}
   SensOn(i)}   d: QM! {LastArr(s,q,p,d), Empty(s,q)}
b: RP! {PkgArr(p,s), Pld(p,i), PDest(p,d)}   e: LM! {Layout Model States}

Package router: building a dynamic model

The model domain is called the queues model. It is built and maintained by the dynamic modeller machine. The phenomena set *c* contains the events in which the machine enqueues and dequeues records in the queues associated with sensors – *Enq(r,q,s)* and *DeQ(r,q,s)* – and the record states that capture the package Id and destination – *RecPkg(r,p,d)*.

The machine maintains the queues in the obvious way. As each package is read and the *SendLabel* event occurs, the machine enqueues its record in the reading station queue. When a package passes the upper sensor of a pipe its record is dequeued from the queue it was in and enqueued in the pipe queue. When it passes the lower sensor its record is dequeued from the pipe queue and either enqueued in the switch queue or discarded because the package has now reached a bin. The static layout model is needed to allow the machine to relate the reading station and sensors to the switches and pipes, and hence to the queues.

The requirement stipulates that the queues model must correspond to the router & packages domain as follows. *Empty(s,q)* is true when the queue *q* corresponding to *s* is empty. *LastArr(s,q,p,d)* holds when a real package with ID *p* and destination *d* has arrived at the sensor *s* associated with the queue *q*, and no package has subsequently arrived at that sensor.

Any questions?

Why do you say 'build and maintain' for the dynamic model, but only 'build' for the static model?

The static model doesn't change. That's what it means to be static.

But won't the organisation that uses the router want to change the layout sometimes?

Yes. We'll come back to that point later. For the moment, we're dealing with the problem of routing the packages; in that problem, the layout is – and must be – regarded as static.

Doesn't the dynamic modeller need to know which way each switch is set?

No. Because there is no overtaking inside a switch, and no resetting of the switch while any package is in it, we can ignore the switch settings. Whichever package enters first, exits first – whichever exit it emerges from.

Why doesn't the dynamic modelling requirement refer to the layout model?

The layout model is used only to associate each newly created queue with the correct sensor. Subsequently, the association is within the queues model.

The identities model is a model of the combined domain of the router and the router control computer. It can be built with the help of a human informant. The problem is straightforward. Here is the problem diagram, without interface annotations:

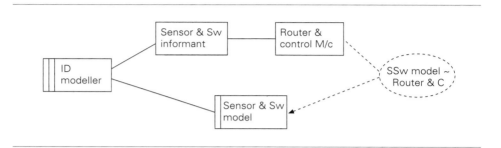

Package router: building an ID model

The model provides information needed by the router control–2, router control–3, and dynamic modeller machines.

10.3.3 Some possible automation

We have used human informants for the destination mapping, the layout model, and the sensor & switch ID model. There's nothing you can do to avoid a human informant for the destination mapping: the information to be captured is in human heads and is simply not accessible to the machine in any other way. But you can avoid using a human informant for the other two models. The machine can be used to build a domain that combines them.

Let's call it the *ports model*. The basic idea is to combine the layout model with the sensor & switch ID model to give a layout model expressed entirely in terms of router controller machine ports. Instead of containing the information:

■   ID model: sensor *s1* is at port *p1*; switch *w2* is at port *p17*;

■   layout model: sensor *s1* is at the entry to switch *w2*,

it will contain only the information:

■   ports model: the sensor at port *p1* is at the entry to the switch at port *p17*.

Let's call the machine in this problem the automatic modeller machine. Here's how the machine can build the model automatically, without a human informant. First, let the machine initialise all the switches to their left positions. Then, by setting just one switch to the right at a time, and checking the resulting *SwPos* states, the machine can associate the *RSw(i)* port for each switch with the *SwPos(i)* port for the same switch. It can do the same for the *LSw(i)* ports. Now the triplets of ports associated with the switches are known. Of course, it is not known which switch is associated with the triplet or where it is in the layout.

Now suppose the operator puts one package on the conveyor, and the machine starts the conveyor. Then first a *SendLabel* event will occur, and then *SensOn(i)* will become true for some sensor *i*. This will be detectable at some port *p1* of the machine. It is now known that the sensor at port *p1* is at the top of the pipe leading directly from the reading station. The next *SensOn* is at port *p2*: the sensor at port *p2* must be the sensor at the bottom of the same pipe. If all the switches have been initially set to *left* by *LSw(i)* events, the following *SensOn* state changes are successively for the sensors at the tops and bottoms of the pipes, taking only left switch exits, all the way to the leftmost bin.

Eventually, by following the progress of a succession of packages, and exploring the combinations of switch settings in a systematic manner, the machine can complete the port model. The problem diagram for automatic modelling is:

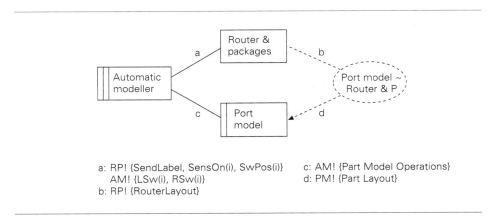

a: RP! {SendLabel, SensOn(i), SwPos(i)}   c: AM! {Part Model Operations}
   AM! {LSw(i), RSw(i)}   d: PM! {Part Layout}
b: RP! {RouterLayout}

Package router: building a layout model automatically

There are two things to say about this automatic model. First, the identities of the router components have not disappeared. You can still think of them as the modelled individuals, but now they are identified with the machine ports at which they share events and states with the machine. Second, because the bins are not represented in the model, the destination mapping must be replaced by a destination-to-port mapping: each destination string must be associated not with a bin, but with the port belonging to the sensor leading directly to the bin.

the domain properties of well behaved packages that are essential to the queues model. So the audit subproblem must itself be decomposed into a model-building and maintaining subproblem and a model-using subproblem.

More ambitious checking might take account of the different apparent sizes of different packages. For example: if package ki takes exactly twice as long as the following package kj to pass the first sensor, but appears to take exactly half as long to pass the second sensor, that gives some reason to suppose that kj has overtaken ki in the topmost pipe. This kind of checking will need a more complete investigation of the physical properties of packages and how they slide through the router, and of the properties of the pipes and switches in the vicinity of the sensors.

When you analyse this subproblem you mustn't be too ambitious. Remember that your central purpose is to detect the most common failures: only a careful investigation of practical experience can tell you what those are. Remember also that over-ambitious checking will be hard to develop, may detect few failures in practice, and will probably give rise to many 'false positives', that is, to spurious detection of failure where none has occurred. A package router that often stops for no good reason will be at least as annoying as one that doesn't stop when it is jammed.

10.3.5   Initialisation

Obviously, the destination mapping, the static model and the identities model must be built first, before the router control machine can be run. That's true whether you choose the automatic modeller or the ID modeller and the static modeller.

Then the router & packages domain can be initialised quite straightforwardly by the router control machine. The machine stops the conveyor, and then allows enough time for any package that may be in the pipes or switches to reach a bin. The router & packages domain is now in a passive initial state, empty of packages. The switches require no initialisation: their settings are accessible to the machine by the shared *SwPos* states, and there is no reason to prefer any particular initial combination of settings over any other. The queues model used by the router control–2 and router control–3 machines, and the dynamic model of the audit machine, can be initialised without difficulty.

10.3.6   Completeness

To address the completeness concern you must consider, among other things, what may be happening in the problem domains while they are not interacting with the machine.

While the router control machine is in operation, all the router equipment is directly connected to it. The packages can't go anywhere except through the pipes and switches. The operator can't do anything except hit the Start and Stop buttons to produce *OnBut* and *OffBut* events for the router control–1 machine. So there's no scope for activity separated from the machine. No difficulty here.

But when the router control machine is not in operation, the router layout may be extended or reorganised. If there are more packages to be handled, finer distinctions will probably be needed among the destinations. That means introducing more bins into the router, with consequent changes to the layout of the pipes and switches. There will also be a need for maintenance and repair. Probably this will involve dismantling some parts of the router equipment, and unplugging them temporarily from the computer ports.

The implications are straightforward: a change to the layout means a change to the models. You must not ignore this. Your operating manual for the package router must cover it fully.

Any questions?

Can't the identities concern be better handled by putting the switches and sensors on a bus?

Yes, that would be easier: the machine would send and receive signals that carry device identifiers. But you would still have to be sure that you quoted the correct device identifiers in the layout model. The static modelling and identities problems haven't gone away.

Can the various models and descriptions not be combined?

Certainly they can. The ports model is already a combination. We're coming to that point in the next chapter.

How can the automatic model be built most efficiently, that is, using the smallest number of packages?

A good question. What do you think? Can you calculate the answer?

Do we really need to address the reliability concern? Won't the operator stop the conveyor anyway when packages get jammed in the router?

Perhaps. But it's better to stop as early as possible. And the other failures – overtaking and undetected packages – will be harder for the operator to recognise before they have caused a lot of misroutings.

10.4 Decomposition heuristics

It's time for a brief review. We have decomposed the package router problem into these subproblems, named according to the names of their machines:

- *router control–1:* starting and stopping the conveyor in response to operator commands, and also to jams detected by the audit machine;

- *router control–2:* correct routing of packages by flipping switches ahead of each package;

- *router control–3:* reporting on packages misrouted when a switch could not be flipped because a package was too close to the preceding package;

- *destination editor:* using a human informant to associate destination strings with router bins (or with sensor ports leading directly to them);

- *dynamic modeller:* building a queues model of the progress of packages through the router, to provide the destination string of each package as it encounters each sensor;

- two versions of static modelling and identities mappings. Either:
  - *static modeller:* using a human informant to build a static model of the router layout;
  - *ID modeller:* using a human informant to associate sensors and switches with machine ports;
    or:

  - *automatic modeller:* building a static model of the layout directly in terms of machine ports, thus making the ID model unnecessary;

- *audit machine:* detecting package jams and other misbehaviour in the router.

So we have reached a point where we have recognised a number of subproblems, sketched their problem diagrams, and discussed them very briefly. The question then arises: how are we going to put it all together? How will the machines we have decided to build cooperate to give a solution to the whole problem?

We're not going to look at this concern now. We'll have something to say about it in the next chapter, on composite frames. In this chapter we're more interested in the process of decomposition.

10.4.1 Simple heuristics

In our decomposition we used some simple and obvious heuristics.

- *Identifying the core problem.* Sometimes a realistic problem seems to have an easily identified core that fits a recognised problem. You can start by taking the

- In the information display frame, the real world may be complex – perhaps requiring an explicit model – but you expect the display domain to be relatively simple: the information machine causes events shared with the display that produce simply-related changes in the display domain states. You expect the requirement to stipulate a simple relationship between requirement and specification phenomena of the real world.

- In the simple workpieces frame, the workpieces domain may be complex, but you expect the user domain to be simple: the user issues a sequence of commands, each one readily interpreted by the editing tool in terms of the workpieces operations that the tool must cause in response.

- In the transformation frame, you expect the inputs and outputs domains to be of roughly equal, moderate, complexity. You expect the IO relation to be satisfiable by one simultaneous traversal of both domains.

Of course, these expectations are not cast in concrete. Some apparent exceptions will still fit happily into the frame and yield to the usual kind of analysis. But an unusually complex domain probably indicates that further decomposition is needed: a further subproblem can be recognised within the basic frame.

We have already seen an example in the package router. The core problem was a required behaviour problem, routing the packages to their correct destination bins. But the controlled domain – the router & packages – had an important complexity: the package destinations are not available when the package passes a sensor. So we had to introduce a model domain to handle this concern. The model was justified by the needs of the report misrouted packages subproblem, but even without the reporting requirement we would still have needed the model for the required behaviour problem alone.

Here's another example. In a transformation problem the IO relation between the inputs and outputs domains may not be satisfiable in a single simultaneous traversal. The commonest and most obvious reason is a difference in the order of data in the two domains. Then you must introduce an auxiliary domain:

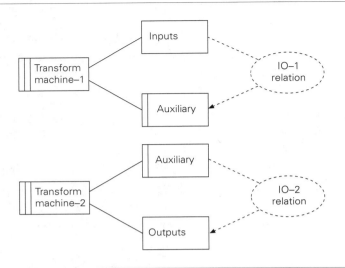

Transformation with an auxiliary domain

Decompose the transformation problem into two transformation subproblems. The auxiliary domain must have the property that it can be traversed both in the order of the inputs traversal and in the order of the outputs traversal.

10.4.5 Modelling the user or operator

In a pure workpieces problem the user domain is treated as an unstructured stream of commands. It is no part of the problem to consider the state of the user, or to distinguish one person acting as user from another. The operator in a commanded behaviour problem, and the informant in a model-building problem, are regarded similarly.

If the individual human user or operator is a domain of interest for its own sake, rather than merely as a source of commands, that is a clear indication of a distinct subproblem. For example, if John and Lucy decide that it's important to know whether a particular entry in the party plan is due to John or to Lucy, that's a fresh information subproblem. The real world is John & Lucy, plus the party editor machine, and the requirement is to display some information about that real world. It may well be that this information subproblem will need a model of John and Lucy, to record their individual editing activities. If so, this model is entirely separate – in the problem analysis – from the party plan itself that they have been editing. If the model and the party plan are merged in the subsequent implementation, that is strictly a solution matter. Merging them in the problem analysis can only cause confusion.

A subtle example

In a system to manage undergraduate degree courses at a university, students enrol for course modules by online interaction with the computer system. The result of these interactions is, of course, to change the states of model domains in the system that model the states of the course modules and of the enrolled students. Other people – administrative staff and faculty members – also use the system. They enter various information about the students and the courses: for example, that an undersubscribed module has been cancelled, or that a student has been awarded a particular grade.

Something is going on here that you mustn't ignore in your problem analysis. There are two different kinds of interaction event:

- a member of the administrative staff or the faculty is playing the part of a user in a workpieces problem or an informant in an information model-building problem; the 'real' event has already happened elsewhere;

- a student enrolling in a module is engaging in the real world action, thus acquiring the right to attend lectures and classes, to submit exercises and tests and have them marked, and to receive academic credit for the module if successful; this is the 'real' event itself.

You can see that these are two distinct things by the different levels of security and authorisation that are surely necessary. The user or informant must be authorised, perhaps by a password, and can then enter information about many different modules and students. But the real world action of enrolling in a module can be authorised only for the enrolling student, and for no one else. There are two subproblems here, and they should be clearly separated.

Any questions?

What does 'effectively static' mean?

In the tennis court problem, 'effectively static' means that you can ignore any changes in membership that may take place during one tennis session. The fast machine will check the membership card before opening the door and switching on the lights; if the card is valid when checked, the machine accepts it and does not check whether its validity will expire during the game. It's acceptable to allow a session that outlasts the player's membership by an extra hour or two.

'Effectively static' doesn't mean that in analysing the fast subproblem you are free to make descriptions with very long time spans that rely on the membership domain not changing at all during that time. If you build a machine that caches all membership information retrieved, and assumes that it remains unchanged, it might allow extra weeks or even years of court use after membership has expired. That would not be acceptable.

Where did the air traffic control example come from?

Daniel Jackson pointed it out to me a few years ago.

Where did the university modular degrees example come from?

From Barry Cawthorne, of the University of the West of England at Bristol.

It seems positively perverse to separate a model of student module enrolment actions from a model of the modules and the students. Why are we doing it?

Because they are about different problems. The student enrolments may be events in a behaviour problem, for example, to ensure that each student enrols in a valid set of modules. The other events are building an information model. It's good to keep the models separate in problem analysis even – or especially – if they will later be combined in the implemented solution.

CHAPTER 11

Composite frames

Realistic problems are composite. They must be decomposed into simple subproblems that fit recognised simple frames. The subproblems have frame concerns and other particular concerns; the interaction among them gives rise to fresh composition concerns. The possible combinations of simple subproblems are unlimited, but many composition concerns can be identified by examining some of the combinations in terms of problem domains common to different subproblems. These concerns include consistency, precedence, interference and synchronisation.

11.1 Introduction

The ideal use of problem frames is when your whole problem perfectly fits a recognised frame, and the frame provides an effective and systematic method of analysis and solution. It doesn't often happen. Realistic problems are too varied to fit any problem frame repertoire of manageable size.

But in some cases, in a highly specialised and refined application area, a large composite frame is developed, and becomes widely accepted as defining a significant class of realistic problems. Typically, the definition is in terms of an appropriate solution structure. This has happened with some object-oriented frameworks. A notable example is the model-view-controller (MVC) pattern or framework.

11.1.1 MVC: a large composite frame

One way to understand the development of MVC – from a conceptual, not a historical, point of view – is as the culmination of successive versions of the workpieces problem frame. The basic workpieces frame is too simple to be useful in practice. The user entering commands can see neither the commands themselves nor the workpieces. Successive improved versions are:

- workpieces with command display. The command text is displayed, character by character, as it is keyed. This development adds an information display subproblem;

- workpieces with commanded workpiece display. A second information display subproblem shows whatever part of the workpieces the user explicitly chooses to display. The commands for this display subproblem are still distinct from those of the workpieces subproblem itself. Primitive line editors were like this. The displayed text appeared in the body of the screen, the command line at the bottom;

- workpieces with required workpiece display. The workpiece display shows whatever part of the workpiece is currently relevant, according to relevance criteria given in the requirement. In the party plan editing problem the relevant part might be determined by the current context – the invitations for a guest, the invitations for a party, or the list of guests and parties;

- workpieces with interactive command display. Commands are selected from pull-down menus. Command variations are chosen by radio buttons and similar schemes. String arguments are entered by selecting an existing occurrence or by keying the argument in a temporary one-line display area;

- workpieces with interactive workpieces display. The workpieces display becomes interactive, allowing direct manipulation. Using the mouse, text can be cut and pasted and graphic objects can be manipulated.

The design of solutions to interactive workpiece problems has received intensive effort since the MVC pattern, implemented in the Smalltalk language, was introduced in the mid-1980s. In the words of one description of the MVC pattern:

> 'The model-view-controller architectural pattern (MVC) divides an interactive application into three components. The model contains the core functionality and data. Views display information to the user. Controllers handle user input. Views and controllers together comprise the user interface. A change-propagation mechanism ensures consistency between the user interface and the model.'

MVC provides a highly evolved decomposition structure for a realistic problem class. The *core functionality and data* is the content of the workpieces. The *information to be displayed to the user* in the views is stipulated in the Information subproblem requirements. The *user input* combines editing and display commands. The change-propagation mechanism ensuring *consistency between the user interface and the model* addresses a composition concern of the editing and display subproblems. The controllers, considered together with the event-handling functions of the operating system, implement combinations of subproblem machines.

The problem to be solved is assumed to be standard, and is not stated explicitly. A developer using MVC is expected to work directly in solution terms: the implementation design is given, and the problem need only be poured into it. Development of the MVC pattern itself has focused on such questions as: Should there be one controller for the whole pattern, or one per view?

Any questions?

Where can I read about MVC?

We mentioned MVC earlier, in Chapter 5. The references given there are repeated here, with two additions. The first reference is to the original published description of MVC; the others are to later discussions. Wolfgang Pree compares MVC with another GUI application framework, ET++.

G E Krasner and S T Pope, *A Cookbook for Using the Model-View-Controller User Interface Paradigm in Smalltalk-80*, Journal of Object-Oriented Programming Volume 1, Number 3, pages 26–49, August/September 1988.

Frank Buschmann, Regine Meunier, Hans Rohnert, Peter Sommerlad and Michael Stahl, *Pattern-Oriented Software Architecture: A System of Patterns*, John Wiley, 1996.

Erich Gamma, Richard Helms, Ralph Johnson and John Vlissides, *Design Patterns: Elements of Reusable Object-Oriented Software*, Addison-Wesley, 1995.

Wolfgang Pree, *Design Patterns for Object-Oriented Software Development*, Addison-Wesley, 1995.

What is direct manipulation?

Instead of entering commands in a special command-language syntax, the user manipulates representations of the objects of interest directly on the computer screen.

Douglas Engelbart, who invented the mouse in the early 1960s, gave an early demonstration in 1968. He showed a task list that could be manipulated by rearranging sections of a graphical model on the screen.

The term *direct manipulation* was originated by Ben Shneiderman. Here are two relevant papers:

Douglas C Engelbart and William K English, *A Research Center for Augmenting Human Intellect*, AFIPS Conference Proceedings of the 1968 Fall Joint Computer Conference, pages 395–410, December 1968. Reprinted in *Computer Supported Cooperative Work: A Book of Readings*, Irene Greif (ed), pages 81–105, Morgan Kaufmann, 1988.

Ben Shneiderman, *Direct Manipulation: A Step Beyond Programming Languages*, IEEE Computer, Volume 16, Number 8, pages 57–69, August 1983.

Don't shrink-wrapped software packages embody useful large problem frames?

Sometimes. And when an application class becomes popular a particular implementation may begin to establish a *de facto* standard. Web browsers and word processors are an example. It's often interesting to study a piece of software or a standardised design and work out its implicit problem frame.

So can I use problem frame ideas to understand a piece of software or to understand a design?

Yes. It's a good way to deal with the traditional software question: if this is the solution, what was the problem?

11.2   Composite problems

If a frame as highly developed as MVC fits your problem perfectly, you should use it. There is no sense in trying to replay the development of MVC in your project. It's ready for use.

But for most realistic problems you won't find a ready-made frame. There's no package router control frame, or library administration frame, or meeting scheduler frame, or home heating frame. You must deal with those problems by decomposing them explicitly into simple subproblems. Each realistic problem is a unique composition of simple subproblems that interact, sometimes in complex ways. These interactions give rise to *composition concerns*. In this chapter we will look at some of the combinations of simple problems that commonly occur, and at the composition concerns that arise.

11.2.1   Common domains

Composition concerns in a pair of subproblems arise chiefly from their different projections of problem domains that they share. Are the two projections consistent? If they are different requirements referring to the same phenomena, can they both be satisfied together? If they are different domain property descriptions, does the domain really possess both properties? If they are different machine behaviour specifications at interfaces with the same problem domain, can the domain engage simultaneously in both behaviours? Can the machine?

If two subproblems don't share any problem domain they can't interact directly. At most they can interact through other subproblems. Consider, for example, two subproblems of the package router control problem: obeying operator commands and reporting misrouted packages. The problem domains in the obeying operator commands subproblem are the operator and the conveyor; in reporting misrouted packages they are the router and packages. There's no direct interaction here because there are no common domains and no common phenomena. If you draw the two problem diagrams together they look like this:

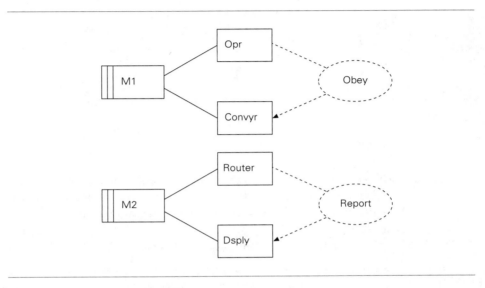

Subproblems that don't interact

There's no scope here for identifying any part of one subproblem with any part of the other. So there's no composition concern.

11.2.2 A non-interacting composition

We're going to show some examples of subproblem compositions that do raise composition concerns. We'll show them as pairs of problem diagrams in this very sketchy form, without annotating the connections. We'll keep the machines and requirements separate, but show common problem domains only once. Here's an example:

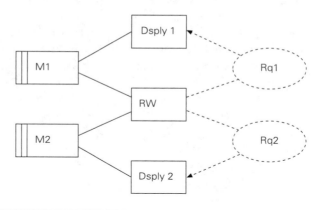

Two-information displays

The diagram shows the combination of two information display subproblems, both displaying information about the same real world domain. The diagram is self-explanatory. The parts of the problem diagram for the first subproblem are the machine M1, the display domain Dsply1, the real world RW and the requirement Rq1. The parts of the second problem diagram are M2, Dsply2, RW and Rq2.

In this example of the two information displays, the two subproblems are *non-interacting*, that is, they don't interact with each other at all in spite of having a common domain.

Here's why. First, the display domains are disjoint, so there's no possibility of interaction there. Second, the real world is autonomous: it must be so in any information problem. So it is unaffected by the behaviours of the two subproblem machines. It follows that neither machine could detect the presence of the other in any way at all: each one is unaffected by the other's behaviour.

It's not hard to find, or imagine, examples of this kind of composition. For example:

- the membership reports and the lending reports in the library administration problem;

- displaying an expected meeting participation and displaying a schedule of meetings in the meeting scheduler problem;

- displaying speed count and distance count in the odometer display problem – treating the two digital displays as different domains.

What composition concerns can arise in this kind of composition? Essentially, only one. In each subproblem development there is a domain properties description of the real world. The two descriptions are made for different purposes. They may have overlapping scopes, that is, there may be real world phenomena that they both refer to. The membership reports and lending reports subproblems will have overlapping scopes if the first is partly concerned with books or the second is partly concerned with members. The meeting participation and schedule of meetings both refer to meeting dates. Both subproblems in the odometer display problem refer to wheel pulses.

Where there are two descriptions with overlapping scopes there is room for inconsistency. We'll come back to this concern later on in this chapter.

Any questions?

Isn't the machine always a common domain?

Two separate subproblem machines will often be combined into one machine – that is, executed on one computer – in the eventual implementation. But this combination isn't in itself a matter for *problem* composition: it's a concern in *solution* composition.

Won't we sometimes need to consider combining the machines in our problem analysis? For example, if they must both traverse the real world domain in sequential traversals, it may be desirable to combine the two traversals into one for reasons of efficiency.

Yes, that's true. But it's still solution composition, not problem composition.

Surely the conveyor and the router do have something in common. If the conveyor is stopped, no more packages will pass the reading station and fall through to the bins.

Well, ultimately, everything is connected to everything else. That's what it means to be in the same universe. But the obey operator subproblem does not mention packages, and the report misrouting subproblem does not mention the conveyor. So a composition concern between them can arise only by a chain of intermediate subproblems. It's dealt with indirectly by addressing the composition concerns of adjacent links in the chain.

Didn't you say in Chapter 3 that it's just too confusing to draw several requirements and several machines in one problem diagram?

Yes. The diagrams we're drawing here are not intended as a substitute for separate subproblem diagrams. They are only an additional help in clarifying subproblem interactions.

11.2.3 Sharing a display domain

Here's a different composition of two information display subproblems:

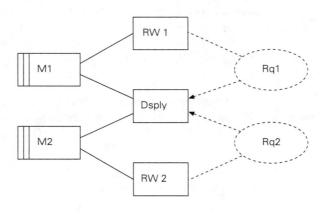

Two information displays

Now the two subproblems have different real worlds. Actually, that doesn't matter very much: we might have retained the common real world of the previous composition. What matters now is that the subproblems have the same display domain. The resources of the display domain must be *shared* between the subproblems.

Allowing for the unimportance of the different real worlds, here are examples of this composition:

- displaying the command line and displaying the edited text in a primitive line editor;

- displaying the 32 voltages in the experimental voltages problem, and displaying the average voltage. Both are displayed on the computer screen;

- displaying furnace equipment malfunctions and displaying current room thermostat settings in the home heating control problem. Both must appear on the control panel;

- displaying out-of-range factors and displaying analog device failures in the patient monitoring problem. Both are shown on the screen of the nurses' station;

- displaying clock information and radio frequency information in a car radio. Both use the same digital display.

Whether a shared domain like this raises a significant concern depends on the domain properties and on the subproblem requirements. Sometimes the sharing is done automatically. For example, the operating system of the machine may provide a window manager. Each display output can be associated with its own window, and the operating system will allow the user to size, position and hide each window at will. In each subproblem that uses the display screen, there is no need to consider other competing subproblems. In the experimental voltages problem the different display windows can be arranged as the experimenter thinks best.

But often there is a significant concern here. In the patient monitoring problem you must decide explicitly how the shared display is to be allocated. You might decide to reserve an area of the screen permanently for each kind of monitoring alarm. No other subproblem that uses the screen of the nurses' station can encroach on this area. In the car radio problem, the display is allocated by time. The radio frequency information is displayed only for the few seconds following each user command that changes the radio's tuning state.

11.2.4 Commanded and required behaviour

We saw a limited example of combining commanded and required behaviour in an earlier chapter. In the operated one-way lights problem the traffic overseer is able to override the required regime of the lights, by extending or curtailing the default required behaviour. This was rather a special case. The operator's commands are interpreted by the machine in the context of the default required behaviour, not of the current state of the controlled domain. That is, the commanded behaviour modifies the required behaviour, it doesn't replace it.

The more general case is like this:

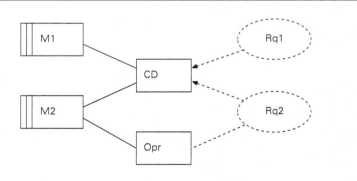

Commanded and required behaviour

In the first subproblem, Rq1 stipulates a required behaviour of the controlled domain CD. In the second subproblem, Rq2 stipulates obedience to the operator's commands. Here are two examples.

- In the airport shuttle problem, the shuttle usually runs without a driver. But there is provision for a driver. The driverless behaviour is the first subproblem; controlling the shuttle in the presence of a driver is the second.

- In the package router control problem, detection of a package jam must cause the machine to stop the conveyor. But in another subproblem the machine is required to stop and start the conveyor in obedience to the operator's instructions.

The two subproblem machines must certainly interact. Each, considered separately, must compel the common controlled domain to satisfy its own requirement. In composing them you must address at least two significant concerns:

- *consistency*: in what respects are the two requirements consistent, in the sense that it is possible to satisfy both? For example, is the shuttle driver to be allowed to drive the shuttle at higher speed than is stipulated for driverless operation?

- *precedence*: in situations where the requirements are not consistent, which should take precedence? For example, if the operator issues a *Start* command while the conveyor has been stopped because of a package jam, should the conveyor be started?

11.2.5 Creating and using a lexical domain

The parts played by lexical domains in basic problem frames and their variants include workpieces, models and descriptions. The frames are different in many respects, but the subproblems they fit are likely to come in pairs: one to create and edit, or maintain, the lexical domain; and another to use it. The same situation arises when a transformation problem is decomposed: the outputs domain of one subproblem becomes the inputs domain of another.

The composition looks like this:

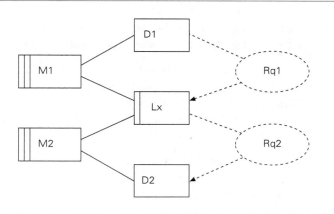

Creation and use of a lexical domain

The lexical domain Lx is created in the first subproblem, and used in the second, perhaps as the model in an information frame, or as the description in a description variant of the required behaviour frame. Examples of this composition are:

- in the patient monitoring problem, the medical staff enter periods and ranges for monitoring each patient. The monitor machine monitors the patients accordingly;

- in the home heating problem, in one subproblem the machine constructs a description of the anticipated behaviour of the occupants, in another it controls the room heating accordingly.

Of course, there will be a consistency concern, checking that the domain descriptions of Lx are consistent in the two subproblems. But this is not the only composition concern, or even the most important.

The second subproblem assumes that the Lx domain is static. For example, in the patient monitoring problem, in analysing the monitoring subproblem you would treat the periods & ranges domain as static. In the home heating problem, the heating control machine uses the description of occupant behaviour, but does not expect it to change while it is being used. This assumption – that a lexical domain that is only being used and is not being created or edited is a static domain – is a necessary and reasonable assumption. How could you read a book that changes under your eyes as you read it?

When the subproblems are composed, the assumption that the common domain is static raises major composition concerns:

- *interference:* you must determine how and where to limit the behaviour of each subproblem machine so that the first subproblem machine can change the common domain as required, and the second can use it as required;

- *synchronisation*: to avoid interference it's necessary to synchronise the execution of the two subproblem machines in some constrained way. What constraints are required? What schedulings are acceptable to your customer? For example, is it acceptable to suspend all patient monitoring while the periods & ranges domain is being edited?

We have introduced these concerns in the context of a common lexical domain. But they can arise equally well in the context of a common causal domain, where one subproblem treats the domain as a controlled domain and the other as an autonomous real world.

Any questions?

Why is it all right to treat the speed count and distance count as different display domains in the odometer speed display problem? They are both in the fascia display domain.

Yes, but we are assuming here that their phenomena are entirely disjoint. The counters are distinct, and so too are the operations that increment and decrement them: they could as easily have been shown as separate domains in the original problem diagram.

Isn't it very limited to consider only pairs of subproblems? Surely we must consider the composition of many more subproblems than that?

That's true. But you have to start somewhere. Also, if you can address the composition concerns in one pair well enough to regard them as a single subproblem, you can compose that single subproblem with another, and so on for as many subproblems as you wish. You can think of that as a kind of bottom-up problem composition.

Are you going to say more about these composition concerns?

Yes. We're going to discuss them in a more general context. We're coming to that right now.

11.3 Composition concerns

We're going to discuss these composition concerns raised by the examples in the previous section:

- *consistency* between different indicative or optative domain descriptions;

- *precedence* between inconsistent domain descriptions;

- *interference* between different interactions with a domain;

- *scheduling* of machines that interact with a common domain.

But first we must address a very general concern about different descriptions of one domain.

11.3.1 Commensurable descriptions

Whenever you describe a domain you are describing some projection of it. You select phenomena and relationships relevant to the purpose in hand, and you make appropriate abstractions to suit that purpose. In analysing different subproblems you have different purposes in mind, so you will probably have chosen different projections, and different abstractions of the phenomena.

That can raise a concern about the descriptions themselves. They may not be *commensurable*, that is, they may not be expressed in terms that allow you to compare them easily, or to compose them if that is necessary. Perhaps you noticed an example in the last chapter.

Abstracting sensor phenomena

When we discussed the package router control problem, we treated the sensor phenomena as *SensOn(i)* states: at any time, for each particular sensor *i*, this state is either true or false. With this abstraction, this is what happens when a package passes the sensor:

(a) before the package arrives, *SensOn(i)* is false;

(b) when the leading edge reaches the sensor, and the package is first sensed, *SensOn(i)* becomes true;

(c) so long as the package is passing the sensor, *SensOn(i)* holds;

(d) when the trailing edge of the package leaves the sensor, and the package is no longer sensed, *SensOn(i)* becomes false.

For some purposes this view of the sensor phenomena is just what you need. In the audit subproblem, where some package jams are detected by carefully checking the

Look at these two descriptions:

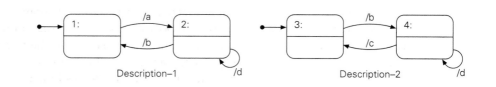

Description–1   Description–2

Two descriptions of one domain

Each describes the behaviour of a domain: the first in terms of *a*, *b* and *d* events; the second in terms of *b*, *c* and *d* events. Are they consistent?

For two state machines, one with *m* states and one with *n* states, the combined description can have up to $m \times n$ states, although not all may be reachable from the initial state. So you can start to make the combined description by setting out the combined states (the combined state '1,3' means that description–1 is in state 1 and description–2 in state 3, and so on), like this:

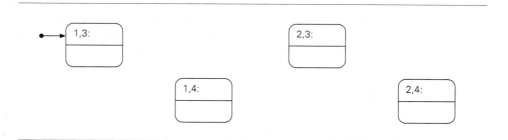

Starting to combine two descriptions

Then, you add the transitions that are shown in the two descriptions. For the common event classes *b* and *d*, discard any transition that does not appear in both descriptions. Here's the result:

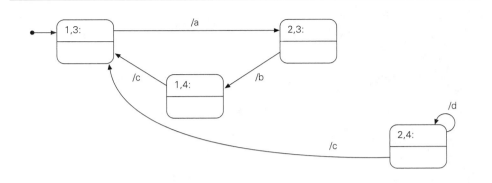

Two descriptions combined

The combined description shows that the combined state '2,4' can't be reached from the starting state, so it can't ever occur. Since *d* events can occur only in that state, it follows that *d* events never occur. The combined description gives the order of events as <a,b,c,a,b,c,a,...>.

Are the two descriptions inconsistent, then? Perhaps. But it depends on what you meant by them.

- You may have meant each description to say that each of its transitions will *definitely happen eventually*. The domain will, sooner or later, get into state 2, and on one of those occasions, sooner or later, it will cause a *d*. And similarly for state 4 and the *d* event there. If this is what you meant, something is definitely wrong. The domain will get into state 2, and it will get into state 4; but no *d* will ever occur because the domain is never in state 2 and state 4 at the same time. The descriptions are inconsistent.

- You may, instead, have meant each description to say that certain undesirable things would *never happen*. There will never be two successive *a* events without an intervening *b*; *d* won't occur after *b* without an intervening *a*; *d* won't occur after *c* without an intervening *b*; and so on. If this is what you meant, there's no inconsistency: *d* will never occur, but then you didn't say it would.

Similar questions arise when you compose descriptions of other kinds, including descriptions of static domains. For example, suppose that two descriptions say that there are zero or more individuals of a certain type; and each description places a different constraint on the individuals. Are the two descriptions inconsistent if there must always be zero individuals because no individual can in fact conform to both constraints simultaneously?

When you write a description you have to know what you mean by it.

Any questions?

Is the difference between describing what will definitely happen and what must never happen the same as the difference between liveness and safety?

Yes. Liveness has been characterised as the property that 'something good will eventually happen', and safety as 'nothing bad will ever happen'. Liveness is harder to think about than safety, because of that intrusive word 'eventually'. If a liveness assertion says that x will happen, and it hasn't happened, how can you know whether (a) it's never going to happen, or (b) it's going to happen, but it just hasn't happened yet? To think about this effectively, you must think of infinite sequences of events. An interesting paper on the subject is Bowen Alpern and Fred B Schneider, *Recognizing safety and liveness*, Distributed Computing, Volume 2, pages 117–126, 1987.

Why can't a d event occur in the state '1,4'?

Because the domain would then be in state 1 where, according to description–1, a *d* event can't occur.

Where does the difference between continuous and discrete descriptions fit into all this?

It's a standard example of the commensurability concern. You have to identify the coarse view with a particular point in the fine view. Here that means identifying each discrete sampling with the value at that point in time in the continuous abstraction.

Direct requirement conflict

Sometimes one subproblem's requirement is in direct conflict with another's. Here's an example:

Secure editing system

A small editing system is required for confidential documents. The editing itself is a straight-forward task of the usual kind, but there is an additional security requirement.

A password file contains passwords arranged in a hierarchy of classes. Only people with appropriate passwords are allowed to perform certain sensitive operations, such as deleting any part of the text of any file, or editing a file whose confidentiality level is above a certain value.

This problem is readily decomposed into a workpieces problem to handle the editing and a required behaviour problem to handle the security. The requirement in the workpieces problem will describe how the documents should change in response to editing commands from the user. For instance, it will stipulate that in response to a *delete* command the currently selected text must be deleted from the currently edited document. The resulting specification describes how the machine achieves this by invoking the workpiece operation *deltext(t)*. But the requirement of the control machine in the security problem will describe restrictions on changes to the documents. In particular, it will stipulate that no text may be deleted unless the user has an appropriate password. In any case where the user does not have the appropriate password, the two requirements are in conflict: one says 'delete', one says 'don't delete'.

Of course, there are many expedients for resolving this conflict. Almost always, the essence of conflict resolution is to give one of the conflicting requirements precedence over the other. In the secure editing problem, security must take precedence over editing.

11.3.3 Precedence

In many behaviour problems different subproblems stipulate different behaviours of the controlled domain. The two behaviours are not consistent, and neither can be properly regarded as a modification of the other. Instead the combined machine must satisfy either one or the other at any time. This is particularly common when the requirement in one subproblem is to respond to the detection of domain failures by an audit subproblem. For example:

- in the sluice gate problem, the required behaviour is to keep the gate open for fixed periods; whenever any failure is detected, such as an apparent overrun of the gate travel, the commanded behaviour is to switch off the motor;

- in a problem to control a lift, the required behaviour is to respond to requests to visit floors; whenever any failure is detected, such as apparent failure of the lift car to move or sensors being *On* simultaneously at different floors, the commanded behaviour is to apply the emergency brakes and switch off the motor;

- in an air traffic control system, the required behaviour is to provide for airplanes to land and take off in an orderly fashion, maintaining the proper spatial separations in the air and on the runways and taxiways. If two planes fail to maintain separation, or one plane fails to respond to the controllers' instructions, successively more radical behaviours are required to avoid collision.

For each possible domain state, the different behaviours are ordered by precedence, and the behaviour with highest precedence is adopted. In many cases it's helpful to think of these different behaviours as different *modes* of operation. In the presence of failure, the whole system switches from one mode to another. In a system with a complex hierarchy of partial failure states, there may be many operation modes.

One way of thinking about the different modes is to think of switching between the different subproblem machines. In one mode the required behaviour machine is controlling the controlled domain; in another, a commanded behaviour machine is in control. To deal properly with this switching, you have to ensure both that the machine relinquishing control is leaving the controlled domain in a permissible state, and that the machine receiving control is able to take over in the current state. Essentially, this is an *interference* concern. We'll discuss interference in the next section.

11.3.4   Interference

Interference is one of the common and most important composition concerns. Two subproblems have a common domain. In at least one of them you regard it as a dynamic domain whose state it can change, for example, as a controlled domain, or a model to be built, or a description to be created or edited. In the other you may either regard it similarly or as an autonomous dynamic domain or even as a static domain.

The interference concern arises because both subproblems are interacting with the domain at the same time. It's helpful to think of their executions as *interleaved*: one subproblem machine executes without interruption – maybe for a very short time, maybe for a very long time – while the other is suspended; then the first machine is suspended and the other executes; and so on alternately. A subproblem machine suffers interference when, on resuming execution, its implicit assumptions about the common domain are invalidated. Typically, the common domain has apparently suffered an arbitrary state change. Although each subproblem machine is correctly specified in isolation, the combination is not correct. For at least one of the two subproblems, the domain does not possess the properties stated in the domain description.

The effect of interference

To see how significant the effect of interference can be, look at these two simple program processes:

```
P1: begin x:=0; for i1:=1 to 50 do x:=x+1; end
P2: begin x:=0; for i2:=1 to 50 do x:=x+1; end
```

Each process executed alone will increment x by 1 to 50 times, giving it an eventual value of 50 when the process terminates. If the two processes are executed together, they will interfere with each other because the variable x is a common domain: both processes update it.

The problem decomposition is:

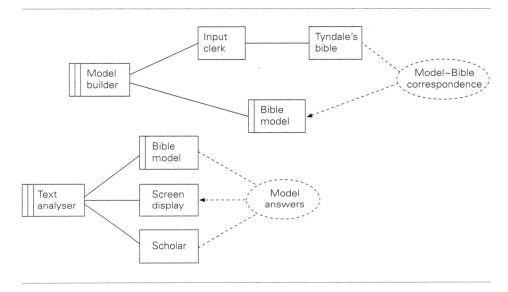

Bible text enquiries: decomposition

The Bible model is held as a database on disk.

At first sight, it may seem obvious that the whole execution of the model builder must be atomic. That is, the complete model must be created before any part of it can be used. That was certainly true of the router layout model in the package router problem: a partially completed model there is of little or no use. But in this problem, the scholars may be keen to use the text analyser on the first book – Genesis – as soon as it has been entered, without waiting for the other four books. It's also possible that the main text may be useful without the marginal notes, the prologues, and other ancillary material. So you should at least consider a finer grain of atomicity for interleaving the creation and use of the model.

Usable states
The essence of an interleaving scheme for the creation and use of a model is the definition of *usable states* of the model. A usable state is one in which the model can be safely used because in that state the model conforms to the model domain description on which the development of that machine was based. There is some circularity here – the domain description takes account of the usable states, and the usable states are defined to support the assumptions of the domain description. That's not surprising: in designing a model domain you must always consider both how it will be created and how it will be used.

There are many possible schemes for dealing with this concern in the Bible text enquiries problem. One scheme is to embody an explicit outline structure – a table of contents – in the model, with provision for indicating, for each component of the structure, whether it is complete or incomplete. The model builder machine maintains this outline structure; the other machine, the text analyser, examines the structure and refuses to answer any query that may involve reference to an incomplete component. In effect, the outline indicates which parts of the model are available and which are not.

Devising a scheme like this does not itself fully define the usable states. It's also still necessary to ensure that the two machines will not interfere with each other. In this case, the model builder must not update the table of contents while the text analyser is traversing it – access to the table of contents, at least, must be atomic in both machines.

Any questions?

Where did the P1/P2 example come from?

From an old ACM self-test exercise. Anthony Hall pointed it out.

Mode switching has uses other than precedence, doesn't it?

Yes. For example, a standard design for engine control software in avionics systems has separate subproblem state machines to provide control in take-off, cruising, landing and other modes. An additional state machine implements the mode switching between them.

Why must we think of execution of the subproblem machines as 'interleaved'. Why can't I just think of their executions as just proceeding in parallel?

Where there is no interference, and the subproblems are effectively executing on independent computers, you can. The idea of interleaving is a good way to get some kind of a grip on the interference concern.

Is database locking, and transaction commit and rollback, something to do with interference?

Yes. Two transactions can interfere with each other in a database in exactly the same way as the editor and controller, or as the *P1* and *P2* processes. The techniques you mention make each transaction effectively atomic.

The idea of usable states of the model seems to be local. It allows some parts to be usable while others are still under construction, as it were. Is that right?

Yes. In many contexts where interference arises this is a standard technique. Think of running a railway. For train operations the track is a static domain. For track maintenance it's dynamic. The idea of local usability is just the obvious idea: don't run the trains on the parts of the track that are being changed. As in database locking, the goal is to lock as much as you must, but no more.

Can local usability be applied to the patient monitoring problem?

Yes. Interference between the editing and the use of the periods & ranges domain, and also of the identities model, can be dealt with in exactly this way. You don't have to stop monitoring all the patients because a new range is being specified for one of them, or because a new patient or a new analog device is being added. Even better, you can continue to monitor a patient's blood pressure while a new period and range is being specified for the same patient's temperature.

It is beginning to seem that addressing composition concerns can lead to changing the subproblem descriptions?

Yes, definitely. This is an illustration of the general rule that development must be iterative.

But doesn't that mean that we should have addressed the composition concerns first, before analysing the subproblems?

No, it doesn't. Until you have analysed the subproblems you don't really know what you're trying to compose.

11.3.5 Synchronisation

Sometimes you find that two subproblems with a common domain are too loosely coupled to cause interference, but you must still concern yourself with their interleaving. And sometimes addressing the interference concern doesn't adequately determine the desired execution interleaving. There are requirements – often unrecognised until quite late in the development – that will place further constraints on subproblem interleaving. We'll call this the *synchronisation concern*.

We have already seen an example of this concern in the tennis court lights problem. We identified – roughly – a membership management subproblem and a lights control subproblem. The domain of members is common to both subproblems: only members in good standing are allowed to use the indoor court and its lights. From the point of view of the lights control subproblem, the members domain is effectively static; for the membership management subproblem it is, obviously, dynamic.

The question arises: what if the indoor court is in use when the player's membership expires? There is no interference concern here: the two subproblems are only loosely coupled in the sense that there is no physical connection outside the machines between the membership expiry and the lighting equipment. But it's easy to see that although there is no interference concern there is another concern: Should a member whose membership expires tomorrow be allowed to start a one-hour game at 11.30pm? The answer to this question must, of course, be given by your customer. It's a straightforward question about the problem requirement. It doesn't arise in either subproblem, only in their composition.

Similar questions arise in many problems that have subproblems of different tempi. In the library administration problem: Is a member whose membership expires tomorrow allowed to borrow a book today? To reserve a book? Is a member whose has some books out on loan allowed to resign before returning them? There is a rich vein of such questions, but they are rarely very difficult. Essentially they are questions about requirement completeness at the level of the whole problem rather than of its individual subproblems.

Adjustable one-way lights again

We haven't finished with the adjustable one-way lights. Our last suggestion was that the processing of each complete phase could be regarded as atomic for both the editor and the controller. But that can't be the whole story. It's inadequate at two levels.

First, making the phases atomic was a careless choice. Suppose the current regime is:

(S1,S2:50; S1,G2:120; S1,S2:45; G1,S2:100;)*

and it is going to be replaced by the regime:

(S1,G2:140; S1,S2:55; G1,S2:110; S1,S2:75;)*

For a certain interleaving of editor and controller, the controller may switch after the first phase. Then one effective instance of the regime body may be:

S1,S2:50; S1,S2:55; G1,S2:110; S1,S2:75;

Two consecutive Stop-Stop phases. Undesired, but not a disaster. But this is also possible:

S1,S2:50; S1,G2:120; G1,S2:110; S1,S2:75;

A Stop-Go phase followed immediately by a Go-Stop phase. This is definitely dangerous.

Second, because of the possibility of interference, the controller must suspend its traversal while editing is in progress. But the road repairer may take a very long time to complete the editing of the new version. Road repairers are not usually noted for their speed and accuracy at the keyboard. While the controller is stopped, at least one of the traffic streams is halted. Is it reasonable to make the traffic wait so long? Almost certainly not.

We are finally reaching the conclusion that you may have been awaiting impatiently since the problem was first introduced in the previous section. There should be two copies of the encoded regime: the *active copy* is for the controller to use, the *reserve copy* is for the editor. Once editing is complete, the active copy is overwritten by the reserve copy. Now the controller can go on working while the reserve copy is simultaneously being edited.

Now we need only decide when the controller can change from the old to the new regime. It can change when it reaches the end of any Stop-Stop phase before it switches to the following Stop-Go or Go-Stop phase. At that point it is always permissible to start using the new encoded regime, regardless of its initial phase.

Building and using a dynamic model

For a dynamic model the concerns are similar to those for a static model, but often with a need for more precision.

One synchronisation concern in a dynamic model is about the *accuracy* of the correspondence between the model and the reality. Once the interference concerns have been adequately addressed, it may still be important to ensure that the model has no states that do not correspond to states of the reality. Such inaccurate model states can arise because a pair of real world events or state changes may be handled by the model builder machine in reverse order.

Suppose, for example, in the library administration problem, a member walks into the library, returns a borrowed book to one assistant, and then hands his membership resignation to another. It's possible that for some reason the assistant dealing with the returned book will be slow to enter it into the computer. There may then be a short period in which the model shows the member as having resigned but not yet returned all his books. This is an inaccurate state of the model: no corresponding state ever held in the modelled reality. In practice, such inaccuracies are often handled by a loose restriction on model usability. Banks, for example, traditionally insist on usability only after the close of business on each day. The balance reported to you at midday by the automated telephone or Web-based enquiry system is not guaranteed to correspond accurately to a state of reality.

Timeliness of a model

Another synchronisation concern in a dynamic model is about the *timeliness* of the information given by the model about the reality. Even if all model states are accurate, they may still lag too far behind the corresponding states of reality to be useful.

The dynamic model used by the package routing subproblem in the package router must be sufficiently timely to give a correct answer to the question: What is the destination of the package that has just passed sensor *i*? For a correct answer you must not only synchronise the model appropriately with the reality, but also synchronise the question with both of them. If the question is asked too early, the model may not yet have been updated; if it is asked too late, another package may already have passed the same sensor. Look at this diagram:

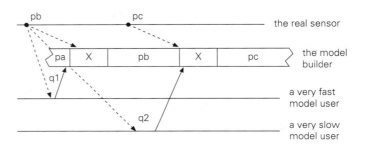

A synchronisation concern

Three successive packages, *pa, pb* and *pb*, pass the sensor. When the model builder machine detects each of these events (we have adopted the coarse abstraction here) it enters an atomic episode of model updating. In this episode the value of the model for the sensor is unavailable to the machine using the model, and is indicated by 'X'. When the update is complete the model has the correct value for the package that has most recently passed the sensor. Because the model lags the reality, this value persists until some time after the next package passes the sensor.

If the model user is fast enough, it may respond to the passage of package *pb* with question *q1*. This question is presented to the model before the model builder has started its atomic updating episode; the incorrect answer *pa* is then given. But if the user is slow enough in detecting package *pb* and presenting the question, it may respond with question *q2*. This question is presented to the model just after the model builder has detected the package *pc*; processing of the question is delayed because the model is being updated; eventually, the incorrect answer *pc* is given.

The subproblem machines must be synchronised to ensure that both the early question *q1* and the late question *q2* are avoided. The simplest way to avoid the early question is to ensure that the model user does not detect the package – and so can not ask the question – until the model has been updated. To avoid the late question it is necessary to ensure that both the builder and the user of the model are fast enough to keep up with the arrival of successive packages. Since all the sensors must be serviced concurrently, this may require careful design. A minimum separation in time between packages passing the same sensor is guaranteed by the physical properties of the router and the packages, but there is no minimum separation between packages at different sensors.

Any questions?

Doesn't interference also arise in mode-switching between subproblems in a behaviour problem?

Yes. Each subproblem machine that relinquishes control must leave the controlled domain in a usable state, that is, one satisfying the domain properties description of the subproblem machine that is receiving control, and respecting the atomicity constraints. However, the concern is insignificant when switching to an emergency stop, as in the lift control example. The brakes can be applied in any state, so there is nothing to do to satisfy the domain properties. And there is no exit from the emergency stop mode: the whole machine must be restarted from the beginning. So it is not necessary to consider a transfer of control in the other direction.

If we must always eventually think about interference and synchronisation, why do we start by treating the common domain as static in one subproblem?

Precisely because you must eventually think about interference and synchronisation. It's much easier to think about them when you know a lot about the subproblems in isolation, and it's much easier to deal with each subproblem without getting mixed up in interference and synchronisation concerns. In a subproblem that uses a model or a description domain it's a tremendously valuable simplification to treat the domain as static.

In the Rational Unified Process it's recommended not to worry about interactions between use cases at run time until the system is designed. Is this the same sort of idea?

To some extent. Perhaps you're thinking of the account in Philippe Kruchten, *The Rational Unified Process: An Introduction*, Addison-Wesley Longman, 1999.

The Rational Unified Process treats concurrency among use cases as a nonfunctional requirement. When you describe each use case originally you 'assume that all use case (instances) can run concurrently without any problem'. That's very like what we have been doing. But the subsequent treatment of interference and other composition concerns is different.

The adjustable one-way lights problem seems rather contrived. Couldn't the conclusion have been easily foreseen?

Perhaps so. But you can't always solve this kind of problem by introducing two versions of the common lexical domain. I have a rather ancient VCR (a video cassette recorder) that allows a sequence of up to six recordings to be programmed in advance. It takes me a while to program the sequence using the very awkward and inconvenient scheme of buttons. You can't be recording anything while you're programming. And funny things happen if the start time for the first recording arrives while you're still programming. I think I'll buy a new VCR.

CHAPTER 12

Grown-up software development

In spite of its 50 year history, software development is a curiously immature affair. To do better we must recognise the great variety in our problems and products, we must think consciously about development risks, we must focus our attention where it matters, we must learn from experience, and we must be masters, not pedants, of development methods.

12.1 The immaturity of software development

The practice of software development is now about 50 years old, if you date it from the invention of the subroutine in its modern form. In many ways, the progress made in the past 50 years has been huge. Today's development tools – programming languages, compilers, integrated development environments, GUI builders – would have astounded our predecessors by their power, efficiency and refinement. Application systems are now commonplace – spreadsheets, modern word processors, telephone systems, the Web – that were scarcely conceivable 50 years ago.

But in other respects we have barely begun to create a mature discipline that could be reasonably compared with the established disciplines of electrical engineering, automobile engineering, civil engineering and many others. Our discipline is still in its infancy. You can see the evidence of our immaturity everywhere around you – in the quality of developed software, and in the naïve way we think and talk about the practice of software development.

12.1.1 Software quality

Notoriously, many software development projects fail completely: they produce no system at all, or one that is never used because it doesn't fit the customer's requirements. But there is another kind of failure that occurs in many projects that are regarded as very successful – a failure of quality.

A hugely successful flagship word processing product, used by millions of people, has hundreds of functional defects. Here are two examples.

- *Outline numbering* is a function that allows headings and paragraphs to be hierarchically numbered – 1, 1.1, 2, 2.1, and so on. The word processor has nine levels of built-in heading styles, all using outline numbering. So outline numbering is a major function of the product. But it doesn't work properly. It's subject to unpredictable disruption: the highest level of numbering is sometimes unexpectedly reset to 0 in the middle of a document, giving 1, 1.1, 0, 0.1, and so on. You can restore the correct numbering by reapplying the heading styles to the affected paragraphs, but the fault may reappear, apparently spontaneously, at any time.

- *Page view* is a function that shows the document as it will be printed. This is the basic WYSIWYG functionality. Its central requirement is to display any graphic objects included with the text, and to handle page breaks correctly. But page breaks are not handled correctly. A newly typed line that should appear at the top of a new page may appear in the top margin; it may be truncated horizontally, showing only the lower half of each character; it may disappear entirely; or it may appear both on the old and on the new page. If a grouped graphic object is selected that is anchored to the first paragraph of a page, a subsequent *ungroup* command – which should show each component in the group individually selected – often causes the whole graphic to disappear entirely.

These are major defects in essential functions, persisting over many versions of the product. The software company has been either unwilling or unable to correct these, and many other, defects. Ed Yourdon wrote about this kind of software:

> *'A pessimist might ... express enormous surprise that we've gotten away with this kind of behaviour for so long, to which an optimist might respond, "That's the price of progress. You're bound to have some rough edges with new, innovative applications that we're building on this year's new, advanced hardware".'*

Count me as a pessimist. However you choose to excuse these failures, they are a sure sign of immaturity in the discipline of software development. At 50 years of age, it's not attractive to be so childish. Similar defects, uncorrected in successive models of a car or a washing machine, would cause a serious scandal. In the world of software development they are unremarkable.

12.1.2 The panacea syndrome

A panacea is a medicine that cures all ills. In software development we have been seeking a panacea for 50 years, greeting each new idea in our field as the magical cure for all our difficulties.

We're still doing it. The published description of a commercially offered development process carries a preface claiming that the process is '... a full-fledged process able to support the entire software development life cycle ... quite simply, the best software process the world has ever seen'. There is no suggestion that the process may be applicable only to some kinds of problem, to the development of some kinds of solution, or to some aspects of development, or even that it may be better suited to some than to others. It is a panacea.

What's wrong is not that this development process has no virtues at all. It may well have some virtues. What's wrong is that it claims every virtue in the book. The snake oil not only cures your cough. It also cures indigestion, restores lost hair, protects against sunburn, lubricates your bicycle chain and makes an excellent salad dressing. The evidence of our immaturity is not in the sellers' claim, but in their confident expectation of the buyers' credulity.

12.1.3 Maturity and mastery

The beginning of maturity in software development is the acknowledgement of variety. This is the central message of this book. There are many kinds of realistic problem. Each is a unique composite of subproblems fitting different frames, each subproblem having many parts and aspects and many concerns to be addressed.

Taking a mature approach to development means dealing properly with this variety. You must recognise the need for many different notations and techniques, and be ready to choose the most appropriate in each situation. You must be ready to consider many different ways of ordering and structuring the tasks that contribute to a development, or to a series of developments over your software career. In short, you must tailor your method, both in the large and in the small, to the problem in hand. One size doesn't fit all.

Don't allow the ideas in any book – and that includes this one – to become an obstacle in your development work. If they are of value, first make sure that you have understood them, and then use them with mastery, not pedantry.

Polya, in his wonderful little book *How To Solve It*, explains the difference between pedantry and mastery:

> *'To apply a rule to the letter, rigidly, unquestioningly, in cases where it fits and in cases where it does not fit, is pedantry. Some pedants are poor fools; they never did understand the rule which they apply so conscientiously and so indiscriminately. Some pedants are quite successful; they understood their rule, at least in the beginning (before they became pedants), and chose a good one that fits in many cases and fails only occasionally.*

> *'To apply a rule with natural ease, with judgment, noticing the cases where it fits, and without ever letting the words of the rule obscure the purpose of the action or the opportunities of the situation, is mastery.'*

It's hard to be a master. You must understand the rules very well indeed before you can break them. And you must learn – and use – the insight and judgment to decide where they apply with full force, and where it's right to break them. In the next sections we'll look briefly at a few aspects of mastery. Then, in the final section, we'll end the book by putting problem frames and their use in a broader perspective.

Any questions?

Didn't Charles Babbage and Ada, Countess of Lovelace, invent the subroutine?

No. Their punched-card technology for representing programs couldn't really support such an idea. The subroutine was invented in the years 1947–1950, when the first general-purpose electronic computers were designed and built. An excellent account is Brian Randell (ed), *The Origins of Digital Computers: Selected Papers*, Springer-Verlag, 2nd edition, 1975.

David Wheeler is credited with inventing the subroutine in its modern form, with a jump and a return address. An early discussion of subroutines and their implications for program structure is M V Wilkes, D J Wheeler and S Gill, *The Preparation of Programs for an Electronic Digital Computer, with Special Reference to the EDSAC and the use of a Library of Subroutines*, Addison-Wesley, 1951.

Where did Ed Yourdon write that comment about optimists and pessimists?

In an article about the implications of – what was then – the looming Year 2000 crisis: Edward Yourdon, *A Tale of Two Futures*, IEEE Software, Volume 15, Number 1, pages 23–29, January/February 1998.

Aren't problem frames a panacea?

No. They're a tool that you can use in combination with a lot of other tools. I'm sorry if I seem to have presented them as a panacea. Not what I intended.

What is Polya's book about, and where can I find it?

It's about solving mathematical problems. It's based on the work of ancient Greek mathematicians, going as far back as Euclid. Polya distinguishes two kinds of problem. A *problem to find or construct*, and a *problem to prove*. An example of a problem to prove is: 'Prove that the area of a triangle is half the product of its base and its height.' An example of a problem to find or construct is: 'Given two intersecting circles, construct a line that touches both.' The book is G Polya, *How To Solve It*, Princeton University Press, 2nd Edition, 1957.

Each kind of problem is rather like a problem frame. It has *principal parts* and a *solution task*. Polya gives many heuristics for problem solving, expressed in terms of the principal parts of each kind of problem. The original idea of problem frames was strongly influenced by Polya's book. There's more about that in Michael Jackson, *Software Requirements & Specifications: A Lexicon of Practice, Principles, and Prejudices*, Addison-Wesley, 1995.

12.2   Risks of development failure

Established engineering disciplines pay a lot of attention to *failure*. In designing any structure or device, the engineer must ask: How will this fail? When will it fail? What will happen when it does? Here is what Henry Petroski has to say:

> '*An idea that unifies all of engineering is the concept of failure. From the simplest paper clips to the finest pencil leads to the smoothest operating zippers, inventions are successful only to the extent that their creators properly anticipate how a device can fail to perform as intended. Virtually every calculation that an engineer performs in the development of computers and airplanes, or telescopes and fax machines, is a failure calculation. In analysing the cantilever beam, even Galileo began by making assumptions about how it would break or fail. Today, in designing a cantilever bridge, the engineer must have an understanding of how much load the individual steel members can safely carry before they pull apart or buckle and how much deflection can be allowed in the center of the bridge.*'

Software components don't fail like physical components. Your machine behaviour specification, and the programs that satisfy it, won't rust or deflect or buckle or break. The risk of failure in a software component – and this is as true of requirements and domain descriptions and specifications as it is of programs – is of failure at development time. The component fails because it's just plain wrong: the specification was wrong; the design was wrong; the program is wrong. The error may not appear for some time – perhaps never, if the condition that reveals it is very rare. But when it does appear, the system will fail in some way or another.

Surprisingly, we don't usually pay much attention to this kind of failure in our development work. We don't usually reason about the consequences of software failure except in the most safety-critical applications.

Why? Partly, because we lack humility. We don't like to confront and acknowledge our own fallibility, however often we see it demonstrated. Another part of the reason is paradoxical. Over the past 40 years some notable researchers have devised and taught us much more reliable methods of making certain kinds of program. Forty years ago most programmers were happy to tell their friends that 'every program has bugs in it', and to bask in the reflected glory of their inexplicably mysterious and esoteric trade. Then the researchers showed that some programs, at least, could be reliably designed without bugs. We began – very properly – to be less proud of our bugs.

But we hadn't learned the right lesson. We thought we had learned that we could produce all our software without errors. But the true engineering lesson is this:

> *'First, you must design all the parts as well as you can. Then you must calculate which are most likely to fail and what will happen when they do.'*

In software development you must do everything you can to eliminate errors. Then you must be constantly asking yourself: What part of my work is most likely to have errors? Where will an error have the greatest consequences? What if this indicative description is false? What if there is a fault in my reasoning in addressing this frame concern? What if this derived machine specification is wrong?

It's important to assess the risk of failure consciously because it helps you to allocate more effort where there's more payoff. Think about the identities concern in the package router problem. That was a central concern. We gave it a lot of attention, and it led to a large part of the work. There was an identities concern in another problem. In the lift position display problem there was an identities concern about the floor sensors, the floor lights and the request lights. How are the floor numbers associated with the specification phenomena? We didn't pay much attention to this one. Was that sensible?

Yes, definitely. First, because the identities mappings were static, so the whole concern was a lot easier. Second, because any error would be quickly revealed at run time. Third, because there were scarcely any consequences for the rest of the development. And fourth, because the static mappings would be easy to fix. That's the basis of assessing the risk of any development failure.

- How hard is it to get this right?

- How surely and quickly will I know if it's wrong?

- How bad will it be if it's wrong?

- How easily can it be fixed if it's wrong?

Risk assessment doesn't justify sloppy work. It justifies designing the greatest strength into the components that bear the greatest weight.

12.3   Shallow requirements

Inadequate requirements are often identified as the commonest cause of project failure. One form of inadequacy is shallowness – a failure to go deep enough into the problem context. If you choose too shallow a problem frame, for the core problem or for an important subproblem, you risk missing important requirements and domain properties.

You can think of problem frames as roughly ordered by their depth in the world outside the computer.

- The shallowest view of a problem sees only the machine, and sees it as a symbol processor. This isn't a problem frame at all because it doesn't even recognise the existence of the domains that provide the machine's inputs and receive its outputs. It's a pure programming point of view. It's reasonable to choose this view if you have been given a fully detailed specification of the machine's behaviour, and your only task is to design and build the program.

- The transformation frame takes you a little deeper. The inputs and outputs are lexical domains, sitting inside the machine, or right next to it on attached devices. When you choose the transformation frame, your problem domains are inert symbolic structures. You're ignoring any meaning that may be attached to those symbols: the problem is simply to satisfy the input/output relation. With the transformation frame, the closest you come to the world outside the computer is a floppy disk or a magnetic tape or a print file.

- The workpieces frame goes a little deeper again. The workpieces domain itself is again lexical, and the meaning of its symbols is again outside the scope of the problem. But the problem is a little richer because you must consider not only the lexical values but also the way those values are changed by the workpieces operations. There's also the user. You must consider the user's behaviour, but only in terms of the editing commands at the machine interface. What the user does when not interacting with the machine, and why the user issues this command or that, is not of interest.

- The information frame takes you deeper still. Your customer wants information about a real world that stretches some distance away from the machine. If it is large and complex, or if it is a remote domain, the requirement phenomena may be a long way from the machine. You must examine the real world to see how the machine can produce information about the requirement phenomena just from the shared specification phenomena. But you're not concerned to know whether producing that information causes any effects in the real world. That is outside the scope of your problem.

■ The behaviour frame goes beyond the information frame. Now you must consider how the domain will behave in response to the behaviour of the machine. When the controlled domain has active states, like the sluice gate or the airport shuttle, you must go a long way into the problem world to understand the domain properties and the requirement and to address the frame concern.

When you tackle any software development problem, you are choosing – consciously or unconsciously, explicitly or implicitly – to locate your work at some point in this ordering. If your choice is too shallow, you are truncating your problem, cutting it off too close to the machine. To avoid this risk, try, at least tentatively, to go one level deeper and see how it feels. Here are three examples.

■ If you have chosen the workpieces frame, ask yourself whether perhaps you are really dealing with an information problem. Then what appears to be a workpieces problem is actually a model-building subproblem: you can't ignore the real world domain of which the workpieces are the model. We have treated party plan editing as a workpieces problem. Although the operations were named *AddGuest*, *AddParty* and so on, they were just operations on the party plan lexical domain. To try one level deeper, ask yourself: 'Should I be considering the real world of John and Lucy's parties, and their guests and invitations? If so, then the party plan is a model of a real world I must explore and describe with care. How are invitations sent out? What if an invitation is lost in the post? Should the party plan contain a model of the guests' replies? Can there be two parties on one day? What if a party is cancelled after the invitations have gone out?'

■ If you choose the transformation frame you are implicitly assuming that there is no indicative relationship between the inputs and outputs domains: they are related only by the optative requirement. Ask yourself: 'Is there, in fact, an indicative relationship between the inputs and outputs domains? If there is, then I should not have treated the inputs and outputs as separate domains. I should combine them. This indicative relationship between them is a property of the combined domain. I must treat this as a behaviour problem: what I had thought of as the input/output relation is actually the required behaviour.'

■ If you choose the information frame you are regarding the real world as autonomous. The question of the machine affecting the real world can't arise. Ask yourself: 'Is part of my purpose that the real world should respond to the outputs produced by the machine? Are we trying to stop library members from borrowing too many books? If so, the information frame is too shallow. I can't describe the real world's desired response to the machine's outputs within the information frame because in that frame there is no optative description of the real world. My problem is, at least partly, a behaviour problem.'

When you try the deeper level like this, you're perfectly entitled to decide that the shallower level is right after all. Is it part of our purpose that the library manager should respond to the membership report? No, it's not. Membership reports is a pure information problem, just as we thought.

But it's good to have tried the water further out. Remember that almost any problem can be forced into a problem frame that's too shallow for it. Programmers traditionally go no deeper than the transformation frame. Some of the most widely used object-oriented methods treat all problems as workpiece problems. If you mean to practice grown-up software development you must do better than this.

12.4 Non-functional requirements

Some requirements are 'non-functional'. What does that mean? It means 'not pertaining to the function (that is, the observable behaviour) of the machine, or to the resulting observable effects in the problem domain'. In this sense, these are non-functional requirements:

- the Ada programming language must be used;

- the software must be delivered by 31 July;

- the computer must be fully ruggedised;

- all software modules must be tested at least up to complete branch coverage;

- the software must be readily maintainable.

You can't express any of these in terms of the behaviour or states of the machine or the problem domain. They are not about the 'function' of the system.

The distinction between functional and non-functional requirements is a reasonable distinction to make, and it's often useful. But there's a serious risk that it becomes an excuse for ignoring important requirements and concerns. It's clearly implied that the non-functional requirements are secondary: their satisfaction won't be checked with the same rigour and determination. If a requirement seems a little vague and subjective, just call it non-functional, and then you can justify giving it only vague and subjective attention.

In a workshop description of the requirements for an office lighting control system, these were classified as 'non-functional requirements':

- the control panels should be easy and intuitive to use;

- no hazardous conditions for persons, equipment or the building are allowed;

- the system issues warnings on unreasonable inputs at its control panels;

- in any case of failure the system shall provide a stepwise degradation of functionality down to manual operability;

- if the outdoor sensor does not work correctly, the control system for room lighting should behave as if the sensor were continuing to show the last correct measurement of outdoor light before the failure.

Most of these requirements are 'non-functional' only in the sense that they have not been analysed – yet. The machine behaviour that can satisfy them has not yet been specified. You might – just might – persuade your customer that 'easy and intuitive to use' is too subjective to describe in more detail. You certainly won't get away without describing the 'hazardous conditions' in full detail and showing how the machine will avoid them: it's a solid requirement in a behaviour problem. The 'unreasonable inputs' are a standard concern in commanded behaviour and in all problem variants with an operator. The 'stepwise degradation' of functionality is a standard treatment of an unreliability concern in a behaviour problem: the system progresses through the precedence order of its different modes. The last requirement is entirely 'functional' and specific, omitting only the detail of how sensor failure is to be recognised – and that's a standard information problem of the auditing kind.

Look sceptically at any classification of a requirement as 'non-functional'. If you allow requirements like these to be relegated to the 'non-functional' category, you risk missing a large part of your problem.

12.5 Amateurism

A major risk in software development is amateurism – failing to consult or use existing specialised knowledge of a problem domain.

We have already mentioned the car cruise control problem. A cruise control system automatically maintains a steady desired speed, selected by the driver, even when the car is travelling over hilly ground. Like the airport shuttle and home heating problems, it's a behaviour problem in which the controlled domain has non-stoppable active states. The machine must continually detect the car's current speed, compare it to the desired speed, and set the car's throttle accordingly.

How would you describe the machine behaviour that sets the throttle? Here are some possibilities, described by Mary Shaw.

- 'On/Off control: *the simplest and most common mode of control simply turns the process off and on. This is more appropriate for thermostats than throttles, but it could be considered. In order to prevent the power from fluttering rapidly on and off,*

off/on control usually provides some form of hysteresis (actual speed must deviate from set point by some amount before control is exercised, or power setting can't be switched more often than a preset limit).

- Proportional control: *The output of a proportional controller is a fixed multiple of the measured error. The gain of a cruise controller is the amount by which the speed deviation is multiplied to determine the change in throttle setting. This is a parameter of control. Depending on the properties of the engine, this can lead to a steady-state value not quite equal to the set point or to oscillation of the speed about the set point.*

- Proportional plus reset control: *The controller has two parts, the first proportional to the error and the second to cause the controller to change output as long as an error is present. This has the effect of forcing the error to zero. Adding a further correction based on the derivative of the error speeds up the response but is probably overkill for the cruise control application.*

For each of these alternatives, mathematical models of the system responses are well understood.'

The fundamental point is clear. There is an established discipline – control engineering – for choosing a control algorithm and calculating the resulting behaviour of the car. If you aren't competent in this discipline, and you mean to practise grown-up software development, you must learn enough to become competent, or get help from someone who is competent, or both. Even the experts don't always get it right. Mary Shaw observes:

'For cruise control, the possibility of runaway feedback is a significant safety concern, as the author's cruise control once vividly demonstrated.'

Expert disciplines exist in many areas. Consider a more demanding version of the traffic lights problem: the machine is required to set the lights to achieve the best possible throughput of traffic in both directions. You may need to draw on queuing theory here. In a critical financial application rigorous auditing of the system is required. Don't think you can invent those auditing rules for yourself. In the home heating problem we mentioned the safety concern in turning the furnace on and off. The rules of thumb we assumed there – the safe procedure for turning on and off – need validation by a professional engineer. Amateurism is not an ingredient of grown-up software development.

12.6 Drowning in complexity

In any realistic problem there's a significant risk of drowning in complexity. The root cause of most complexity in software development is premature composition. The separate pieces that you have to consider are very rarely complex; the complexity of the system comes from their composition. Here is Fred Brooks' comment about software complexity, from his famous talk *No Silver Bullet*:

> *'The complexity of software is an essential property, not an accidental one. Hence descriptions of a software entity that abstract away its complexity often abstract away its essence ...*
>
> *Many of the classical problems of developing software products derive from this essential complexity and its non-linear increases with size ... From the complexity comes the difficulty of enumerating, much less understanding, all the possible states of the program, and from that comes the unreliability ...'*

This is combinatorial complexity, and it comes from composition. The *non-linear increase* of complexity with size is the effect we saw in Chapter 11 when we briefly discussed the composition of two state machines. If you compose four state machines, each with five states, the composed machine may have as many as 625 combined states. Six machines with six states give 36,656 combined states. The number of states of the successful word processing product mentioned earlier in this chapter is unthinkably huge. That's why the people who built it probably couldn't fix the error in the outline numbering function, even if they wanted to. The space of possibilities to explore is too large.

The key to protecting yourself against this complexity is postponing composition until you have mastered the components. That means postponing the solution until after you have analysed and understood the problem. In software development, solution is, above all, composition: a single machine to embody the behaviours of all the subproblem machines; a single model to combine all the subproblem information models and all the identities models; a single model object to combine all the projections of each real world entity. The result will be vastly more complex. You can check it against your much simpler subproblem projections. But only if you postponed composition long enough to make them.

Any questions?

Where is the Petroski quote about failure from?

Henry Petroski, *Invention by Design: How Engineers Get from Thought to Thing*, Harvard University Press, 1996.

Who are the researchers who taught us reliable methods of programming?

You can read some of their papers in O-J Dahl, E W Dijkstra and C A R Hoare, *Structured Programming*, Academic Press, 1972.

Surely there are many other aspects of requirements – for example, identifying all the stakeholders – than the two or three you have mentioned here?

Yes, of course. There are many. This isn't a book about requirements or requirement elicitation. Try:

Ian Sommerville and Pete Sawyer, *Requirements Engineering*, John Wiley and Sons, 1997.

Ben Kovitz, *Practical Software Requirements,* Manning, 1998.

Suzanne Robertson and James Robertson, *Mastering the Requirements Process*, Addison-Wesley, 1999.

Where was the lighting control system project?

It was done for a university, and used as an example in a research workshop. Participants produced many different descriptions and analyses of the requirements.

Where can I read Mary Shaw's paper?

The discussion of control algorithms is in Mary Shaw, *Beyond Objects: A Software Design Paradigm Based on Process Control*, ACM Software Engineering Notes, Volume 20, Number 1, pages 27–38, January 1995.

There's a discussion of 11 different design solutions to the cruise control problem in Mary Shaw, *Comparing Architectural Styles*, IEEE Software special issue on Architecture, Volume 12, Number 6, pages 27–41, November 1995.

Where can I read Fred Brooks' famous paper?

Frederick P Brooks Jr, *No Silver Bullet – Essence and Accidents of Software Engineering* in Information Processing 86: Proceedings of the IFIP 10th World Computer Congress, pages 1069–1076; North-Holland, 1986.

You should also read Wlad Turski's reply: Wladyslaw M Turski, *And No Philosopher's Stone, Either* in Information Processing 86: Proceedings of the IFIP 10th World Computer Congress, pages 1077–1080; North-Holland, 1986.

Brooks' paper but not, unfortunately, Turski's reply is reprinted in: Frederick P Brooks Jr, *No Silver Bullet – Essence and Accidents of Software Engineering*, IEEE Computer, Volume 20, Number 4, pages 10–19, April 1987.

12.7 Focused attention

An essential part of mastery is focusing your effort and attention on what's important. In software development, the touchstone of effort and attention is *description*.
Descriptions are the working medium of software development. If you're uncertain
how much attention you, or your colleagues, are really giving to a subject, look for
the descriptions about it. But you must look with clear eyes. There are many ways
of deceiving yourself, and you must be critical and demanding. If you decide not to
describe something, that may well be the right decision. But deceiving yourself
about what you're describing is never right.

12.7.1 Direct description

If there is no description – pictures or text, formal or informal, handwritten or
machine-readable – about a topic, then you aren't paying it any attention. Don't
tell yourself that you're thinking about it in the background. Background thinking
isn't accessible to anyone else, it doesn't get any critical appraisal, and you'll have
forgotten it by tomorrow.

If you mean to pay serious attention to something, you must describe it, and
describe it directly. The scope of the description must include all the relevant phenomena of the subject to be described. There are several ways of failing to make a
direct description. One way is to describe the machine behaviour at an interface
instead of describing the problem domain on the other side of the interface. A
description of the behaviour of the lights controller machine isn't at all the same
thing as a description of the properties of the light units domain: the lights controller has no state corresponding to the broken state of a light unit.

Describing the model

The classic case of failing to make a direct description, of course, is describing a
model instead of the real world that it models. The widespread use of the word
'model' in the sense of 'description' encourages the common but self-deceiving
statement 'we are modelling the problem domain'.You are invited to think that it
means 'we are describing the problem domain'. But it really means 'we are describing our computer model of the problem domain'. Not at all the same thing. Just to
remind you:

■ the model ignores some real world phenomena. The library model of *book* has
   attributes ISBN, author, title and publisher. A real book may have more than
   one printing – with text and design changes – under the same ISBN. The first
   and second printings of *Software Requirements & Specifications* are different books
   in the real world, but in the model they are copies of the same book;

- the model has some phenomena that model nothing in the real world. The electrical circuit domain has nothing corresponding to the deletion of voltage records in the circuit model. The lift & buttons domain has nothing corresponding to the lift model transition 3.3 seconds after a button is pressed while the lift is serving a floor;

- the model may be only approximate. The voltages in the circuit model domain are discrete values measured at five millisecond intervals. In the electrical circuit they vary continuously. The lift model assumes fixed timings for the behaviour of the real world lift and its doors, but the real behaviour is subject to significant variation;

- a dynamic model lags behind the real world. The queues model of the router & packages is sometimes out of date. When two packages arrive nearly simultaneously at different sensors, the order of events and state changes in the model does not correspond in any simple way to the behaviour of the packages and sensors;

- real world defined terms may correspond to designated phenomena in the model. In the circuit the maximum and minimum voltage at each point are defined state phenomena, but the machine that builds the model must change these states explicitly as distinct phenomena.

Your description of the model can't serve as your description of the real world simply because the two are different domains.

Direct description
Another failure of direct description is ignoring a remote domain. Here's an example. In a video rental problem development you may see a scenario like this:

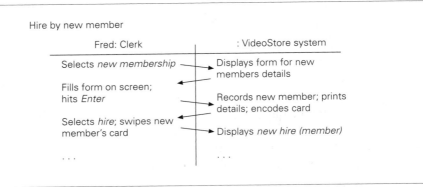

Beginning of a scenario

Is this scenario a description of 'How a new member hires a video'? Definitely not. There is nothing here about the member or about the video. The scenario is just about the interaction between the clerk and the machine. For a direct description you need something more like this:

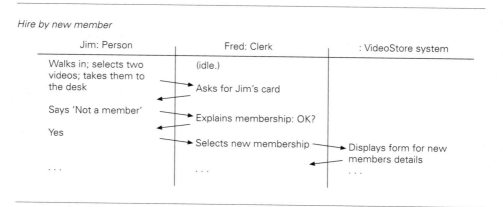

Hire by new member

Beginning of another scenario

This scenario could be a direct description of 'How a new member hires a video'. It describes what the customer does, quite explicitly.

Compact description

If you are paying proper attention to a subject your description of it will be *compact*. The subject is covered in one document. It's not good enough to distribute the description over many documents. You need to be able to see the description in one place, then you know that you've got it all, and can reason about the whole of it.

This is one reason why the technique of describing the whole requirement in terms of use cases can't ever be sufficient for any system. The use cases are fragments of several behaviour descriptions with larger time spans. Essentially, there is one larger behaviour for each participant in the use cases. There's a behaviour of a video rental customer; there's a behaviour of a video rental tape; and there's a behaviour of a video rental clerk. If you don't make a compact description of the behaviour of each participant, all you have is a distributed description. You have to try to piece it together from the several use case descriptions. That won't be easy.

Examined description

If a topic is important you must examine your description carefully and subject it to serious review. Perhaps it needs to be inspected or reviewed with other developers; or compared with existing documentation such as technical or procedure manuals; or presented very carefully to your customer, to users, or to other people with special knowledge of the domain. Perhaps you need to go out and examine the domain directly, comparing what you find with what you have asserted in your descriptions.

It's hard to do this well because you have to abandon the usual basis of human discourse. You must question even the most obviously correct assumptions. Well, actually, it's the obviously correct assumptions that you must question most aggressively. Obviously correct assumptions are often false. Did you see the movie *Titanic*? When the ship was approaching the iceberg, the iceberg was on its starboard – that is, on its right – side. The order was immediately given: 'Hard to starboard.' Obviously, this order was disastrously wrong, and was largely responsible for the collision. Obviously, the order should have been 'hard to port'.

Wrong. The order was perfectly correct. The conventions of helmsman's orders at sea were established around the 14th century when a ship was steered by a tiller attached to the rudder post. If you move the tiller to the right, the rudder moves to the left and the ship steers to the left. So, in accordance with this convention, the order 'hard to starboard' was an order to steer the Titanic to its port side – to its left – away from the iceberg. The convention survived the replacement of the tiller by the ship's wheel, and persisted until 1934, when it was changed by international agreement. It was still in force when the Titanic went down in 1912.

Any questions?

Why do you keep repeating the point about models?

First, because it's really important. Second, because it's largely ignored in most people's development practice. And third, because it's entirely ignored in most books about development method. But I'm sorry to have annoyed you. I won't do it again.

What is 'the transition in the lift model that occurs 3.3 seconds after a button has been pressed while the lift is serving a floor'?

It's the transition in the model that means that 'for purposes of the model we will now assume that the button press request has been satisfied'.

Where does the video store scenario come from?

It's adapted, with some minor changes, from Desmond F D'Souza and Alan Cameron Wills, *Objects, Components and Frameworks with UML: The Catalysis Approach*, Addison-Wesley Longman, 1999.

D'Souza gives the fuller version, showing the customer explicitly. There are many good things in this book.

Why is it so important to include the customer and the video – they don't interact with the machine at all, do they?

They are what the problem is about. To see the effect on a video rental system of ignoring everything except interactions with the machine, look at Peter G. Neumann, moderator, *The Risks Digest: Forum on Risks to the Public in Computers and Related Systems*, Volume 12, Issue 51, Wednesday 16 October 1991, ACM Committee on Computers and Public Policy.

It contains a sad tale of a video rental customer. The customer returned the video but the clerk failed to check the return into the computer. The result is that the customer can't rent any more videos from the store. At the time of writing this book, the sad tale is on the web at:

http://catless.ncl.ac.uk/Risks/12.51.html#subj3

You're joking about port and starboard in the Titanic, aren't you?

No. It's true. It's a spectacular example of a very common kind of ambiguity. Whenever a term can have exactly two interpretations, in opposite senses, there's scope for this ambiguity. My fax machine has a slider control marked 'Darker' and 'Lighter'. Does it mean 'Darker Original' or 'Darker Output'? I have a pair of duvets, one marked by a red border, the other by a blue border. Does red mean 'this one is warmer', or 'use this one in warmer weather'? These *binary terms* always need careful explicit designations.

12.8 Problem frames in perspective

Essentially, problem frames give you a way of classifying software development problems. They can provide a structure for capturing your growing experience and knowledge. They can help you to anticipate the concerns that you must eventually address, and to put them into context. They can help to guide problem decomposition by showing a repertoire of subproblem classes that you know how to handle. The granularity of a problem frame is important: much bigger than an object class; bigger than a typical design pattern; smaller than almost any realistic problem. Big enough to represent a significant portion of the whole problem; small enough for each subproblem domain and interface to be manageably simple.

Problem frames emphasise physical domains and physical phenomena and interfaces, because the point of software development is to build machines that interact with the world and change it. In the final analysis, satisfaction of the requirement comes down to observable effects in the world.

12.8.1 Not a panacea

The problem frames approach doesn't work for every kind of problem in every situation. For some problems the emphasis on physical phenomena is a major disadvantage. If you are faced with a problem in pure mathematics, you won't be much concerned with physical domains and interfaces. If your problem is to build a graphical user interface, you should probably use some kind of interface builder to go straight to a solution in a standardised style. If you're building a compiler, the most important help will probably come from established texts on compiling and on formal languages. The only problem frames you will be using are the frames that are implicit in the compiler literature.

12.8.2 Finding more frames

The set of problem frames we have discussed in this book is certainly not definitive or canonical. If you find the problem frame approach helpful you may want to find more frames to add to your personal repertoire. There are several situations that may suggest new problem frames.

- You are dealing with a small problem that seems to need no decomposition, but fits no existing frame. Perhaps it's an example of a new frame. Don't be too hasty, though. If the recalcitrant problem results from decomposition of a larger problem, you should probably try a different decomposition first.

- You are studying a software development method. There may be a useful new problem frame hidden in it. The way to winkle it out is to identify the assumptions that the method is making about the problem and the problem domains.

- You are reading a book about software architecture. Software architecture is about solutions rather than problems. But it can be illuminating to ask yourself: what kind of problem could be solved using this architecture? You may find a new problem frame there.

- You are reviewing a design or an implementation that has been made without benefit of problem frames or, perhaps, of any explicit problem analysis. Can you recognise the problem to which this is the solution? Sometimes this kind of reverse engineering is worth the trouble, and may reveal a new problem frame.

When you're using a problem frame, you should always be critically aware of how well it fits – or doesn't fit – your problem. Sometimes you have an uneasy feeling that the fit isn't as good as it should be. Perhaps you can identify a new frame variant that would fit your problem better. Perhaps you need a completely new frame.

12.8.3 Learning from experience

The indispensable precondition for maturity in any discipline is learning from experience. That is what has brought the established engineering disciplines to the level of competence they have achieved. When a major failure happens – such as the Challenger shuttle disaster of 1986, or the collapse of the Hartford Coliseum space-frame roof in 1978, or the spectacular destruction of the Tacoma Narrows bridge over Puget Sound in 1940 – the engineers are compelled to submit to a public enquiry. The results are published, widely disseminated, and incorporated into a growing, highly structured, body of engineering knowledge.

It's important that this body of knowledge is highly structured. Every lesson learned can be understood at many levels, from the most particular to the most general. The lesson of the Tacoma Narrows bridge was a general engineering lesson about going too far beyond existing practice. It was also a lesson about bridges. It was about suspension bridges. It was about wind deflection of roadways in suspension bridges. It was about the combination of horizontal and vertical deflections. When a lesson can be precisely located in the body of knowledge, it becomes both more useful and more accessible.

You should do no less in your software development. Problem frames can furnish an essential dimension of the structure.

Any questions?

Are the ideas about concerns still useful even if I'm not using problem frames for a particular development?

I hope so. Don't think of this, or any other, approach to software development as a single doctrine that must be swallowed whole or not at all.

Where can I read about engineering failures?

There's a lot written about this topic. For an excellent account of the Challenger and Tacoma Narrows disasters, you could try C Michael Holloway, *From Bridges and Rockets, Lessons for Software Systems*, Proceedings of the 17th International System Safety Conference, Orlando, Florida, pages 598–607, 1999.

If you want to read about an earlier generation's efforts, 200 years ago, to deal with the 'rough edges with new, innovative applications that we're building on this year's new, advanced hardware', see Nancy G Leveson, *High-Pressure Steam Engines and Computer Software*, IEEE Computer, Volume 27, Number 10, pages 65–73, October 1994.

For many good insights into engineering successes and failures, see:

Henry Petroski; *Design Paradigms: Case Histories of Error and Judgement in Engineering*, Cambridge University Press, 1994.

Henry Petroski, *Engineers of Dreams: Great Bridge Builders and the Spanning of America*, Alfred A Knopf, 1995.

Henry Petroski, *Invention by Design: How Engineers Get from Thought to Thing*, Harvard University Press, 1996.

What about software failures?

There's less written about software failures than there should be. One notable report is Nancy G Leveson and Clark S Turner, *An Investigation of the Therac-25 Accidents*, IEEE Computer, Volume 26, Number 7, pages 18–41, July 1993. The Therac-25 was a radiography machine whose software failed disastrously, delivering lethally excessive doses of radiation.

Another report, on the notorious failure of the Ariane rocket, is *ARIANE 5 Flight 501 Failure; Report by the Inquiry Board,* Chairman of the Board, Prof J L Lions, Paris, 19 July 1996. At the time of writing, the Ariane report is available at:

http://www.esa.int/htdocs/tidc/Press/Press96/ariane5rep.html

If problem frames can furnish one dimension of the knowledge structure, what are the other dimensions?

One is certainly provided by the large body of knowledge about computer science. Another is knowledge of particular domain types. Architecture is another. The structure of knowledge can have many dimensions. For a strongly held view on knowledge in software development, see D L Parnas, *Software Engineering: An Unconsummated Marriage*, Communications of the ACM, Volume 40, Number 9, page 128, September 1997.

Appendix 1: notations

1 Context diagrams

Basic context diagram

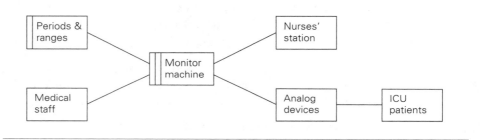

Context diagram symbols

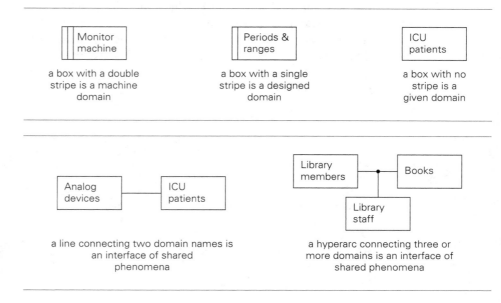

a box with a double
stripe is a machine
domain

a box with a single
stripe is a designed
domain

a box with no
stripe is a
given domain

a line connecting two domain names is
an interface of shared
phenomena

a hyperarc connecting three or
more domains is an interface of
shared phenomena

Context diagram annotations

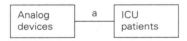

a: Skin resistance

an identifier on an interface line
or hyperarc denotes a set of
shared phenomena

an annotation indicates
the phenomena of the
identified set

2 Problem diagrams

Basic problem diagram

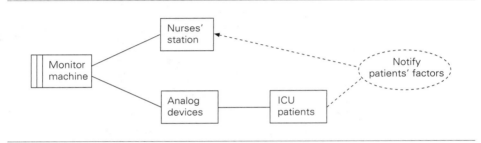

Problem diagram symbols

Monitor machine	Periods & ranges	ICU patients
a box with a double stripe is a machine domain	a box with a single stripe is a designed domain	a box with no stripe is a given domain

a dashed oval is a
requirement

Lights
regime

a solid oval is a
physically represented
description

Lights
regime

a striped solid oval is
a designed physically
represented description

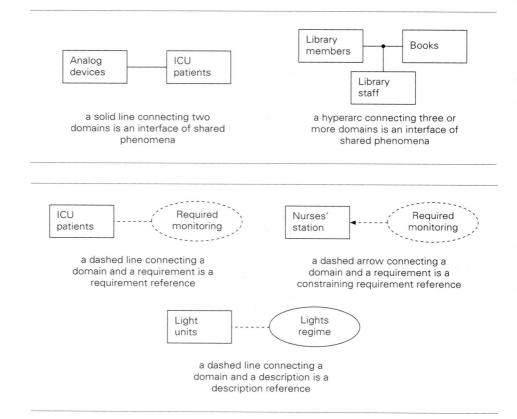

a solid line connecting two
domains is an interface of shared
phenomena

a hyperarc connecting three or
more domains is an interface of
shared phenomena

a dashed line connecting a
domain and a requirement is a
requirement reference

a dashed arrow connecting a
domain and a requirement is a
constraining requirement reference

a dashed line connecting a
domain and a description is a
description reference

Problem diagram annotations

an identifier on an interface line
or hypererc denotes a set of
shared phenomena

an identifier on a description or
requirement reference denotes a
set of phenomona referred to

b: HR! {Temperature, TempKnob,
Occupancy Sensor }
HC! {Valve Settings}

an annotation names the controlling
domains and the set of phenomena
controlled by each one

3 Problem frame diagrams

Frame diagram
Same as for problem diagrams.

Frame diagram symbols
Same as for problem diagrams.

Frame diagram domain markings

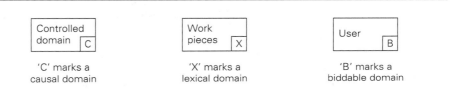

'C' marks a
causal domain

'X' marks a
lexical domain

'B' marks a
biddable domain

Frame diagram interface markings

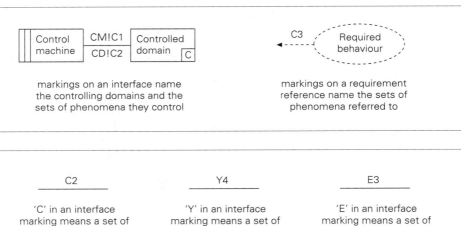

markings on an interface name
the controlling domains and the
sets of phenomena they control

markings on a requirement
reference name the sets of
phenomena referred to

C2

'C' in an interface
marking means a set of
causal phenomena

Y4

'Y' in an interface
marking means a set of
symbolic phenomena

E3

'E' in an interface
marking means a set of
event phenomena

4 State-machine diagrams

Basic state-machine diagram

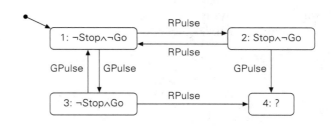

State-machine symbols

a blob-headed
arrow marks the
initial state

each state is identified (3:)
and may be marked with
state phenomena that hold

an arrow is a
transition between
two states

Events and actions

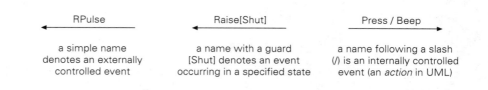

a simple name
denotes an externally
controlled event

a name with a guard
[Shut] denotes an event
occurring in a specified state

a name following a slash
(/) is an internally controlled
event (an *action* in UML)

Transitions

a transition on an implicit
event (3.5 secs has elapsed
since entering the source
state)

a transition on an
implicit event (the
state Shut has
become true)

multiple internally
controlled events may
follow a slash (/); they
occur in sequence

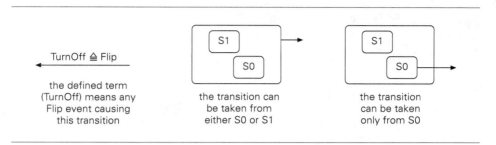

TurnOff ≜ Flip

the defined term
(TurnOff) means any
Flip event causing
this transition

the transition can
be taken from
either S0 or S1

the transition
can be taken
only from S0

State annotations: state

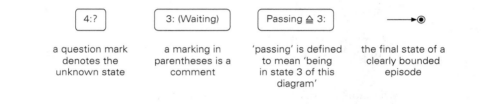

a question mark
denotes the
unknown state

a marking in
parentheses is a
comment

'passing' is defined
to mean 'being
in state 3 of this
diagram'

the final state of a
clearly bounded
episode

State annotations: events

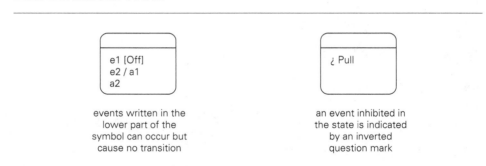

events written in the
lower part of the
symbol can occur but
cause no transition

an event inhibited in
the state is indicated
by an inverted
question mark

5 Tree diagrams

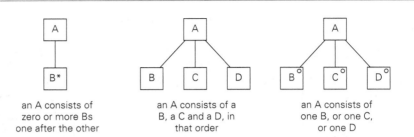

an A consists of
zero or more Bs
one after the other

an A consists of a
B, a C and a D, in
that order

an A consists of
one B, or one C,
or one D

6 Logical symbols

a $\wedge$ b	a $\vee$ b	$\neg$ a	a $\rightarrow$ b	a $\leftrightarrow$ b
a and b	a or b	not a	a implies b	a if and only if b

$\forall$ a $\bullet$ p(a)	$\exists$ a $\bullet$ p(a)	$\exists$! a $\bullet$ p(a)	p(a) $\triangleq$ q(a) $\wedge$ r(a)
for all a p(a) holds	for some a p(a) holds	for one a p(a) holds	p(a) is defined to mean q(a) $\wedge$ r(a)

Appendix 2: glossary

abstraction
  Taking away detail considered unnecessary for the purpose in hand. Treating a chess move as an atomic instantaneous event is an abstraction because it ignores the movement of the player's hand across the board, and the picking up and putting down of the piece moved.

active
  A *domain* is active with respect to a subset of its *event* or *state phenomena* if it initiates event occurrences or state changes without external stimulus from another domain.

analysis
  To analyse a *simple problem* is to identify and address its *frame concern* and the other concerns that it raises. A problem that is not simple must first be *decomposed* or *structured* into simple problems.

atomicity
  An operation or an episode in a *domain* is atomic if it cannot be regarded as a sequence of smaller parts, especially for purposes of interleaving with another domain's behaviour.

audit problem
  A problem of checking that a *domain* complies with a stipulated behaviour, and reporting deviations.

basic problem
  A problem fitting a *problem frame* in its simplest form, with the smallest possible number of *domains*. For example, a basic *information problem*.

behaviour problem
  A problem of achieving and maintaining a required behaviour in a particular part of the world.

boundary
  See *problem boundary*.

breakage concern

A concern in which it is necessary to ensure that the *machine* does not cause a *problem domain* to enter an *unknown state*.

causal phenomena

Phenomena that can cause other phenomena and can be controlled, that is, *events*, *states* and *roles*.

characteristics

See *domain characteristic*s.

commanded behaviour problem

A behaviour *problem* in which the behaviour to be achieved and maintained is chosen by an operator at run time.

commensurability concern

A concern that may arise for two *descriptions* of the same *domain*. The descriptions are commensurable if they use the same *abstractions* for the *phenomena* to which they both refer.

completeness concern

To address a *completeness concern* is to ensure that a *description* is complete.

composition concern

A *concern* arising from the composition of *subproblems* of the same problem.

conceptual concern

A *concern* arising from the use of intangible concepts that the developer must define correctly in terms of observable *phenomena*.

concern

A concern is an aspect of a problem demanding the developer's attention, for example, a *completeness concern,* or an *initialisation concern.*

connection

A connection is an *interface* or a *reference* in a *problem* between the *requirement* and a *domain* or between two or more domains.

connection domain

A domain that is interposed between the *machine* and a *problem domain*. For example, the Post Office might be a connection domain in a mail order problem, interposed between the machine and the customers domain.

consistency concern

To address a consistency concern is to show that two *descriptions* of a *domain* can both be true simultaneously.

constraint

See *requirement constraint.*

context diagram

A diagram showing the structure of the problem context in terms of *domain*s and *connection*s between them. A context diagram always has one *machine domain.*

continuous phenomena

A *phenomenon* is continuous if for any pair of distinct possible observations there is another observation that lies between them. For example, electrical voltage at a point in a circuit is continuous because if V1 and V2 are distinct possible observed voltages, then (V1+V2)/2 is also a possible observed voltage.

control

Control of a *causal phenomenon*. For an *event* this is the ability to initiate its occurrence. For a *state* it is the ability to initiate a change from true to false or vice versa. For an *event* role it is the ability to determine which *individual* should participate in the event.

control characteristics

The characteristics of a *domain* pertaining to the *control* of its *phenomena*, for example, whether it is *active.*

control prefix

A prefix of the name of a set of *phenomena* on an *interface* in a *frame diagram*, indicating which *domain* controls the *phenomena.*

customer

A notional person representing all the people who are entitled to contribute to the r*equirement* in a *problem.*

deadlock

A situation in which nothing can happen because neither of two *domains* or *entities* can progress until the other progresses first.

decomposition

A decomposition of a problem is a structuring into two or more *simple problems.*

definition

A statement of the meaning of some terminology. The meaning is given in terms of *designated phenomena* and previously defined terminology.

description

A description may be a *development description,* for example, a *specification* or a *requirement*, or a description of the properties of a *domain*. Or it may be the content of a machine-readable *description domain*. A description may be *indicative* or *optative.*

description domain

A *domain* in a problem whose *problem role* is that it describes another domain, for example, a *manufacturing plan* domain describes the behaviour of a *factory* domain.

description reference

A reference by the *requirement* or by a *description domain* in a subproblem to some *phenomena* of another domain of the same subproblem. It is represented in the *problem diagram* by a dashed line from the requirement or a description domain to the other domain.

designation

A statement associating a class of *phenomena* with the term used to denote it. The designation states: the term to be used; kind of phenomenon, for example, *event* or *state*; and an informal recognition rule by which instances of the phenomenon can be reliably recognised.

designed domain

A designed domain is the physical realisation of a *description* or *model* that the developer is free to design.

development description

The descriptive content of a document produced during development. For example, a *requirement,* a *specification,* or a description of domain properties.

discrete phenomena

A *phenomenon* is discrete if it is not *continuous.*

domain

A set of related *phenomena* that are usefully treated as a unit in problem *analysis,* and represented as a unit in a *context diagram* or in a *problem diagram.*

domain characteristics

The characteristics of a *domain* that are significant in a particular problem or subproblem. They may be *control characteristics* or *structural characteristics.*

domain flavour

Two *domain*s have different flavours if their properties descriptions need different languages or notations.

domain properties

The expected and assumed relationships among the *phenomena* of a *domain.*

entity

A kind of *phenomenon.* An *individual* that can undergo change over time, for example, a motor car.

event

A kind of *phenomenon*. An *individual* that is an occurrence at some point in time, regarded as atomic and instantaneous: for example, a keystroke.

event-reactive

A *domain* is event-reactive if it reacts to a class of externally controlled events by causing events.

event role

A kind of *phenomenon*. A *relationship* that is the participation of one or more *individuals* in an *event*, for example, the participation of a data record in a write event.

failure

Failure of a domain to exhibit its described properties or behaviour.

frame

See *problem frame*.

frame concern

The central concern for problems of a class defined by a *problem frame*.

frame diagram

A diagram describing a particular class of problem. It takes the form of a generic *problem diagram*, with some special naming and annotation conventions.

given domain

A *domain* that is given in a particular problem, that is, it is not the *machine* and not a *designed domain*.

heuristic

A rule of thumb that helps to find something that is being sought, for example, a problem decomposition.

identities concern

Ensuring the correct association between multiple entities in one *domain* and the phenomena *shared* by them and another domain.

identity projection

A *projection* of a *domain* or *interface* or *requirement* in which nothing is omitted.

indicative

An indicative *description* describes *domain* properties and behaviour that hold irrespective of the behaviour of the *machine* in a problem. By contrast, an *optative description* describes domain properties and behaviour that the machine must guarantee.

individual

An individual is a *phenomenon* that can be named and is distinct from every other individual: for example, the number 17, George III, or Deep Blue's first move against Kasparov.

informal domain

A *domain* for which no exact description of *domain properties* is true without exception.

information problem

A problem in which the requirement is to produce information about a *real world problem domain*.

inhibition

The ability to inhibit a *controllable phenomenon*. For example, to prevent an *event* or a *state* change from occurring.

initialisation concern

Ensuring that the *machine* and the *problem domains* are in appropriate states at the start of execution.

interface

A *connection* among two or more *domains* consisting of *phenomena* that they all share.

interface annotation

A list, in a *frame diagram* or *problem diagram*, of the *phenomena* of an *interface*, showing which domain controls each one. In a frame diagram, the kinds of the phenomena are also shown.

interface phenomena

The *phenomena* of a *domain* that it shares with other domains, especially with the *machine*.

interference concern

The possibility that the interaction of one *subproblem machine* with a *domain* will interfere with the interaction of another with the same domain.

liveness

A domain property or requirement that some specified event or state change will definitely happen.

machine

In a software development problem the machine to be built by the developer. It is built in the form of software, and deployed by running the software on a general-purpose computer. The machine is a *domain*.

made domain

A *domain* in a particular problem that is made when the *machine* runs, for example, a report.

model

A *designed domain* whose purpose is to provide an analogy or surrogate of another domain.

mood

The function of a description or piece of description. For example, *indicative* or *optative*.

multiplex domain

A domain containing isolated multiple instances of a class of phenomena.

null projection

A *projection* of a *domain* or *interface* or *requirement* in which nothing is included.

observable phenomena

Phenomena that can, in principle, be observed in the physical world.

optative

An optative *description* describes *domain* properties and behaviour that the machine in a problem must guarantee. By contrast, an *indicative* description describes domain properties and behaviour that are known to hold irrespective of the behaviour of the *machine*.

overrun concern

Choosing and describing appropriate treatment of *shared* events that are caused by one *domain* before a sharing domain is ready to react to them.

parsing concern

Ensuring that the parts of a sequence of *phenomena* are correctly interpreted according to the structure of the sequence as given in *descriptions* or *definitions*.

partial description

A *description* that leaves a part of its declared subject matter undescribed. For example, a *state-transition diagram* with an *unknown state*.

passive

A *domain* is passive with respect to a subset of its *event* or *state phenomena* if it does not initiate event occurrences or state changes without external stimulus from another domain.

phenomenon (plural: phenomena)

An element of what we can observe in the world. Phenomena may be *individuals* or *relations*. Individuals are *entities, events,* or *values*. Relations are *roles, states,* or *truths*.

precedence concern

A *composition* concern that arises when two *requirements* cannot both be satisfied. To address the concern is to determine which should take precedence in each situation.

problem

A task to be accomplished by software development. A *subproblem* of such a task.

problem boundary

An imaginary contour dividing the parts of the world that are in the *problem context* from those that are not.

problem class

A class of *problems* defined by a *problem frame*.

problem context

The parts of the world in which the *problem* is located. The context is structured as a number of *domains* connected to each other and to the *machine*. The problem context is shown in a *context diagram*.

problem diagram

A diagram describing a particular problem. It shows the problem parts: the *requirement,* the *domains,* and the *interfaces* and *references* among them.

problem domain

A *domain* in a *problem* other than the *machine domain;* especially, a *given domain*.

problem frame

The definition of a problem class. A problem frame consists of a *frame diagram, domain characteristics,* and the *frame concern*.

problem role

The participation of a *domain* in a problem. A domain may appear in a problem as a *given domain*, as the *machine domain*, or as a *designed domain*. A given or designed domain may be a *description domain*.

process

A collection of *events* ordered in time.

projection

A version or description of a *domain* or *interface* or *requirement* in which only those *phenomena* and properties are included that are of interest for a particular purpose in hand.

properties

See *domain properties*

real world

The chief *problem domain* in an *information problem*, about which information is to be produced.

reference

A *connection* between a *requirement* and a *domain* or between a *description* domain and another domain: The connection consists of references to phenomenon of the domain.

relation

A set of *relationships* of the same type: for example, *Mother(x,y)*.

relationship

A kind of *phenomenon*. An association among two or more *individuals*, for example, *Mother(Lucy,Joe)*. Also, generally, any pattern or structure among phenomena of a *domain*.

reliability concern

Dealing appropriately with the possibility that a *domain* will fail to behave in accordance with its described *domain properties*.

remote domain

A *problem domain* that has no interface of *shared phenomena* with the *machine*, but is indirectly connected to it by a *connection domain*.

required behaviour problem

A behaviour *problem* in which the behaviour to be achieved and maintained is described by the requirement.

requirement

The requirement in a problem is a condition on one or more *domains* of the *problem context* that the *machine* must bring about, for example, a stipulated correspondence between a report and the reality it concerns.

requirement constraint

A *requirement reference* that constrains the *domain* to which it refers. If a requirement reference constrains a domain, the *machine* must ensure that the state or behaviour of that domain satisfies the requirement.

requirement phenomena

The *phenomena* of a problem or a *domain* that are the subject of *requirement references*. To be distinguished from *specification phenomena*.

requirement reference

A reference by the *requirement* to some *phenomena* of a *domain*. It is represented in a *problem diagram* by a dashed line between the requirement and the domain. If the line has an arrowhead (pointing to the domain) the requirement reference is a *requirement constraint*.

role

See *event role* and *problem role*.

run time

The time at which the developed software for a problem is executed.

safety

A domain property or requirement that some specified event or state change will definitely not happen.

scheduling

To schedule two *subproblem machines* is to determine how their executions should be interleaved.

scope

The scope of a *description* is the set of *phenomena* to which it refers.

shared phenomena

A phenomenon is shared by two or more *domains* if they all participate in it. For example, both the hammer and the nail participate in the event *Bang*.

simple problem

A simple *problem* is one that need not be decomposed into *subproblems*.

simple workpieces problem

A *workpieces problem* in which the only problem domains are the workpieces and the user.

span

The span of a *description* is its extent in some structural dimension of the described domain. For example, the description time span.

specification

An *optative* description, produced during development, of the desired behaviour of the *machine* in a subproblem.

specification phenomena

The *phenomena* of a *problem* or a *domain* that are shared with the problem *machine*. To be distinguished from *requirement phenomena*.

state

A kind of *phenomenon*. A *relationship* among two or more *individuals* that can be true at one time and false at another, for example, *Married(Fred,Ann)*. Also, an element of a *state-transition diagram*.

state-reactive

A *domain* is state-reactive if it reacts to a class of externally controlled events by changing its state.

state-transition diagram

A diagram showing behaviour in the form of a set of states with transitions between them.

structural characteristics

The characteristics of a *domain* concerned with the structure of its *relationship phenomena*: for example, whether a particular *relation* forms a tree.

structuring

To structure a problem is to decompose it into two or more *simple problems*.

subproblem

A part of a *problem*, having its own *requirement* and its own *problem context*.

synchronisation concern

A *composition concern*. To address a synchronisation concern is to determine how two *subproblem machines* should be *scheduled*.

tag

A name created to identify a *process* and so allow *events* and *states* to be associated with it.

total description

A *description* that leaves no part of its declared subject matter undescribed. For example, a *state-transition diagram* with no *unknown state*.

transformation problem

A *problem* in which a *lexical* input *domain* is to be used to create a lexical output domain.

traversal

A traversal of a *domain* is a structured progression in which all or some of its *phenomena* are accessed by a *machine*.

truth

A kind of *phenomenon*. A *relationship* among two or more *individuals* that is either true at all times or false at all times. For example, *GreaterThan(5,3)* is always true, and *LessThan(5,3)* is always false; both are truth phenomena.

union domain

A *subproblem domain* formed from the combination of two separate domains in the larger *problem context.*

unknown state

A state in which the subsequent behaviour and properties of a *domain* are entirely unknown. A domain that has entered the unknown state can not subsequently leave it.

value

A kind of *phenomenon.* An *individual* that can not undergo change over time, for example, the character 'X', or the number 23.

variant frame

A variant of a basic *problem frame* in which an additional *problem domain* is introduced, or the control characteristics of an interface are changed, for example, an operator variant, or a control variant.

workpieces problem

A *problem* of developing a tool to support creation and editing of text or other machine-readable objects.

References

Ackoff, R L, *Scientific Method: Optimizing Applied Research Decisions,* Wiley, 1962.

Alpern, Bowen and Schneider Fred B, *Recognizing Safety and Liveness*, Distributed Computing, Volume 2, pages 117–126, 1987.

Anon, *An Analysis of Three Mile Island*, IEEE Spectrum, Volume 16, Number 11, pages 32–34, November 1979.

ARIANE 5 Flight 501 Failure, Report by the Inquiry Board, Chairman of the Board: Prof J L Lions, Paris, 19 July 1996.

Balzer, Robert M, Goldman, Neil M and Wile David S, *Operational Specification as the Basis for Rapid Prototyping*, ACM SIGSOFT Software Engineering Notes, Volume 7, Number 5, pages 3–16, December 1982. Reprinted in *New Paradigms for Software Development*, W W Agresti, IEEE Tutorial Text, IEEE Computer Society Press, 1986.

Boehm, Barry W, *Unifying Software Engineering and Systems Engineering,* IEEE Computer,Volume 33, Number 3, pages 114–116, March 2000.

Booch, Grady, *Object Oriented Design with Applications,* Benjamin/Cummings, 1991.

Booch, G, Rumbaugh, J and Jacobson, I, *The Unified Modeling Language User Guide*, Addison-Wesley Longman, 1999.

Brooks Jnr, Frederick P, *No Silver Bullet – (Essence and Accidents of Software Engineering*, in Information Processing 86: Proceedings of the IFIP 10th World Computer Congress, pages 1069–1076; North-Holland, 1986. Reprinted in IEEE Computer, Volume 20, Number 4, pages 10–19, April 1987.

Buschmann, F, Meunier, R, Rohnert, H, Sommerlad, P and Stahl, M, *Pattern-Oriented Software Architecture: A System of Patterns,* John Wiley, 1996.

Cameron, John, *JSP & JSD: The Jackson Approach to Software Development,* IEEE CS Press, 2nd Edition, 1989.

Cook, Steve and Daniels, John, *Designing Object Systems: Object-Oriented Modelling with Syntropy,* Prentice Hall International, 1994.

Krasner, G E and Pope, S T, *A Cookbook for Using the Model-View-Controller User Interface Paradigm in Smalltalk-80*, Journal of Object-Oriented Programming, Volume 1, Number 3, pages 26–49, August/September 1988.

Kruchten, Philippe, *The Rational Unified Process: An Introduction*, Addison-Wesley Longman, 1999.

Leveson, Nancy G, *Software Safety: What, Why and How*, ACM Computing Surveys, Volume 18, Number 2, pages 125–163, June 1986.

Leveson, Nancy G and Turner, Clark S, *An Investigation of the Therac-25 Accidents*, IEEE Computer, Volume 26, Number 7, pages 18–41, July 1993.

Leveson, Nancy G, *High-Pressure Steam Engines and Computer Software*, IEEE Computer, Volume 27, Number 10, pages 65–73, October 1994.

London, P E and Feather, M S, 1986; *Implementing Specification Freedoms* in *Readings in Artificial Intelligence and Software Engineering*, C Rich and C E Waters (eds), pages 285–305, Morgan Kaufmann, 1986.

Maiden, N A M and Sutcliffe, A G, *Analogical Retrieval in Reuse-Oriented Requirements Engineering*, Software Engineering Journal, Volume 11, Number 5, pages 281–292, September 1996.

Meyer, Bertrand, *Object-Oriented Software Construction*, Prentice Hall International, 1988.

Minsky, Marvin, *Computation: Finite and Infinite Machines*, Prentice Hall International, 1972.

Neumann, Peter G, moderator, *The Risks Digest: Forum on Risks to the Public in Computers and Related Systems*, Volume 12, Issue 51, Wednesday 16 October 1991, ACM Committee on Computers and Public Policy.

Nijssen, G M, *A Framework for Advanced Mass-Storage Applications* in Medinfo 1980, Proceeding of the Third World Conference on Medical Informatics, North-Holland, 1980.

Nijssen, G M and Halpin,T A, *Conceptual Schema and Relational Database Design, a fact oriented approach*, Prentice Hall, 1989.

Parnas, David Lorge and Madey, Jan, *Functional Documents for Computer Systems*, Science of Computer Programming, Volume 25, Number 1, pages 41–61, October 1995.

Parnas, D L, *Software Engineering: An Unconsummated Marriage*, Communications of the ACM, Volume 40, Number 9, page 128, September 1997.

Petroski, Henry, *Design Paradigms: Case Histories of Error and Judgement in Engineering,* Cambridge University Press, 1994.

Petroski, Henry, *Engineers of Dreams: Great Bridge Builders and the Spanning of America,* Alfred A Knopf, 1995.

Petroski, Henry, *Invention by Design: How Engineers Get from Thought to Thing,* Harvard University Press, 1996.

Polya, G, *How To Solve It,* Princeton University Press, 2nd Edition, 1957.

Pree, Wolfgang, *Design Patterns for Object-Oriented Software Development,* Addison-Wesley, 1995.

Randell, Brian (ed), *The Origins of Digital Computers: Selected Papers,* Springer-Verlag, 2nd Edition, 1975.

Randell, B, *The Origins of Digital Computers: Supplementary Bibliography* in N Metropolis, J Howlett, and Gian-Carlo Rota (eds), *A History of Computing in the Twentieth Century,* Academic Press, 1980.

Reubenstein, Howard B, and Waters, Richard C, *The Requirements Apprentice: Automated Assistance for Requirements Acquisition,* IEEE Transactions on Software Engineering, Volume 17, Number 3, pages 226–240, March 1991.

Robertson, Suzanne and Robertson, James, *Mastering the Requirements Process,* Addison-Wesley, 1999.

Rumbaugh, J, Jacobson, I and Booch, G, *The Unified Modeling Language Reference Manual,* Addison-Wesley Longman, 1999.

Sedgewick, Robert, *Algorithms*, Addison-Wesley, 2nd Edition, 1988.

Shneiderman, Ben, *Direct Manipulation: A Step Beyond Programming Languages*, IEEE Computer, Volume 16, Number 8, pages 57–69, August 1983.

Shaw, Mary, *Beyond Objects: A Software Design Paradigm Based on Process Control,* ACM Software Engineering Notes, Volume 20, Number 1, pages 27–38, January 1995.

Shaw, Mary, *Making Choices: A Comparison of Styles for Software Architecture*, IEEE Software, special issue on software architecture, Volume 12, Number 6, pages 27–41, November 1995.

Sommerville, Ian and Sawyer, Pete, *Requirements Engineering;* John Wiley and Sons, 1997.

Stevens, W G, Myers, G J and Constantine, L L, *Structured Design*, IBM Systems Journal, Volume 13, Number 2, pages 115–139, 1974.

Swartout, William and Balzer, Robert, *On the Inevitable Intertwining of Specification and Implementation*, Communications of the ACM, Volume 25, Number 7, pages 438–440, July 1982.

Turski, Wladyslaw M, *And No Philosopher's Stone, Either* in Information Processing 86: Proceedings of the IFIP 10th World Computer Congress, pages 1077–1080, North-Holland, 1986.

van Lamsweerde, A, Darimont, R and Massonet, Ph, *Goal-Directed Elaboration of Requirements for a Meeting Scheduler: Problems and Lessons Learnt* in Proceedings of RE95, the Second IEEE International Symposium on Requirements Engineering, pages 194–203, May 1995.

van Lamsweerde, Axel and Leiter, Emmanuel, *Integrating Obstacles in Goal-Directed Requirements Engineering* in Proceedings of the 20th International Conference on Software Engineering, April 1998.

van Schouwen, A J, Parnas, D L and Madey, J, *Documentation of Requirements for Computer Systems* in Proceedings of the IEEE International Symposium on Requirements Engineering, pages 198–207, January 1993.

Verheijen, G M A and Van Bekkum, J, *NIAM: An Information Analysis Method in Information System Design Methodologies: A Comparative Review*, T W Olle, H G Sol and A A Verrijn-Stuart (eds), pages 537–589, North-Holland, 1982.

White, S, *Panel Problem: Software Controller for an Oil Hot Water Heating System* in Proceedings of COMPSAC 86, pages 276–277, October 1986.

Wilkes, M V, Wheeler, D J and Gill, S, *The Preparation of Programs for an Electronic Digital Computer, with Special Reference to the EDSAC and the use of a Library of Subroutines*, Addison-Wesley, 1951.

Wing, Jeannette M, *A Study of 12 Specifications of the Library Problem*, IEEE Software, Volume 5, Number 4, pages 66–76, July 1988.

Yourdon, Edward, *Modern Structured Analysis*, Prentice Hall International, 1989.

Yourdon, Edward, *A Tale of Two Futures*, IEEE Software, Volume 15, Number 1, pages 23–29, January/February 1998.

Zave, Pamela, *Secrets of Call Forwarding: A Specification Case Study* in Formal Description Techniques VIII (Proceedings of the Eighth International IFIP Conference on Formal Description Techniques for Distributed Systems and Communications Protocols), pages 153–168, Chapman & Hall, 1996.

Index

DATE DUE

04/29/05			